Culture Shock

Culture Shock

Psychological reactions to unfamiliar environments

ADRIAN FURNHAM
AND STEPHEN BOCHNER

With a Foreword by
WALTER J. LONNER

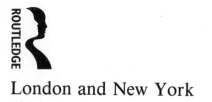

London and New York

First published in 1986 by
Methuen & Co. Ltd

Reprinted 1989, 1990
by Routledge
11 New Fetter Lane
London EC4P 4EE

Simultaneously published in the
USA and Canada by Routledge
a division of Routledge,
Chapman and Hall, Inc.

© 1986 Adrian Furnham and
Stephen Bochner

Set by Hope Services, Abingdon
Printed in Great Britain at the
University Press, Cambridge

*British Library Cataloguing in
Publication Data*

Furnham, Adrian
Culture shock: psychological
reactions to unfamiliar
environments.
1. Culture shock
I. Title II. Bochner, Stephen
155.9   GN517

*Library of Congress Cataloging-
in-Publication Data*

Furnham, Adrian.
Culture shock.
Bibliography: p.
Includes indexes.
1. Culture shock.
I. Bochner, Stephen.   II. Title.
GN517.F87   1986
303.4'82   86-8376

ISBN 0-415-04523-1

For Michael Argyle,
whose hobby is travel.

Contents

PART IV
Culture learning and management   219

List of figures

List of tables

Acknowledgements

We are of course indebted to a number of people who have helped us and shaped our thinking on the topic of culture shock. These include Michael Bond (Chinese University of Hong Kong), Peter Collett and the late Jos Jaspars (Oxford University) who are to be thanked for useful conversations. Also we should mention the tireless efforts of Louise Kahabka and Vera Thompson in Sydney and Elsie Banham in London, who patiently retyped chapter after chapter. We are also indebted to the Australian Studies Centre at the Institute of Commonwealth Studies for providing the first author with a Commonwealth Visiting Fellowship so that he could discuss finer points of the book with the second author on a yacht in Sydney Harbour. Any responsibilities for errors, omissions, misjudgements may be attributed to a combination of the excellent white wine and the swell in Port Jackson.

ADRIAN FURNHAM
STEPHEN BOCHNER

The authors and publishers would like to thank the following individuals, journal editors, organizations and publishers for permission to reproduce copyright material that appears on the pages below. Although every effort has been made to trace copyright holders, they apologize in advance for any unintentional omission or neglect and will be pleased to insert the appropriate acknowledgement in any subsequent edition of this book.

Pergamon Press for Tables 2.1, 2.2 and 2.3, from *Cultures in Contact: Studies in Cross-Cultural Interaction* (1982)   *21, 24, 25*

W. Peterson and *American Sociological Review* for Table 3.1   *43*

New Community for Table 3.2   *46*

P. Rack and Tavistock Publications for Table 3.3, from *Race, Culture and Mental Disorder* (1982)   *52*

R. Cochrane and Longman Group Ltd. for Tables 3.4 and 4.7, from *The Social Creation of Mental Illness* (1983)   *53, 86*

W. B. Gudykunst, *The International Journal of Intercultural Relations* and Pergamon Press for Table 3.5   *57*

Charles A. Price and the Department of Demography, Australian National University for Table 4.1   *68*

A. Richardson, Australian National University Press and Pergamon Press, Australia for Table 4.2, from *British Immigrants and Australia: A Psycho-Social Inquiry* (1974)   *70*

C. Bagley and *The Journal of Biosocial Science* for Table 4.4   *79*

R. Cochrane, *Social Psychiatry* and Springer–Verlag for Tables 4.5 and 4.6   *80–1, 82*

H.B.M. Murphy, *Psychological Medicine* and Cambridge University Press for Table 4.8   *93*

H.B.M. Murphy, M.B. Kantor and C.C. Thomas for Table 4.9, from *Mobility and Mental Health* (1973)   *94*

Charles Zwingmann for Tables 5.1 and 5.2 and Figure 5.1a & b *113, 120, 127*

I.E. Babiker, *Social Psychiatry* and Springer–Verlag for Table 5.3   *122*

P.S. Adler, *The Journal of Humanistic Psychology* and Sage Publications for Table 5.4   *130*

I. Torbiorn and John Wiley and Sons Ltd. for Figs. 5.2 and 5.3, from *Living Abroad: Personal Adjustment and Personnel Policy in the Overseas Setting*   *133, 134*

P.L. Pearce and Pergamon Press for Tables 6.1, 6.2 and 6.3, from *The Social Psychology of Tourist Behaviour* (1982)   *142–3, 144–5, 146*

B. Weiner and CBS College Publishing for Table 7.1   *168*

T.H. Holmes, R.H. Rahe and *The Journal of Psychosomatic Research* for Table 8.1   *179*

D. Gish and *The Journal of Psychology and Theology* for Table 10.2   *228*

Foreword

When Professors Furnham and Bochner kindly invited me to write a foreword to this book, I was in a good setting to do so. I had recently arrived in Germany, where I was to spend nearly a year on a sabbatical leave from my university, with additional support from the Fulbright Program and German sources. My wife and three teenagers accompanied me. What better way to make comments about a book on adjustments to other cultures than during the process of a five-member family adapting to a set of other-culture circumstances? We also had the additional perspective of reflecting on our previous sabbatical, spent in Mexico seven years earlier, and comparing the two experiences.

While my wife, especially, and I were quite familiar with Europe in general and Germany in particular, our children were not. And even my wife and I were only slightly familiar with our sabbatical locale of the Saarland, a beautiful part of south-western Germany which has rich historical ties with France. Here my wife and I could monitor our own and each other's adjustment to the subtle nuances of subjective culture, and both of us could watch our apprehensive offspring absorb and accommodate a new culture and language. This family adventure was in part designed to help us see ourselves against the backdrop of a different culture – perhaps the last time we could do this while the children were still legally under our control. A bonus to this family and professional outing was, as mentioned above, how it could contribute to this foreword.

The manuscript did not reach me until after our return home, and that was an advantage. The delay gave me plenty of time to reflect on what I knew would be a central part of my comments: how helpful, in fact, can a book on culture shock be to those who are anticipating or even going through an experience where some degree of discomfort is expected? Or, how helpful might such a book be to those who are trying to aid others as they struggle with the problems of human adaptation to unfamiliar environments? A more general question was also of interest: because adaptation to any unfamiliar situation is highly dependent upon enormous variations in both situations and persons, is it possible to develop a taxonomy or a set of guidelines which could embrace all these variations in a credible, consistent and beneficial way?

'You're off for a year of adventure!' These words are shouted from the cover of the *1984 Orientation Handbook* prepared by the Fulbright Commission (otherwise known as the Council for International Exchange of Scholars). The Fulbright people, world-wide, have had a lot of practice in helping to prepare professors, teachers, students and others to live abroad. They give tips about schools, shopping, common customs, medical procedures, characteristic cultural misunderstandings, and so forth, all based upon the experiences of hundreds of culture travellers that preceded them. In one of their unofficial publications they in fact devote a few pages to culture shock and explain its symptoms, phases and resolution. Summarized are the major features of Kalervo Oberg's description of 'culture shock', that well-worn and (like its time-orientated counterpart of 'future shock') perhaps frequently misused phrase which Oberg introduced into the English language, apparently in 1954. Oberg's catch-phrase was and continues to be interesting and very influential. Implied in its use is a sort of axiom that adjustment to another culture is assumed to follow a 'natural' course. The ebbing and flowing of exhilaration, anxiety, frustration, hostility, bewilderment, homesick-ness, denial, lethargy, and other reactions to situational stress, are supposed to subside and eventually settle into a calming sea of relative adjustment to, and acceptance of, the other culture as just another way of construing reality. In other words, we voluntarily or involuntarily confront an unfamiliar set of rules about how life should be lived, we eventually learn the rules, and we go on living happily, or maybe grudgingly, ever after. That is, until the next time. It's as simple as that, so it seems.

During the early part of our sabbatical, my wife would occasionally consult the Oberg reference. She enjoyed 'checking on where we were' with respect to our adjustment. While it was true that we slept longer than usual during our first two weeks, and that the children were justifiably anxious about attending school (they initially knew little German), I was convinced that Oberg's notion was only minimally relevant for our situation. After all, everyone seems to suffer a bit from jet-lag and the rigours of last-minute packing, and all children seem to have at least a little anxiety about school. How much of our reaction was really attributable to the stresses and strains of confronting another culture?

Smugly and with academic aplomb I insisted that we were not candidates for a valid case of culture shock. Some adjustments were necessary, of course, but actual *shock*? No, I demurred, 'shock' seems to imply something serious, like tonic immobility, and should therefore be reserved for the special case. We had plenty of things to cushion us against a text-book type of shock. For instance, my wife and I had visited

Germany several times and had even lived there for a combined total of about nine years. We actually felt at *home* there, much of the time. The language, especially for my wife, posed no serious problems, despite the fact that I am convinced that one can never *really* know a culture until one masters its language. Our multilingual friends and colleagues made it easier for us, as they do with most Americans, by speaking English. And we were well within the range of the American Forces Radio and Television Network, allowing us to tune in on mainstream America almost any time we wished. Our financial resources were quite satisfactory, allowing us to buy a new automobile. This is culture shock?

I argued that for Oberg's, or anyone else's, model of culture shock to work, we would have to be in a rather different set of other-culture circumstances, with stressors that challenged our adaptive resources. We could not be temporary sojourners, somewhat insulated from most anxiety-arousing circumstances and therefore inoculated against real stress, and expect to feel the full force of a classic case of culture shock. If we were to qualify as a text-book case of this debilitation, we could not be, as we were under our rather enviable circumstances in Germany, capable of almost immediate escape from nearly any unpleasant situation. I further argued that our experiences in Mexico much more closely approximated conditions which would permit the consideration of Oberg's original notion and the common use of 'culture shock'. It was there, on the Yucatan Peninsula, where we experienced significant discrepancies between social realities and our own well-learnt template of how things 'should be' between people and things and people and people.

Many things impressed and affected us in Mexico: the cheerful fatalism of very friendly people; abject poverty and occasional wealth; the Spanish language (which we could not handle as well as German), not to mention the infinitely more complex Mayan language; family and friendship patterns and customs that at times appeared baffling; collegiate relationships which were strained because of mutually desired but chronically unmet perfection in interpersonal interaction; the rush of the market-place, the hot and humid weather, the inability to comprehend fully the incredible accomplishments of the ancient Maya, the occasional resentment of 'rich Americanos', the unpredictability of the 'floating' peso, and so on. Worse yet, from a culture-shock perspective, but somehow strangely satisfying and memorable, were my experiences in a rural Mayan village. Things there were *really* different, and I was indeed a stranger in a strange land. And even more graphic were other experiences: short stays in places like Istanbul, Calcutta, Tokyo, Bogotá, where one gets a feel for truly striking cultural differences; where one is perhaps ill-equipped even to know how to look for the basic, whopping differences to which one would have to become adjusted if a semblance of psychological survival was to be expected.

As the weeks and months passed in Germany, I continued to ponder our relatively easy situation, and how it could not qualify as a very florid case of culture shock. The closest we got to the bouquet of emotions which surround culture shock involved an ugly legal hassle with our landlord; in that controversy our nearly complete ignorance of German rental laws and the court system made us appreciate the many things in Germany that we *did* understand. Amid our frequent feelings of helplessness, how empathetic we felt toward the millions of immigrants and other culture travellers who either had to understand local laws, but *quick*, or sink fast!

By the time we were ready to end our 'great adventure', I had developed a good case against culture shock as a unitary phenomenon and as a term that can be bandied around with the same ease that we use terms like 'measles', 'influenza', or even the related concept of 'fatigue'. My patient wife had long since stopped listening to the details of my rationale, and so when I could not get others (e.g. our well-adjusted children) to listen to my arguments, the dialogue was internal. The core of my argument was that culture shock has to be considered and understood as a complex and interactive phenomenon. Just as there is no fixed number of types of persons who are candidates for the unpleasant effects of culture shock, there is no set number of situations which reliably trigger this common problem of adaptation. One has to consider which person, which situation, which behaviour and which desired outcome. Subscribing generally to the social-learning paradigm(s) in psychology, I would tell those within earshot that every case of *everything* in the mammoth arena of human behaviour, including culture shock, has to be considered in the context of its own configuration of actors and settings. Categorizing people (for example, as catastrophizers, extroverts, independents) as well as types of situation (such as the academic sojourn, forced migration, ethnic segregation) works only to a limited extent. Beyond the point of limited explanatory power afforded by categories, one must consider the whole configuration – including the hard-to-measure subjective evaluation of the complete process as experienced by the 'victim'.

I explained to my wife that I now knew Furnham and Bochner's book would simply have to take into account these person-by-situation factors. A very wide-ranging presentation of considerations involving culture shock would have to be included if the book were to make a genuine contribution to the literature on adaptation to other cultures.

The manuscript finally arrived, a few weeks after I returned home and had been struggling with the effects of 'reverse' culture shock (but let's not get into *that* troublesome concept!). My high expectations about the manuscript were met, and exceeded. The approach taken by the authors is generally consistent with basic principles of social-learning theory. The book is comprehensive, extremely well referenced, and clearly organized and written. Its broad coverage will be welcomed by researchers and practitioners in psychology, anthropology, international education, psychiatry, epidemiology, and international management, or by anyone who needs to know about human variations in coping with unfamiliar cultural settings. And unlike any other available book on this topic, Furnham and Bochner have stressed social skills as a means both to avoid certain aspects of culture shock and to deal with the effects once they are experienced.

The authors' main point in emphasizing social skills is that the best way to cope with an unfamiliar environment is to learn *behaviours* which are appropriate for the social situation in question. One can learn about another culture passively and cognitively, perhaps in this way starting the coping process by anticipating how one will adjust. The print and electronic media as well as seminars, classes and conversations with fellow travellers all help in this regard. Although not trivial, this is an abstract and indirect process. To understand the consequences of culture shock, and to know what has to be done to resolve them, will require action in *both* the cognitive and behavioural spheres. Such is the general aim of the social-skills approach for the reduction of unpleasant consequences of learning how to behave properly in an unfamiliar setting.

While Furnham and Bochner emphasize social skills as an effective way to help ameliorate the negative side of behaving awkwardly or incorrectly in a foreign milieu, their book is not just one of applied behaviourism. On the contrary, it is a remarkably well-researched and broad-banded book, and gives a thorough overview of the topic. For instance, at least seven different 'theories' or 'explanations' (their quotation marks) are outlined and critically appraised. The authors also cover a wide range of conditions which may induce culture shock – from the simple, brief sojourn of the camera-toting tourist, to the trauma of being a refugee or the victim of forced migration.

Had I the pleasure of writing such a solid book, it would have been tempting to devote a section to the numerous factors which determine how seriously a *specific* person may be affected by culture shock. Before anyone's reactions to a new culture can be completely understood, an assessment of these factors will be needed. At least six classes of 'predictor variables' seem important enough to merit individual consideration:

1. *Control factors.* How much control does one have over *initiating* the other-culture experience? This could range from complete control (as in an idyllic vacation to a sun-swept island) to absolutely no control (such as forced and permanent relocation for political or economic reasons).
2. *Intrapersonal factors.* These would include the person's age, extent of previous travel, language skills, resourcefulness, independence, fortitude, capacities to tolerate ambiguities and frustrations, appearance and similar personal characteristics.

3. *Organismic–biological factors.* Included here would be one's overall physical condition, special medical or dietary needs and general ability to tolerate physically the demands of stressful disruptions in the tempo of one's familiar routine.

4. *Interpersonal factors.* The nature and extent of one's support group, both at home and abroad, including whether one is travelling alone, would be important. Ability to call others for urgent assistance (medical, financial, legal) or just a friendly visit over a cup of coffee or glass of beer would be affected by one's support group. The mutual expectations of all parties concerned – before, during, and after the sojourn – would also affect how one behaves.

5. *Spatial–temporal factors.* Where on earth is one going, and when, and for how long? An extended trip to the Arctic in winter will not be the same as a short trip up north in the summer.

6. *Geopolitical factors.* The current level of international, national, regional or local tensions, which can change in an instant depending upon whose 'side' one is on (perhaps correctly or incorrectly perceived by others), can critically affect the individual. These factors and what one may or may not say about contemporary events would have to be handled very carefully.

Considerations such as the above are implied by the authors throughout the book. Stating them in this way, however, will underscore the multidimensionality of the interesting phenomenon of culture shock. These comments may be of some assistance in comprehending the valuable scope of this book.

In concluding my remarks, I want to congratulate the authors for a job very well done, and to thank them for asking me to contribute some thoughts on the topic. I learnt a great deal from reading the manuscript. Their volume is an impressive review and analysis of just about every piece of literature published in the English language (and maybe a few others) on culture shock. It also gives prescriptions for practical ways of handling it. Furnham and Bochner's book will be one of the first things that I pack for my next trip to a new and different place; it will also be the first book that I recommend to my anxious and apprehensive sojourning friends. Anyone interested in the varieties and vicissitudes of human adaptation to unfamiliar cultures will find it to be a thoughtful and thorough piece of scholarship. It will also be, for many, a practical resource for those whose work involves assisting others who are rendered temporarily ineffective by all the factors that are embraced under the simple, riveting concept of culture shock.

WALTER J. LONNER, PhD
Department of Psychology
Western Washington University
Bellingham, Washington
USA

Part I
Psychology of intercultural contact

1 *Introduction and overview*

The aim of this volume is to describe and explain the psychological consequences of exposure to novel, unfamiliar cultural environments. The book sets out to look at the assumptions people hold about such experiences, describe the theories that have been proposed to account for the effects of contact with new cultures and list some of the actual consequences which have been revealed by systematic research. The final sections of the book will describe some of the means of coping with unfamiliar environments, and the techniques and procedures that have been employed to prepare cultural travellers for their new experiences. The emphasis throughout will be on presenting the findings of empirical research from a variety of disciplines, including anthropology, demography, psychology, psychiatry and sociology. Thus, where appropriate, accounts of the surveys, studies and experiments that have dealt with the effects of culture contact are reported, as distinct from the many myths that abound in this area. The book aims to be interdisciplinary as well as critical.

. The book is divided into four parts. Part I provides a general introduction to the social psychology of cross-cultural interaction. After the present overview, Chapter 2 describes the process of cross-cultural contact, or what is entailed when individuals from different cultural backgrounds interact with each other, and what are likely to be some of the outcomes of such meetings. The scene is set by listing some of the main parameters of intercultural interaction. These include the history of culture contact; the various purposes for which persons travel abroad (e.g. to study, trade or settle); the varying durations of typical sojourns (e.g. long, medium or short term); the direction of movement (e.g. from developed countries to the Third World and *vice versa*); and the assumed as well as actual effects of these movements on the individuals concerned, and on the sending and receiving societies taking part in the exchange.

In this section the potentially stressful effects of exposure to unfamiliar cultures is discussed. Two quite opposite assumptions have prevailed in this field. On the one hand, experiencing a second culture is held to be beneficial, since such exposure is said to broaden one's perspective, promote personality growth and provide insight into the culture of origin through a contrast with other world-views. At the very least, exotic places are assumed to provide a welcome change from the tedium of familiar, routine activities, and the tourist and entertainment industries have used that argument to induce millions of travellers to leave home in search of that goal, real or imagined, attainable or not. In addition to its educational and entertainment value, second-culture exposure is also promoted on the grounds that it should result in greater mutual understanding between the peoples of the world and thus lead to better international relations and less inter-group friction and hostility.

There is certainly evidence that culture contact can have beneficial effects on those participating in it. However, there also exists an opposing point of view, based on the central assumption that exposure to an unfamiliar culture may be, and often is, stressful and hence potentially harmful. Rather than expanding the mind and providing a satisfying and interesting personal experience, the hypothesis states that unfamiliar environments create anxiety, confusion and depression in individuals so exposed. In extreme cases, physical illness may be a direct consequence. Rather than creating better mutual understanding, culture contact often leads to hostility and poor interpersonal relations among those involved in the interchange. There is a good deal of evidence to support this pessimistic view of the consequences of culture contact, and in reviewing the literature the major terms and concepts are introduced. These include the core notion of culture shock and its derivatives, role shock, role strain, role ambiguity and culture fatigue. In the concluding portion of the chapter the two conflicting outcomes of the sojourn experience are reconciled, by invoking a cost–benefit model of cross-cultural contact – that is that inevitably the process will have some positive and some negative consequences – and by referring to the conditions under which either positive or negative consequences may be expected to occur, the obvious implication being that the more favourable the cost–benefit ratio, the more successful a particular sojourn is likely to be.

Chapter 3 aims to describe some of the motives that cultural travellers have for their geographic movement. This is a complicated and messy area of research as any theorist interested in human motivation knows. People often have multiple, interdependent reasons for travelling. Furthermore, many are not able to report fully on their motives, so making research difficult. More importantly perhaps, as the literature from both student sojourners and some migrants attests, there are often very conflicting motives for travelling. There are often contradictions between the explicit 'official' reasons for movement and implicit 'unofficial' motives that makes this topic, although clearly very important, extremely difficult to research.

Chapter 3 also attempts some definitions and categorizations of the different ways in which travellers may be grouped. From the innumerable dimensions possible – motives, country of origin, destination, and so on – four dimensions are isolated which are seen as most parsimonious. Purely for illustrative purposes these dimensions are considered two at a time: amount/quality of change versus geographic distance; and length of stay versus motives for migration. From these dimensions various groups of cultural travellers may be described, some of which are examined in greater detail in the following section. Finally, as some of the literature in the field (see Ch. 4) relies heavily on mental-health admission records, some of the problems of using these as data will be considered.

Part II of the book is devoted to a detailed description of the experiences of three large and distinct groups of culture travellers. Chapter 4 deals with permanent or long-term second-culture exposure, of which the best example is migration. Chapter 5 deals primarily with overseas students, international businesspersons and their dependants, and other medium-term sojourners, and Chapter 6 describes the experiences of tourists and business people abroad. This section is therefore organized in terms of the duration of the sojourn and the sojourners' commitment to it. There is another dimension that co-extends with sojourn-length and commitment, namely the degree of psychological distress associated with each type. The evidence, which is extensively reviewed, suggests that by and large the persons subject to the greatest stress are the migrants, followed by those on extended sojourn (with some exceptions, such as the wives of businessmen, who seem particularly at risk). Tourists in the main experience the least difficulty, although again there are notable exceptions to be found in the literature.

This section of the book illustrates very clearly the way in which the general literature on culture shock has been neatly but artificially carved up between different disciplines. The extensive, long-established and cross-national literature on mental health and migration has been almost exclusively the territory of social psychiatrists and epidemiologists. A smaller, more recent, but in some senses more analytic, literature on the psychology of the sojourn, and more particularly the experience of overseas students and Peace Corps workers, has been of particular interest to cultural anthropologists and social and clinical psychologists. The relatively little research on tourism or business travellers, on the other hand, has been executed by sociologists and management scientists, respectively. Despite the great differences in terminology, methodology and theoretical orientation, there is a surprising coherence in the results. Furthermore, within each area there are some interesting counter-intuitive examples of adaptation. Thus, whereas migration has always been associated with distress and mental illness, and tourism (and upward social mobility) with enjoyment, pleasure and success, the literature suggests that in some instances migrants are more healthy than the natives and clearly benefit from their move, while tourists experience illness and unhappiness instead of relaxation and pleasure.

Each chapter (4, 5 and 6) in this section has had to be somewhat selective in describing the empirical studies as in most instances they are numerous. But it is not only empirical studies that are reported. Researchers in every area have made some attempts to offer a theoretical explanation for their findings. Many of these 'theories' or 'models' or 'explanations' are really no better than descriptions of the process and offer little or no new theoretical insights or implications for remedial action. However, there are some hypothesis-testing, theory-building studies, which are highlighted.

Part III of the book looks at some of the ways in which researchers have attempted to explain the relationship between geographic movement to unfamiliar environments and consequent psychological reactions. Culture shock has been variously ascribed to a sudden shift in the contingencies that customarily reinforce social behaviour; to a lack of knowledge or uncertainty about mutual expectations; to rigid personalities unable to accept change; to value-differences leading to negative evaluations of the new culture; to status loss; to the noxious effects assumed to be inherent in change *per se*; to difficulties with diet; to the lack of social-support systems in the new culture; and to other factors that make life in the new society, particularly the interpersonal side of it, uncertain, unpredictable and generally unpleasant. Either explicitly or implicitly, each of these explanations of culture shock carries some implications for remedial action. As we have said, many of the accounts of culture shock are merely descriptive rather than explanatory, leaving open the aetiology of the condition; and many of the remedies may be ineffective, impractical and, in some cases, counter-productive. Various culture orientation and training programmes have been employed with varying degrees of success. These include cognitive training or providing information about the new culture, usually about its social rules; the raising of self-awareness, where the assumptions of one's own culture are made explicit and the sojourner is exhorted to become a cultural relativist; attribution training, where participants are taught to explain behaviour from the perspective of another culture; learning-theory-based approaches where participants are taught to seek reinforcement or to reinforce themselves for culturally appropriate behaviour; and behavioural training, where participants role-play life in simulated environments, such as a mock Asian village built in Hawaii to train prospective Peace Corps volunteers for service in the Far East. None of these methods has met with unqualified success in preparing persons for life, work and play in new cultural settings, possibly because they are not theoretically well-founded.

Chapter 7 looks at three popularly used but rather simplistic descriptions of culture shock in terms of grieving, beliefs about control and selective migration. These concepts are drawn from widely disparate academic traditions but can and do add new insights into the reactions of cultural travellers. However, they cannot explain the numerous differences in reactions, and for all three the extant empirical findings offer only weak support for the theories.

Chapter 8 considers three more recent 'explanations' for culture shock; these draw most from clinical/medical and social psychology. The negative life-events and social-support literature both offer complementary and overlapping (not competing) explanations or full descriptions of how, when and why cultural travellers experience distress. Although these theories have not been directly or extensively used to test findings in the culture-shock area, some studies within each of the two traditions point to the usefulness of the idea. The third research area concerns value differences and their relationships to misunderstandings and distress. The virtue of this area is that very clear, testable hypotheses can be formulated simply by knowing the respective value systems of the country (group or area) from which the traveller came and to which he or she moves. All three research areas offer new insights into this complex area of psychological reactions to unfamiliar environments.

In Chapter 9 there is offered a model which overcomes some conceptual and practical problems by combining the notion of culture shock with that of social skills. The core idea is that a sojourner can be regarded as a person who is lacking or deficient in the social skills of the new society. This formulation provides a very precise and definable account of the sojourn experience; it places the problem of the sojourn squarely where it belongs (i.e. in the interpersonal sphere); it emphasizes social difficulties of the everyday, mundane sort and de-emphasizes the exotic that is so often associated with other formulations of culture shock thereby heightening the anxiety of the sojourner; it removes the stigma attached to traditional accounts, with their implications of personal inadequacy, by emphasizing that coping with another culture is just a skill, rather like playing tennis, which can be learnt under appropriate circumstances and where no blame attaches to a person ignorant of the game. In short, this formulation takes culture shock out of the clinical field into the area of education and learning. Finally, the model provides quite specific guidelines for preventive and remedial action, based on the procedures developed for social-skills training, a method that has been used successfully in a variety of areas.

The final section of the book (Part IV) is concerned with two problems. In Chapter 10 some attempt is made to evaluate the various theories and explanations for the existence of culture shock. Apart from the obvious criteria of any theory – well founded, internally logical, testable, extensive – they are judged by how well they fit the data presently available. As will become apparent, many of these theories are overlapping and complementary, though they do have rather different implications for the management of culture travellers. Again, as in

Chapter 9, the advantages of the social-skills approach will be highlighted.

Chapter 11 looks in more detail at training programmes that are based on the social-skills model. In particular, a three-stage sequence is proposed. The initial phase is a diagnostic one in which those specific skills that a particular sojourner lacks are determined. This is followed by a training sequence in which these skills are imparted, using a variety of techniques, by a trainer who is familiar with both cultures – that of the sojourner and that of the receiving society. Finally, the effectiveness of the intervention can be evaluated against performance by the person in real-life situations where the sojourner had previously experienced difficulty. Although general in scope, culture orientation based on social-skills training can be tailor-made to specific individuals and to particular instances of sojourner-society/host-society combinations. At the same time, since many of the problems are likely to be shared by a number of sojourners (e.g. Australian businessmen in Japan), the method lends itself to the construction of some packaged training programmes that most participants would benefit from.

Chapter 12 ends the book, bringing the various strands together and draws certain conclusions about the management of psychological reactions to unfamiliar environments. In particular, there is a clear need for institutions in the business of sending or receiving culture travellers to provide systematic orientation and support for their people, based on the principles and techniques that are available and which have been reviewed in this book. This would not only smooth the path of the average culture traveller but, perhaps more importantly from the point of view of these institutions, reduce the financial and political costs represented by disappointed, disillusioned and demoralized students, migrants and failed businesspersons.

2 Intercultural contact: processes and outcomes

Contact between culturally diverse individuals has an ancient tradition. Observers of contemporary race relations tend to ignore the fact that cross-cultural interchange is as old as recorded history. Since the beginning, persons brought up in one culture have travelled to other lands, to trade, teach, learn, convert, succour, settle or conquer. Perhaps the reason why culture contact is often treated as a modern phenomenon is that psychology, sociology and anthropology, the disciplines most concerned with the topic, are themselves relatively young sciences and are perhaps regarded as having 'discovered' the field. But long before social scientists began to describe and speculate about contact with exotic cultures, there appeared accounts written by explorers, travellers, adventurers, refugees, charlatans, traders, and even tourists, that dealt with what today would be labelled as cross-cultural phenomena. Indeed, probably the best accounts of culture contact come not from contemporary social science but from such sources, or from novelists and playwrights recreating past intercultural exchanges. For instance, among the original writers, the journals of Captain Cook, Marco Polo, Xenophon, Columbus, Drake, Burton, and Lafcadio Hearn provide excellent eyewitness accounts. Among the novelists, most of whom appear to have taken real historical events as their theme, Clavell's *Shogun*, Michener's *Hawaii* and Gore Vidal's *The Creation* are only some of the writers who provide extraordinarily perceptive analyses of culture contact, as does Attenborough's recent film about Gandhi.

Perhaps the biggest difference between the early days and contemporary culture contact is that now travellers tend to fit into more specialized role categories. They are tourists or traders or settlers or foreign students, and their purposes and time-frames differ depending on which of these roles they are enacting. In the pre-jet age, when it used to take several years to travel say from England to Asia or Australia, the travellers tended to be much more rounded in their interests and aims. Many were scientists, students, soldiers, traders, missionaries and often settlers all rolled into one. In that sense, the specialized disciplines of migration studies, tourism studies, international student-exchange studies, international trade studies, the sorts of headings that will be used in this book to summarize the data, are a modern phenomenon, being the concomitant of a more complex world where role and occupational specialization intrude into all spheres of human endeavour. However, the elements that distinguish these various groups of travellers today have probably always existed, albeit as part of a less-differentiated syndrome than was shared by most of those who ventured abroad.

During the last three or four decades social scientists have become increasingly interested in the area of culture contact. Several reasons in conjunction have been responsible for this burgeoning research effort. A major factor has been the sheer increase in the incidence of cross-cultural contacts, partly due to a shrinking world as a result of the jet and silicon-chip age, but largely also due to government intervention. The post-war reconstruction period saw an unparalleled rise in the number of international aid schemes, educational exchange programmes, migrant and refugee resettlement plans, 'Peace Corps' initiatives and the military occupation of large parts of Europe and Asia. These programmes were all supported by government funds, either directly or indirectly. Later, the private sector entered the field of cross-cultural relations as multinational companies and international trade rapidly expanded in conjunction with the post-war boom. Common to every one of these international programmes, at the sharp end there occur interactions between culturally disparate groups and individuals. In addition, both experience and research have shown that such interactions by their very nature are potentially stressful, that cross-cultural life was not meant to be easy. Applied psychology responded to the challenge and began to develop the theoretical constructs and remedial methods that now enable us to comprehend and facilitate culture contact. This research will be described in greater detail later in this book. Our purpose here is to provide an initial broad overview of the processes inherent in cross-cultural exchange, the problems that arise and some of the solutions that have been proposed.

There are four ways in which intercultural contact can be described, corresponding to four different approaches in the literature. First, it is possible to categorize the research by the sorts of individuals or groups who have been studied. For instance, there exist large specialist literatures on foreign students, migrants, tourists, and so forth. Second, the psychology of the contact experience can be analysed in terms of variables such as its purpose, time-span and type of involvement, and these variables can be related to particular groups of participants. Third, outcomes of contact can be classified in terms of their impact on the participating groups. And fourth, the effect of contact on individuals can also be described and categorized.

Cutting across all these classifications is an important issue that requires clarification, namely whether we have in mind a one-way or two-way model of influence. Most of the earlier literature has a distinctly unidirectional flavour in its implicit assumptions about who should be the 'targets' of research. For instance, many investigators have studied the adjustment problems of overseas students or migrants but failed to ask whether these migrants or students had any impact on the host society and its members, as if these host individuals were impervious to the influence of the strangers in their midst. This is a serious conceptual and empirical error, as common sense and more recent research have shown. A major theme of this book is that all contact has two-way reciprocal consequences, although the extent to which each party is affected by the interaction depends on a variety of factors, many of which will be reviewed later.

We will now briefly discuss the four approaches to intercultural contact. Much of this material will be treated more fully later in this book in sections specifically devoted to the issues here being introduced.

Substantive areas of research

International education
Since the Second World War, governments and foundations have supported a huge number of students as well as senior scholars, enabling these persons to spend varying lengths of time attending overseas institutions. In addition, many privately funded students have swelled the ranks of academic exchange. Foreign scholars, often a highly visible minority, constitute about 10 per cent of the student population on many campuses throughout the western world (Bochner and Wicks, 1972), although many non-western, so called less-developed countries also support and encourage foreign students (e.g. Zaidi, 1975). It has been estimated that world-wide at any moment there may be up to half a million students and scholars attending institutions of higher learning abroad (Edgerton, 1976; Klineberg, 1976).

Three waves of research can be discerned in this field. As the programmes gained momentum in the 1950s, it became clear that many foreign students were experiencing serious psychological difficulties. When this was realized, a great deal of research, much of it of dubious quality, was initiated to address the issues. Undoubtedly the most important studies were those supported by the Social Science Research Council and published by the University of Minnesota Press, inquiring into the adjustment problems of foreign students in the United States (Bennett, Passin and McKnight, 1958; Lambert and Bressler, 1956; Morris, 1960; Scott, 1956; Selltiz, Christ, Havel and Cook, 1963; Sewell and Davidsen, 1961). In Britain, too, research with a similar objective was beginning to appear (Carey, 1956; Singh, 1963; Tajfel and Dawson, 1965).

The second wave constituted a veritable flood of research reports, scattered throughout the literature. For example, an annotated bibliography compiled in 1964 (Parker, 1965) contained 915 entries, and a selected bibliography by Shields (1968) listed 495 items. The problem with these studies is that many of them were a-theoretical, and used what Brislin and Baumgardner (1971) have called 'samples of convenience' rather than properly constituted representative groups of subjects. The preferred methodology was to administer a questionnaire that included a variety of items about the respondents' adjustment problems and attitudes to the host country. Control groups were notable by their absence and very few of these studies included a host-group sample. This literature is difficult to interpret and summarize. Reviews that did make an attempt to integrate some of the findings include those of Bochner and Wicks (1972) and Eide (1970).

The third wave, to some extent overlapping with the second, comprises a continuous effort to bring order to this chaotic field, through the development of theoretical models capable of guiding research and accounting for the findings in a systematic, integrated way. The problem here is that many of the theories that were proposed have a rather low level of conceptual sophistication, tending to be more descriptions than explanations. Nevertheless, at least there is a conscious attempt to place events and phenomena into some sort of conceptual framework, which is to be commended as a useful first step. Since many of the concepts are not restricted to international educational exchange but are equally relevant to many if not all types of contact situations, the theoretical constructs will now be briefly mentioned here, to foreshadow more extensive treatment elsewhere in this book.

The early models concentrated on the more noxious aspects of cross-cultural contact. The view that cross-cultural interaction is stressful and requires a clinical approach was established by the pioneers in the area, and this pseudo-medical model has persisted to the present day (e.g. Eitinger and Schwarz, 1981). A major early influence was Stonequist (1937), who drew on the work of Park (1928) to publish a widely cited book called *The Marginal Man*, dealing with the problems encountered by persons caught between two cultural systems, not belonging to or fully accepted by either group. The concept has been criticized (e.g. Mann, 1973), but it is still used by many writers to explain the adjustment difficulties of culture travellers.

Another concept, also in the clinical mode, was the notion of culture shock, introduced to the literature by Oberg in 1960 and subsequently elaborated by a great many followers. The term refers to the idea that entering a new culture is potentially a confusing and disorientating experience, and this concept has been widely used (and misused) to 'explain' the difficulties of the cross-cultural sojourn. As this is one of the main themes to be addressed in this book, 'culture shock' will be given a more extensive and systematic treatment later.

A third concept, again with negative connotations for the psychological welfare of the sojourner, and introduced at about the same time (i.e. in the late 1950s) was the notion of the U-curve of adjustment, or the idea that cross-cultural sojourners progress through three main phases: an initial state of elation and optimism, replaced by a period of frustration, depression and confusion (presumably the period labelled by Oberg as 'culture shock') and finally followed by a gradual improvement leading to feelings of confidence and satisfaction with the new society (Coelho, 1958; Deutsch and Won, 1963; Du Bois, 1956; Gullahorn and Gullahorn, 1963; Jacobson, 1963; Lysgaard, 1955; Selltiz and Cook, 1962; Sewell, Morris and Davidsen, 1954).

More recently, theoretical models of the sojourn experience have been proposed that eschew the clinical flavour, with its assumptions of breakdown in the normal healthy psychological functioning of the individual, and the attendant stigma of failure and weakness on the part of the sojourner that is implicit in an approach that recommends therapy and counselling for those unable to cope with cross-cultural experiences. The new models liken cross-cultural exposure to a learning experience and, instead of therapy for the traveller, propose programmes of preparation, orientation and the acquisition of culturally appropriate social skills (Bochner, 1982; Furnham and Bochner, 1982; Klineberg, 1982).

For instance, Klineberg (1981) has suggested that the academic sojourn should be regarded as a life history. Klineberg points out that pre-departure experiences, levels of competence and degree of preparation will affect what happens to the person while abroad, which in turn will have an impact on the individual's life after return to the home country. The various stages in the life history of the sojourn may be conveniently listed as selection for study abroad; preparation, including the provision of practical and cultural information about the host society and language training; the academic experience while abroad, particularly whether this leads to formal success or failure; general adaptation to the new environment, including the making of friends with host members; and finally the return home, including the extent to which the person is accepted back into the culture of origin and provided with support in the form of a suitable job, status recognition, and so forth. Later in this book we will review empirical evidence regarding each of the life stages of the academic sojourn. Here we simply wish to make the point that the merit of this approach is to show that any difficulties sojourners might have, including contracting 'culture shock', are not due simply to intrapsychic, within-skin deficiencies and weaknesses but are the product of a complex set of social, psychological, between-skin influences played out over a long period of time. For instance, as Klineberg has pointed out, the seeds of many during-sojourn disasters are sown years previously because the 'wrong' people were selected to go abroad. We will have occasion to refer to the social psychology of culture shock in later sections of this book.

The concept of 'adjustment' is frequently used in the sojourn literature. There are two problems with this formulation. The first is its already discussed clinical flavour, implying that the failures and problems that sojourners experience are the symptoms of some underlying pathology which requires treatment. Klineberg's life-history approach has shown the inappropriateness of regarding the sojourn in this light. The second problem is that 'adjusting' a person to a new culture has connotations of cultural chauvinism, the implication being that the newcomer should abandon the culture of origin in favour of embracing the values and customs of the host society. We will return to this issue later, which in the broadest sense concerns the vital question of cultural preservation. Our purpose in raising it here is to introduce an alternate theoretical model of cultural accommodation that does not rely on the concept of adjustment. Bochner (1972; 1981; 1982) has called this process 'culture learning'. The model states that the major task facing a sojourner is not to adjust to a new culture but to learn its salient characteristics. Unlike the notion of adjustment, learning a second culture has no ethnocentric overtones. There are many examples in life when it becomes necessary, or at least advisable, to learn a practice even if one does not approve of it, and then abandon it later when circumstances change. Well-brought-up English persons will soon learn to push and shove their way on to a Tokyo subway car or remain forever on the platform, but will presumably resume their normal queuing practice after returning home, or suffer the consequences of social opprobrium. The possession of a particular skill by itself carries no value judgement – the performance attracts notice only when the appropriate skill is lacking or when the act is performed in inappropriate circumstances.

Bochner's culture-learning model has recently been extended to incorporate two further concepts. One is to combine the idea of social skills (Argyle, 1979; 1980) with cross-cultural competence (Furnham and Bochner, 1982). The second has been to draw attention to the importance of the social-support system of the sojourner as the context in which appropriate culture-learning can take place (Bochner, Buker and McLeod, 1976; Bochner, Hutnik and Furnham, in press; Bochner, McLeod and Lin, 1977; Bochner and Orr, 1979; Furnham and Alibhai, 1985a; Furnham and Bochner, 1982).

It was Argyle and Kendon (1967) who first suggested that the behaviour of people interacting with one another can be regarded as a mutually organized, skilled performance. Interpersonal difficulties arise when this performance breaks down or cannot be initiated in the first place. Subsequent empirical research has identified some of the interpersonal skills that socially incompetent persons lack or perform unsatisfactorily. These include expressing attitudes, feelings and emotions;

adopting the appropriate proxemic posture; understanding the gaze patterns of the people they are interacting with; carrying out ritualized routines such as greetings, leave-taking, self-disclosure, making or refusing requests; and asserting themselves (Trower, Bryant and Argyle, 1978). In sum, socially inadequate individuals have not mastered the social conventions of their society: they may be unaware of the rules of social behaviour that regulate interpersonal conduct in their culture or, if aware of the rules, unable or unwilling to put them into practice.

Thus it could be said that socially unskilled persons are often like strangers in their own land. This perspective leads to the idea that people newly arrived in an alien culture or subculture will be in exactly the same position as the socially inadequate individuals referred to earlier, since there is empirical evidence showing that the elements of social interaction listed above vary across cultures (Argyle, 1982; Furnham, 1979, 1983c; Hall, 1959, 1966; Hall and Beil-Warner, 1978; Leff, 1977). An ironic twist is that individuals in this predicament, such as foreign students, business people, diplomats, and so forth, often tend to be highly skilled in the verbal and non-verbal practices of their own society and find their unaccustomed inadequacy in the new culture particularly frustrating and embarrassing.

Later in this book we will present empirical evidence illustrating the sorts of ordinary, everyday situations that sojourners find difficult. One main purpose here is to introduce the culture-learning/social-skills model of cultural accommodation and to note that it carries clear implications for the comprehension and management of cross-cultural difficulties. Cross-cultural problems arise because sojourners have trouble negotiating certain social situations. Therefore it is necessary to identify the specific social situations which trouble a particular sojourner and then train the person in those specific skills that are lacking. This is quite a practical idea, based on evidence from intracultural studies that subjects who are incompetent in their culture of origin will generally respond favourably to remedial social-skills training (Argyle, 1979).

However, since most sojourners are unlikely to undertake formal training in social skills, it is important to ascertain under what actual conditions does culture-learning occur (or not occur, as the case may be). The answer to that question, supported by theoretical as well as empirical considerations (Bochner, 1981) is that a major source of cultural information will be those host nationals who function as culture friends and informal trainers. One important condition must be satisfied before such culture-learning can proceed, namely that sojourners must have close, perhaps even intimate, links with members of the host society who are able and willing to act as culture friends and mediators. This question has led Bochner and his colleagues to investigate the friendship patterns and social networks of foreign students. These studies, summarized most recently in Bochner, Hutnik and Furnham

(1986) consistently show that overseas students typically belong to three distinct social networks, each serving a distinct psychological function. The three networks are monocultural, bicultural and multicultural, respectively. The monocultural network consists of bonds with fellow compatriots, and its function is to provide a setting for the rehearsal and expression of ethnic and cultural values. The bicultural network consists of bonds with host nationals, and its function is to facilitate instrumentally the academic and professional aspirations of the sojourner. The multi-cultural network consists of bonds with other non–compatriot foreign students and its function is recreational, as well as providing mutual support based on a shared foreignness. Consistently, the studies show that the least salient network is the bicultural one. For instance, Furnham and Bochner (1982) found that close links with British people accounted for only 18 per cent of the friendships of 150 foreign students in Britain. American data show a similar trend, with only 29 per cent of the relationships of the foreign students consisting of bonds with host-culture members (Bochner, McLeod and Lin, 1977). Klineberg (1982) and Klineberg and Hull (1979) in an investigation of foreign students in eleven different countries have come up with similar results, reporting that a majority of their subjects stated that their 'best friend' (a measure also used by Bochner) was either a fellow-national or another foreign student. The evidence is overwhelming that many overseas students do not know a single host national intimately, even after many years of residence in the country being visited, and are therefore quite isolated socially from the host society. This separation creates a vicious circle, since the lack of host-culture friends diminishes the sojourner's opportunities for learning those cultural skills that might facilitate entry into the local society, thereby rendering it even more inaccessible.

We have dwelled at some length on the academic sojourn, partly because the literature in that area is voluminous, but mainly because the topic provides a vehicle for introducing some of the issues, principles, concepts and controversies that characterize the process of culture contact generally, not just with respect to overseas students. Since the same conceptual and theoretical points arise with respect to other forms of contact, the discussion henceforth will be limited to listing the remaining substantive areas of research, without undue repetitive elaboration of the contextual issues.

Migration
Studies of immigrants have been conducted in most of the major receiving countries. For instance, research has taken place in the United States (Gordon, 1964), Great Britain (Watson, 1977), Canada (Kosa, 1957), Israel (Hertz, 1981) and Australia (Taft, 1966; Stoller, 1966). Most of these studies suffer from the methodological and conceptual problems already discussed, namely that they tend to be a-theoretical, consist

mainly of surveys and concentrate on the adjustment problems of the migrants to their new surroundings, ignoring any impact the newcomers might have had on the receiving society. Some of this literature will be reviewed later in this book.

International aid

The last thirty years have seen a great increase in the incidence of technical assistance and international aid. For a variety of reasons, not all of them altruistic, the wealthier countries of the world have provided aid to those nations less well endowed with material prosperity. Initially this involved outright gifts of food, clothing or medicine, but increasingly international aid has taken the form of transferring technical know-how from the industrialized to the less-developed world. Some of the assumptions underlying these programmes were naive, to say the least, and it soon became obvious that the transfer of technology from one cultural system to another created a variety of problems, many of them psychological (e.g. Bochner, 1979, 1981; Kumar, 1979; Seidel, 1981). A voluminous literature exists and will be referred to later in this book.

One particular form of aid that attracted the notice of social scientists from its inception was the Peace Corps. When the programme was set up, psychologists were involved in the selection and training of many of the volunteers; and when subsequent programme evaluations found that neither selection nor training criteria predicted performance in the field, these same psychologists began to speculate about the reason for this failure and about some of the wider dynamics of culture contact (Guthrie, 1975, 1981; Textor, 1966). This literature, also, will be referred to later in this book.

International business

After international aid followed international business, though it should be pointed out that international ownership and overseas control of companies was common before World War II. As the world became more prosperous, international commerce developed and grew. International business contacts take several forms. A highly visible phenomenon is the multinational corporation, where managers from one culture have to co-ordinate and motivate a workforce whose members come from a variety of cultures. Another important group are the international brokers and negotiators, who act as links in the export and import of goods and services across national boundaries. A special feature of the lives of people engaged in international commerce is that, unlike in many of the other areas of cross-cultural contact, their success or failure as cultural negotiators can be measured more immediately and with greater objectivity than is the case say with international education, migration or aid. Based on purely commercial criteria, the bottom line in the annual balance sheet provides a pretty good index of cross-cultural effectiveness as a commercial mediating person.

Cross-cultural training

The many instances of failure in interpersonal relations between culturally disparate individuals led to a burgeoning literature on training (for reviews, see Brislin, 1979; Brislin and Pedersen, 1976). This literature will be discussed in detail later. Suffice to say at this stage that many of the programmes and their rationales lack acceptable empirical support, and this area is still in the process of being developed.

Tourism

The growth of tourism has sparked off a spate of psychological investigations, and there is now quite a respectable literature in existence (for a review, see Pearce, 1982a,b). A noteworthy characteristic of this literature is that, unlike in the other substantive areas reviewed, there are a number of writers who have consciously adopted an interactionist stance, meaning that they have set out to look at the reciprocal effects that tourists and host members and their societies have on each other. This is a natural concomitant of one of the major concerns in this area, as the impact of tourism on previously untouched parts of the world becomes apparent.

'Third' cultures

A number of studies have been conducted of so-called 'third culture' networks, that is of individuals who in addition to their culture of origin, belong to a global community, a world system with which they identify and from which they derive their values (Useem and Useem, 1967, 1968; Useem, Useem and Donoghue, 1963; Useem, Useem and McCarthy, 1979; Useem, Useem, Othman and McCarthy, 1981). These are the people who carry out global programmes, who relate segments of one society with segments of other societies and thus serve as mediating persons (Bochner, 1981) in their professional lives. Typically, they work for international agencies such as UNESCO or the World Health Organization, and in the private sector for the global multinationals. Many diplomats, although primarily identified with their own countries, also have a foot in the door of their third culture, to the extent that they are genuinely concerned to improve international relations. In some ways the future of humankind depends on the third cultures that link human beings together into world-wide systems, but this literature is still relatively meagre and awaits further development.

This completes the overview of the substantive topics. Many of these topics will be revisited later in this book. We now turn to the second approach, an analysis of the main dimensions of the contact experience.

The psychological dimensions of contact

In a review of the contact literature, Bochner (1982) identified the psychological variables that were most frequently mentioned as affecting the outcome of the interactions, and from this developed a general typology of contact situations. The present discussion is an extension of that analysis, which is linked to the nature of the societies that provide the behaviour settings (Barker, 1968, 1979) for the contact. Societies can be classified according to two dimensions. First, societies differ in the extent to which they are *internally* homogeneous. Societies are complex systems, and the criterion of homogeneity can be applied to any or all of their facets, such as their physical features, class structure, climate, material resources, languages, and so on. Our present interest is in the extent to which a society can be regarded as culturally homogeneous or heterogeneous. To avoid fruitless disputes about the meaning of these terms, the concept is being used here to refer to the ethnic and/or cultural identity of an individual (DeVos, 1980) and is ultimately anchored to the empirical operation of asking people what cultural group they belong to. For example, in Australia many persons of mixed Aboriginal and European descent are now asserting that they are Aborigines, although this is not obviously apparent from their physical appearance. Nevertheless, it is reasonable to regard such individuals as Aboriginal, irrespective of their light skin and previous identification with the white group in Australian society.

Theoretically, culturally homogeneous societies are made up of members who all have more or less the same ethnic identification. Although there probably does not exist a society today that is completely homogeneous culturally, it has been argued that a country like Japan comes close to that condition. At the other end of the continuum is a nation like the United States, which has always regarded itself as culturally diverse, although within an overall umbrella of being 'American'. Nevertheless, the list of hyphenated Americans is quite extensive.

Before leaving the dimension of internal homogeneity/heterogeneity, it should be noted that the *salience* of cultural diversity – that is the extent to which it matters whether one does or does not belong to a particular group – interacts with the diversity dimension. Thus in some societies the differences between various groups are not regarded as important, whereas in other societies such differences are highly salient (Bochner and Ohsako, 1977). For instance, the black–white distinction is likely to be more salient in South Africa than South America. Likewise, the Catholic–Protestant distinction is more salient in some parts of Ireland than say Australia.

The theoretically expected relationship between salience of diversity, on the one hand, and degree of diversity, on the other, is complex, and probably curvilinear, although there is no evidence to support this hypothesis. Thus it would be reasonable to predict that in highly heterogeneous societies ethnic identity is regarded as trivial, since being different is not unusual and hence is unremarkable. On the other hand, it could also be argued that in such societies people develop a high degree of sensitivity to their own and the others' cultural membership. This question can only be resolved by empirical research, and the outcome will probably depend on other variables such as the relative numerosity, status and power of the various groups. It is an important issue, though, because to some extent the quality of the contact between culturally diverse individuals depends on the extent to which they regard such differences as salient (Bochner and Perks, 1971).

The second way in which societies can be classified is in the extent to which they differ *externally* from each other, again on a variety of dimensions, such as their climate, geography, economic resources, and socio-cultural patterns. There have been several attempts to develop yardsticks that can be used to compare the cultural aspects of different societies. For instance, an early approach tried to classify cultures according to whether they were 'simple' or 'complex' (Freeman and Winch, 1957). Pelto (1968) used categories such as 'tight' or 'loose' to describe cultures, and Witkin and Berry (1975) contrasted cultures in terms of the extent to which they were differentiated. No doubt there exist conceptual and empirical problems in carrying out such comparisons, but it is in principle feasible to think and speak of cultural dimensions along which societies can be ordered (Boldt, 1978; Boldt and Roberts, 1979). Furnham and Bochner (1982) used this idea to develop an index of culture distance, in which foreign students from twenty-nine different countries attending English universities were classified into three categories: whether their culture was 'near', 'intermediate' or 'far' from British society. In a study testing this scheme, it was found that the categories predicted the degree of social difficulty encountered by the students in England. The results showed that as the distance between the culture of origin and the host society increased, so did the social difficulty of the students. This is one of the few studies that has provided empirical confirmation for the hypothesis that culture distance appears to be a major determinant of 'culture shock', an idea that had previously been largely an unexamined assumption. Thus, when we compare societies *externally* with each other, the underlying dimension that is of special concern to the psychology of contact is the extent to which the cultures can be regarded as close or distant, since their relative location on this dimension will affect the ease with which the respective cultures can be learned by those coming into contact with them.

In the preceding discussion we identified the broad societal variables that provide the context within which culturally disparate individuals interact. Next, it may be useful to describe and categorize those variables that relate more immediately to the personal psychology of the individuals concerned. These include: on whose territory the interactions take place (home, foreign or joint); the time-span of the interaction; its purpose; the type of involvement; the frequency of contact; and the degree of intimacy, relative status and power; the numerical balance; and the distinguishing characteristics of the participants. The model is presented in detail in Table 2.1.

When we relate the personal variables to the societal ones, it becomes evident that within-society cross-cultural interactions differ in several

Table 2.1 Main dimensions of cross-cultural contact

Contact variables	Types of cross-cultural contact and examples			
	Between members of the same society		Between members of different societies	
	Type	Example	Type	Example
Time-span	Long term	Subcultures in multi-cultural societies	Short term	Tourists
			Medium term	Overseas students
			Long term	Immigrants
Purpose	Make a life in	Subcultures	Make a life in	Immigrants
			Study in	Overseas students
			Make a profit	Traders
			Recreate	Tourists
Type of involvement	Participate in society	Subcultures	Participate	Immigrants
			Exploit	Traders
			Contribute	Experts
			Observe	Tourists
			Convert	Missionaries
			Serve as a link	Diplomats
Summary concept	Majority minority	White and black Americans	Host sojourner	Overseas students

Source: S. Bochner, *Cultures in Contact: Studies in Cross-Cultural Interaction*, Oxford, Pergamon, 1982.

important respects from between-society contacts. Permanent members of multicultural societies, or those intending to become permanent (such as immigrants), will meet on territories that are joint and often include institutional settings such as schools, the work place, amusement centres and legal and administrative bodies. Their commitment is total and long term, and there will be frequent contacts with dissimilar persons, although whether these relations attain intimacy will depend on a variety of other variables, such as the relative status, distribution and size of the participating groups. For instance, although many multicultural societies have a numerically and politically dominant majority, such as in Australia or the United States, there are countries like South Africa where the dominant group forms a minority. There are also societies that contain several different ethnic groups who are relatively equal in number and in the wealth and power they control. For instance, in Hawaii there are three dominant groups – Japanese, Chinese and Caucasian – each with its own sphere of influence, with the Japanese dominating the civil service, the Chinese active in commerce and the Caucasians in finance (Daws, 1968). In Fiji, the Fijians and Indians are approximately equal in population and political influence (Chandra, 1975), although here too there is a specialization of functions, with the Indians predominantly involved in commerce and finance while the Fijians gain their wealth from land use and agriculture.

The analysis of between-society contacts reveals a somewhat different set of dynamics. These interactions are all affected by the fundamental distinction that both actors and observers make between the social role of host and the social role of visitor. The expectations and occasionally the dispensations that are associated with the status of visitor/stranger have long been of interest to sociologists (e.g. Heiss and Nash, 1967; Nash and Wolfe, 1957; Rose and Felton, 1955; Schild, 1962). In the present context, the main characteristics relate to those individuals having 'come later', in contrast to the established 'owners' of the territory, hence the interaction will seldom take place on joint territory but rather on home or foreign ground depending on whether we are speaking of the host or of the sojourner. Also, with the exception of immigrants, the expectation is that the visitors will at some stage return to their country of origin, hence their commitment to the host country is not perceived as being permanent; indeed, in many instances these strangers may be seen and see themselves as holding their primary allegiance to their country of origin, even if their sojourn is extensive, examples being overseas students, business persons and 'guest workers' (Boker, 1981). Often too, there may be a status imbalance between host and visitor, in some cases favouring the hosts, in others favouring the visitor. All of these conditions will vitally affect the quality of the contact between hosts and visitors.

Finally, affecting both within- and between-society contacts are the visible characteristics that distinguish different cultural groups, and the salience of these characteristics (Bochner and Ohsako, 1977; Bochner and Perks, 1971; Hartley and Thompson, 1967). Markers such as race, skin colour, language, accent and religion (Bochner, 1976; Klineberg, 1971) tend to evoke both in the actor and in the observer a categorization of the participants into an 'us' versus 'them' classification, which in turn colours any interaction between persons so categorized (Sherif, 1970). Usually, once the categorization has been made, it leads to some form of discriminatory behaviour in favour of those people classified as belonging to the in-group (Tajfel, 1970). It is true that under some conditions strangers or oppressed minorities will be treated more leniently and/or favourably than the in-group (e.g. Bochner and Cairns, 1976; Dutton, 1971, 1973; Feldman, 1968; Schild, 1962), but so-called incidents of reverse discrimination tend to be the exception rather than the rule. The evidence is overwhelming that out-group members, once they have been recognized and labelled, usually on the basis of some visible or audible characteristic, will be regarded and treated less favourably than members of the in-group (Bochner, 1980, 1982).

Outcomes of contact

When culturally disparate groups come into contact with each other, they will have an impact on each other's social structures, institutional arrangements, political processes and value systems. The nature and extent of these changes will depend on the conditions under which the contact occurs (e.g. whether peaceful or in conquest), the relative power of the interacting groups, and a host of other variables. Likewise, the actual accommodation between the groups can take a great variety of forms. In addition, the individuals caught up in the contact also have an impact on each other. Normally, most commentators leave it at that, that is they point out (correctly) how vastly complex these processes are, imply that this complexity defies any attempt to construct a conceptual system that will unify the large array of phenomena under consideration, and then list some of the specific processes and outcomes that they are particularly interested in.

This somewhat unsatisfactory state of affairs prompted Bochner (1981, 1982) to develop a set of principles that can be used to classify all of the empirically observed outcomes of cultural contact within a single overall framework. The principles were developed so that they would have maximum generality. Thus the same principles can be used to categorize contact at the group level, as well as to describe the psychological reactions of individuals caught up in cross-cultural contact. Finally, the model can be applied to contact between different groups in the same society, as well as to contact between different societies. Table 2.2 presents this schema as it applies at the group level,

Table 2.2 Outcomes of cultural contact at the group level

Contact outcomes	Between groups in the same society Examples	Between different societies Examples
Genocide of original inhabitants by outsiders	—	Australian Aborigines in Tasmania American Indians
Genocide of newcomers by insiders	Nazi Germany	—
Assimilation of out-groups by in-group	Migrants in 'melting pot' societies	Diffusion of western innovations 'Cocacolonization'
Segregation of out-groups by in-group	USA before Second World War South Africa Imperial India	White Australia immigration policy
Self-segregation of out-group	Tribal lands Enclaves in Alaska, the US south-west, Australian centre	East Germany during Cold War Mainland China during Cultural Revolution
Integration	Emerging pluralistic societies such as Australia, New Zealand, Hawaii	Emerging transnational institutions such as the United Nations, the East–West Center and 'third cultures'

Source: S. Bochner, *Cultures in Contact: Studies in Cross-cultural Interaction*, Oxford, Pergamon, 1982.

and Table 2.3 sets out the various categories of responses that exhaust the varieties of individual reactions to contact. A brief discussion of these principles and their application now follows.

Group effects

A historical overview of the various outcomes of inter-group contact shows that they can be classified into four, more or less mutually exclusive categories. These are genocide, assimilation, segregation and integration (Bochner, 1979, 1982).

Table 2.3 Outcomes of cultural contact at the individual level: psychological responses to 'second culture' influences

Response	Type	Multiple-group membership affiliation	Effect on individual	Effect on society
Reject culture of origin, embrace second culture	'Passing'	Culture I norms lose salience Culture II norms become salient	Loss of ethnic identity Self-denigration	Assimilation Cultural erosion
Reject second culture, exaggerate first culture	Chauvinistic	Culture I norms increase in salience Culture II norms decrease in salience	Nationalism Racism	Inter-group friction
Vacillate between the two cultures	Marginal	Norms of both cultures salient but perceiveds as mutually incompatible	Conflict Identity confusion Over-compensation	Reform Social change
Synthesize both cultures	Mediating	Norms of both cultures salient and perceived as capable of being integrated	Personal growth	Inter-group harmony Pluralistic societies Cultural preservation

Source: B. Bochner, *Cultures in Contact: Studies in Cross-cultural Interaction*, Oxford, Pergamon, 1982.

Genocide

There are many recorded instances in ancient as well as recent history where one group, usually in the majority or possessing superior technological resources, has killed or attempted to kill all members of another group with whom they came into contact. Genocide tends to be justified by the perpetrators on the grounds that the group being eradicated are not really human, an argument that is not shared by those who are the victims of this process. There can be nothing more terrifying than belonging to an ethnic group being systematically exterminated. The effect on those doing the killing is more difficult to gauge, since the appraisal of their own behaviour is likely to undergo the self-justificatory distortions that individuals employ to reduce the dissonance that is aroused by acting repugnantly (e.g. Aronson, 1976).

Assimilation

Assimilation is the term used to describe the swallowing up of one culture by another. This occurs when a group or a whole society gradually adopt, or are forced into adopting, the customs, values, life-styles and often the language of a more dominant culture. The process can be observed to occur both within societies as well as internationally. Until quite recently, many societies adopted a deliberate policy of assimilation with respect to existing minority groups, or newcomers such as immigrants (Bochner, 1981). Intraculturally, after a few generations of assimilation, minority members tend to become culturally and usually also physically indistinguishable from the mainstream, resulting in the virtual disappearance of the minority culture. The effect on the majority culture is more difficult to gauge. In some cases the dominant culture remains steadfastly unmoved by all the foreign influences it has ingested. Other cultures undergo subtle modifications that are reflected in a more cosmopolitan, 'softened' version of the original mainstream ethos. It is very difficult to provide hard evidence of these changes, and the definitive study of how mainstream cultures are affected by immigrants and other newcomers has yet to be conducted.

At the international level, the post-war years have seen an irreversible push towards global homogeneity in cultural manifestations (Bochner, 1979). The dominant influences have come from the west, leading Lambert (1966, p. 170) to refer to this process as 'cocacolonization'. The overall effect is that differences between cultures become eroded, the diversity in life-styles is reduced and many traditional patterns will disappear for good. It is not usually acknowledged that assimilation policies and practices are racist, implying as they do that the dominant culture is superior in relation to the minority, or 'lower status', practices it is swamping. Sometimes, of course, these attitudes are made explicit, as when the culture being absorbed is described as being backward, primitive and overdue to join the twentieth century, a comment for instance made by Inkeles (1975, p. 323) in relation to the desirability of transferring western technology to the underdeveloped regions of the world. Pressures to assimilate can arouse feelings of inferiority, self-rejection and even self-hatred (Bettelheim, 1943; Lewin, 1941).

Segregation

Segregation refers to a deliberate policy of separate development. Since such policies are usually unsuccessful in practice, their main value in the present context lies in shedding light on the psychology of those advocating such a course. It is thus interesting to note that at the intra-societal level, the impetus for segregation can come either from the dominant majority seeking the exclusion of certain minority groups from mainstream positions, institutions and territories; or the minority groups themselves can actively demand separate states, cultural enclaves, special schools, land tenure based on ethnic background, territorial reserves, sanctions against intermarriage, and so forth.

Internationally, similarly, protectionist policies are pursued whose aim is to isolate societies from each other. Thus nations so inclined will develop practices aimed at keeping unwanted people, information and influences out of their countries, and will also place restrictions on their own citizens' travel abroad, in order to prevent them from becoming contaminated by foreign ideas.

In practice, segregation, whether of the enforced or self-imposed kind, is largely doomed to failure as the world becomes increasingly interdependent and as the flow of information through global radio and television systems brings the various peoples of the world into almost instant communication with one another. However, the *attitudes* towards segregation – that is, the idea, however empirically untenable, that segregation is desirable and possible – has important consequences for cross-cultural relations.

Integration

As we mentioned earlier in this chapter, there is general consensus that life was not meant to be easy for persons in contact with members of other cultures. Both theoretical considerations and the empirical evidence overwhelmingly support this conclusion, and later in this book we will be reviewing some of the literature pertaining to the difficulties of the cross-cultural traveller. Here, however, we would like to make one important point, to which we shall return on several subsequent occasions in this book. The point relates to the manner in which people have tried to resolve the difficulties associated with cross-cultural contact. The 'methods' that have just been reviewed all have one thing in common: they 'solve' the problem of contact between culturally diverse peoples by either eradicating the people who are different (genocide); by eradicating the differences (assimilation); or by eradicating the contact (segregation). In other words, these 'solutions' propose to resolve the difficulties of cross-cultural contact by eliminating it. The real issue, which is how to improve relations between members of different cultures, is ignored.

Cross-cultural relations, as a problem to be solved, can only begin to be tackled when it is explicitly acknowledged that human groups differ in their respective cultural identities, that they have a right to maintain their idiosyncratic features if they so wish and that this principle applies to diversity both within and between societies. This first step, obvious and simplistic though it might seem, has some very important and far-reaching consequences. In its most basic form the principle rules out genocide and assimilation as acceptable forms of cross-cultural 'relations'. But more significantly, it raises the following question: if groups do and should be allowed to differ, what is the consequence of this cultural diversity on the fabric of society? Does it necessarily follow that the greater the cultural diversity (whether within or between societies), the greater the resulting friction between them, or is there no necessary connection between diversity and inter-group harmony? Stated in this way, the issue now becomes an empirical one and also, of course, a theoretical one in the sense of seeking explanations for the observations. In other words, the basic question this approach raises is whether different groups can live together in harmony and, if so, what the nature of such a relationship might be. The other approaches either ignore this question or assume that the answer is in the negative. However, if one starts with the premise that at least in principle cultural diversity does not inevitably lead to conflict, then this opens the way to research and theorizing about the contact conditions that either enhance or impede cross-cultural understanding. The subsequent chapters of this book all directly or indirectly address themselves to this issue.

The contact model that provides a useful conceptual framework for such an approach draws on the principle of integration to describe the structure of culturally pluralistic societies. The term 'integration' is sometimes erroneously used as interchangeable with 'assimilation', but it needs to be emphasized that the two terms have quite different meanings and describe totally different processes. 'Integration' refers to the accommodation that comes about when different groups maintain their respective core cultural identities, while at the same time merging into a superordinate group in other, equally important respects. Both within-culture as well as between-culture integrated arrangements exist. For instance, it has been suggested that Hawaii is an example of a successful, integrated multiracial society (Daws, 1968) where the various ethnic groups maintain their distinct identities and cultures, yet within a general framework of Hawaiian-Americanness that binds them together, and where the law, at least in principle, upholds equal opportunity and mutual tolerance. It should be noted that this benign appraisal of Hawaii is by no means unanimous and perhaps should only be treated here as an illustration of what might be, instead of as an example of what has been, achieved.

The evidence is stronger in regard to global integrated systems. Here we can draw again on the work of the Useems (Useem and Useem, 1967, 1968; Useem, Useem and Donoghue, 1963; Useem, Useem and McCarthy, 1979; Useem, Useem, Othman and McCarthy, 1981) with 'third culture' individuals. These persons and their networks are 'integrated' in the sense that we are using this term here, in that they identify with the particular society that they work and live in but at the same time also belong to a global social network which they respect and value. A very good example of this dual pattern of identification is the international scientific community.

Individual effects

In the preceding sections we have been considering the results of inter-group contact from a sociological perspective, particularly the varieties of changes in group structure and norms that may occur during and after contact. In the next section we will briefly describe the various alternative ways in which individuals respond to contact. Thus the analysis now shifts to the psychology of the individual caught up in a cross-cultural situation, the kinds of responses that individuals have been observed to make and the psychological effect of these different forms of accommodation on the individual as well as on the person's wider society. Four types of response styles describe most of the possibilities, though there may be exceptions, and in the present discussion these styles will be referred to as 'passing', chauvinist, marginal and mediating.

As noted earlier, the dependent variable that we regard as central in any study of second-culture influences is the change that may occur in people's ethnic identity. More precisely, the basic idea is that individuals exposed to multicultural influences, whether through birth or circumstances, can either become or resist becoming multicultural. Translated into the sorts of empirical questions that have been investigated in this area, we come up with the four response styles referred to above: (1) Often individuals, particularly in contact situations in which the second culture has a higher status, may reject their culture of origin and adopt the new culture, an effect that is sometimes referred to as 'passing'. (2) Occasionally, though, individuals, after coming into contact with a second culture, will reject those influences as alien, retreat back into their culture of origin and become militant nationalists and chauvinists. (3) A third response, also quite common, is for individuals to vacillate between their two cultures, feeling at home in neither, an effect that has been referred to as the 'marginal syndrome'. (4) Finally, some persons seem to be able to synthesize their various cultural identities, the equivalent of integration at the personal level, and acquire genuine bicultural or multicultural personalities. Such individuals are relatively rare, and Bochner has referred to them as 'mediating persons'.

Each of the response styles will now be described in greater detail, together with some evidence for the existence of each type of outcome.

'Passing'

This term was initially introduced into the literature in the 1930s, particularly in the United States, where among other things it referred to the 'passing' of light-skinned blacks into white society, that is blacks passing themselves off as whites. In its heyday, the process has been a major preoccupation of racists, demographers, novelists and some sociologists and psychologists. For instance, Stonequist (1937) devoted an entire chapter of *The Marginal Man* to 'passing'. In the contemporary literature, the word is no longer popular, but the idea persists. For instance, when writers talk about the acculturation or assimilation, say of migrants (e.g. Taft, 1973), they are in reality describing the 'passing' or attempted 'passing' of these individuals into the wider community. Thus there are many conceptual similarities between the constructs of passing and assimilation.

The problem has also arisen in a more practical way in connection with international education exchange schemes. There have been many instances of overseas students unwilling to return to their countries of origin after completing their studies abroad, due to having become acculturated to the society in which they attended university (Adams, 1968). A more subtle manifestation of the same process can be seen at work in those overseas-trained professionals who, after returning home, tackle the problems of their societies with the knowledge, techniques, values and solutions they acquired overseas, without any attempt to modify these foreign procedures to make them appropriate to the local culture. Alatas (1972, 1975), writing about South-east Asia, has called this phenomenon the 'captive mind' syndrome, which 'is the product of higher institutions of learning, either at home or abroad, whose way of thinking is dominated by western thought in an imitative and uncritical manner' (1975, p. 691).

Exaggerated chauvinism

There is ample evidence for the occurrence of a response that is the opposite of 'passing'. Some individuals react to second-culture influences by rejecting them, often in a fairly exaggerated manner, and become militant nationalists and chauvinists. There are probably as many western-educated professionals in Asia and Africa who detest the country in which they received their training as there are captive minds, if studies such as those by Morris (1960), Tajfel and Dawson (1965) and Terhune (1964) are representative. Similarly, there are quite a few studies in the area of race relations showing that it is not all that uncommon to find inter-group friction increasing directly with the amount of contact (cf. Amir's 1976 review; Bloom, 1971; Mitchell, 1968).

The marginal syndrome

As we indicated earlier, the notion of marginality was introduced to the literature by Park (1928) and Stonequist (1937). Despite some criticisms about how the concept should be formulated (e.g. Mann, 1973) there is little doubt about the widespread existence of this syndrome, although there is some argument as to whether marginality should be regarded as wholly noxious or whether there are some positive consequences stemming from being in a marginal position. We will return to this issue later in this book. Here we are concerned with the original formulation of this concept. Descriptively, it refers to those individuals who are members, or aspire to membership, of two racial or cultural groups which have mutually incompatible norms, values or entrance qualifications. Stonequist used the term 'marginal' to refer to the location of such individuals with respect to the two groups they wanted to belong to. According to Stonequist, since these people are unable to become full members of either group, they will find themselves on the margin of each. Unless they can resolve their conflict, marginal persons are doomed to vacillate between their two cultures, unable to satisfy the contradictory demands of their respective reference groups. Thus, according to Stonequist, the marginal syndrome has a noxious or at least stressful effect on those caught up in the conflict. There is certainly evidence to suggest that this may be true in some cases. For instance, one of the world's most famous marginal men, J. Nehru, wrote in his autobiography that 'I have become a queer mixture of the east and the west, out of place everywhere, at home nowhere . . . I am a stranger and alien in the west. I cannot be of it. But in my own country also, sometimes, I have an exile's feeling' (1936, p. 596).

However, there is also evidence to suggest that under some conditions, marginal men and women, due to their position in society, may become quite successful, by the usual ways in which success is measured, and may also adopt innovative and divergent social roles. It is quite possible, however, that these so-called marginal persons are really mediating men and women, the topic of the next section.

Mediating persons

The fourth category refers to those relatively rare individuals who respond to second-culture influences by selecting, combining and synthesizing the appropriate features of their respective social systems, without losing their cultural cores or 'myths' (Ritchie, 1981). Bochner (1981) has called such individuals mediating persons because they appear to have the capacity to act as links between different cultural systems. In particular, mediating persons bridge cultural gaps by introducing, translating, representing and reconciling the respective societies to each other.

Comment on the personal psychology of cross-cultural contact

Before concluding, it is appropriate to make several comments on the preceding discussion regarding the effects of cross-cultural contact on the individuals concerned. First, the process of becoming heterocultural (or resisting this change) has an analogy in the field of second-language learning (Taft, 1981). For instance, persons raised in a linguistically homogeneous environment will learn the language of that society as their first language. If they then study abroad in another country, or marry a person from another linguistic group, or emigrate to a distant land, they may or may not acquire a second, third or nth language, to varying criteria of competence, and in so doing may or may not forsake their first language. There are also people who start out in life with more than one language; they may be born into a multilingual society, as is the case in Switzerland, or they may be the offspring of mixed marriages, or they may be second-generation immigrants. Again, such bilinguals may or may not retain both their languages, learn further languages or gradually become monolingual in one of their tongues, shedding the others for practical or psychological reasons.

Second, the analogy between language acquisition and developing a heterocultural personality provides further support for the utility of the concept of culture-learning referred to earlier in this chapter. Given the close links that have been shown to exist between culture and language (cf. the reviews by Bickley, 1982, and Taft, 1981), there may well be parallels between the acquisition of a second language and becoming a multicultural person.

Third, leading on from the previous point, an unresolved issue in the area is the crucial question of what determines the various types of responses. Why do some individuals react to multicultural influences by becoming marginal while others become mediating persons; why do some become chauvinists while others attempt to 'pass' into the second culture? Most existing research is unable to answer these questions, except in a *post hoc* manner. Adopting a culture-learning/social-skills approach, which in turn draws on some of the principles of second-language acquisition, and combining these ideas with the social psychological model that underlies much of the discussion in this chapter, may lead to a better theoretical understanding of how and why different people react in the various ways that they do.

Finally, the various responses of individuals to culture contact share one important similarity with the group effects discussed earlier in this chapter. It will be recalled that we made the point that genocide, assimilation and segregation were pseudo-solutions to the problem of improving cross-cultural relations, since they simply did away with the contact altogether, and that only integration addresses the actual issue. The same point can be made about the first three types of psychological reactions to contact. Thus a person who 'passes' from one culture to another, or remains stubbornly monocultural even when bombarded with second-culture influences, has 'solved' the problem by evading it, by pretending that it does not exist. Marginal persons certainly know that they have a problem, but lack the strategies that would enable them to come up with a solution. Only the mediating response provides a genuine framework for the acquisition of multicultural responses, skills and self-perceptions.

Chapter summary

The topic of intercultural contact can be approached in four different ways. First, the material can be classified according to the different groups of persons who have been studied. Second, the contact experience can be analysed in terms of its constituent variables. Third, the effect of contact on the participating groups can be categorized. And fourth, how individuals respond to contact can be described. In the past, each of these approaches has been employed, and each has generated a large literature. A comprehensive view must combine all of these strands and also make explicit the assumption that all contact has two-way reciprocal consequences, with both parties affected by the interaction, although not necessarily to the same extent.

The major substantive areas of research have included international education, migration, international aid, international business, tourism, 'third' cultures and cross-cultural training. There is general consensus that cross-cultural contact is inherently stressful, but there is substantial disagreement about the nature and determinants of cross-cultural stress and how it might be alleviated. Earlier models were described as being pseudo-medical in assuming that those unable to cope with cross-cultural experiences had somehow broken down and required therapy and counselling. More recent models have likened cross-cultural exposure to a learning experience, ascribed cross-cultural stress to a lack of the appropriate social skills and based remedial action on preparation, orientation and social-skills training.

Another advantage of the culture-learning model is that it does not rely on the notion of 'adjusting' sojourners to a new culture, an idea that has undesirable clinical and ethnocentric overtones. The model also draws attention to the need for adequate social-support systems as contexts for culture-learning, particularly in the light of evidence that most sojourners are isolated in their daily lives from their host culture.

The constituent psychological elements of the contact experience were discussed in relation to some of the structural aspects of the societies that provide the behaviour settings for the contact. Thus the extent to which societies are internally culturally homogeneous or heterogeneous will have an important influence on the nature and quality of the contact experiences of its residents. Another variable is the salience of cultural diversity – the extent to which ethnic identification matters and is responded to. Similarly, the extent to which societies differ externally from each other will affect the relations between their members, the evidence suggesting that as the psychological distance between cultures increases, so will the difficulties experienced by newcomers attempting to accommodate to the host society.

The psychological variables that make up the contact experience include the territory on which the interaction takes place, the time-span of the interaction, its purpose, type of involvement, frequency of contact, degree of intimacy, relative status, numerical balance, the distinguishing characteristics of the participants, the expectations and dispensations connected with the social role of visitor/stranger, and the in-group/out-group differentiation, with its associated discrimination in favour of those classified as belonging to the in-group.

The outcome of contact on the participating groups can take one of four different forms: genocide, assimilation, segregation and integration. Only the last-mentioned form can be considered as a genuine attempt to solve the problem of harmonizing cross-cultural relations. Similarly, the effect of contact on the participating individuals can also take one of four different forms: 'passing', exaggerated chauvinism, marginality and cultural mediation. These four different styles reflect changes in the individual's ethnic identity as a consequence of exposure to second-culture influences. Only the mediational response will lead to the acquisition of multicultural skills.

Learning a second culture, or 'forgetting' one's first, is rather like learning a language or letting a language fall into disuse. Finally, the determinants of the various response-styles of intercultural contact are not yet fully understood, but a model that combines a culture-learning with a social-skills approach seems to hold some promise in providing an account of this problem.

3 Motives and definitions: reasons for, and consequences of, geographic movement

Introduction

A convenient starting point from which to begin the study of psychological reactions to unfamiliar environments is to consider what motivates people to travel in the first place. Human motivation as an area of research has attracted psychologists from many different research traditions for a number of years (Weiner, 1980), yet it is not an easy topic to study. Motives are often complex, having biological, psychological and cultural determinants. Furthermore, stressful behaviours may be the result of a host of complementary and competing motives, which are often difficult to disentangle.

From a methodological point of view the study of social motives is limited because of the unreliability of self-report (for a review of the literature on the relationship between verbal self-reports and behaviour, see Bochner, 1980). There are numerous reasons why people will not or cannot report on their true motives: there may be memorial or other response biases which distort reports of past behaviour; subjects may be loath to admit to researchers their real reasons and motives for travel, particularly if these conflict with official stated or funded reasons; also, as many clinicians have pointed out, people often cannot, even if they want to, report on their motives for various actions, particularly in the area of social motivation (Atkinson, 1958). Despite these difficulties, researchers have attempted to describe the motives of cultural travellers and link them systematically to different patterns of coping with culture stress.

The motives for travel will be discussed under headings which correspond with various chapters in Part II. The motives of tourists and business people, students and voluntary workers, and migrants, respectively, will now be considered.

The motives of tourists and business people

According to Pearce (1982a), research into the motives of tourists poses various problems. First, it is wrong to regard tourist motivation as a short-term process isolated from the rest of a person's activities and concerns. People often plan and work for their holidays far in advance of the actual event and apparently derive as much satisfaction from this planning as they do from the travelling itself. Furthermore, the decision to go to a particular place, for a particular time, with particular associates cannot be separated from the wider, long-standing motivation of individuals.

Second, there is the problem associated with whether motives are measured before, during or after travel. There are numerous reasons for supposing that motives recorded before travelling, in order to predict specific reactions to specific places, are rather different from a *post hoc* descriptive account of travel motivation, which is usually more general. Other difficulties stem from the belief that travel is supposed to be intrinsically satisfying, and hence motivations that are offered are often tautological.

In his analysis Pearce (1982a) draws on several theoretical areas – including the hierarchy of needs, attribution theory and achievement motivation – to account for tourist motivation. For instance, it is suggested that the motives of tourists may be linked to their level on Maslow's (1966) hierarchy of needs. Thus some may travel to fulfil needs for love and belongingness, others to achieve higher self-esteem and still others to 'self-actualize' themselves. Alternatively, one's need for achievement may dictate to what extent travel may be used as pure 'time-out', relaxation or an opportunity to better oneself materially and mentally. Pearce reviews two studies that have used this perspective to account for tourist motivation. Dann (1977) has distinguished between two types of tourists: those wishing to escape and 'get away from it all' in order to reduce the feelings of anomie prevalent in many western cultures, and those primarily in pursuit of 'ego-enhancement'. From data collected in Barbados, he concluded that anomie tourists were married and middle class while ego-enhancers were of lower socio-economic status, female and older. The former, he suggested, needed to feel they belong to a caring, integrated, emotionally rewarding community, while the latter needed an elevated social position and power. Despite obvious problems with this study, it does highlight the very different motives of different groups travelling on holiday to the same place.

Crompton (1979) has offered a fairly comprehensive analysis of the motives for tourism. From both a review of the previous literature and an empirical study, he identified nine motives for a 'pleasure vacation'. Seven of these motives were classified as *socio-psychological* and included escape from a perceived mundane environment, exploration and evaluation of self, relaxation, prestige, regression, enhancement of kinship relationships and facilitation of social interaction. Two of the motives were labelled *cultural* and include novelty and education. Whereas the socio-psychological motives were unrelated to attributes of the destination, the cultural motives were related, at least partially. The actual destination served only as a medium through which these various psychological needs could be satisfied. Methodologically, Crompton noted that the interviews caused many of the thirty-nine respondents to confront for the first time their 'real motives' for going on holiday. Crompton noted that his study may have implications for destination promotion and market segmentation.

Cohen (1979) derived various motives for travel after making a distinction between five modes of tourism: recreational, diversionary, experiential, experimental and existential. Each of these is quite different and presupposes different destinations, activities and adaptations.

In contrast to market research, a psychological perspective leads to the view that tourists are not motivated by specific factors associated with their destination (beaches, hotel facilities, arranged amusements) but rather by the broad suitability of a place to meet particular psychological needs:

> Conceptualizing holiday destinations, according to their capacity to fit human needs, may produce some strange and novel mental maps of travel destinations. Instead of distance, culture and climate being used to classify destinations, one can envisage clusters of vacation centres which are predominantly self-exploratory, or social interaction, or indeed sexual arousal and excitement. (Pearce, 1982a, p. 65)

The motives for travel are imperfectly understood, complex and manifold. In specific instances, however, where they are known, they may easily account for how and why tourists experience their holiday as fulfilling, pleasant, relaxing; or tiring, disappointing and aggravating. Often no amount or type of travelling can satisfy the desires of some travellers (for self-actualization, enlightenment, etc.) while many holiday destinations make promises of facilities and activities that may appear to, but cannot, fulfil certain needs.

Whereas there is limited psychological research on tourists' travel motives, there is even less on the motives of business people moving from one locale to another. While the reasons for companies posting their employees to foreign places may be fairly easy to understand (Torbiorn, 1982) the motives of individual business persons moving abroad and back again remains relatively unexplored territory. It is generally assumed such moves are simply motivated by economic rewards (Bartel, 1979), yet, as Torbiorn (1982) found in his study of Swedish business people, the motives were much more complex than this. He found both 'push' or negative motives relating to dissatisfaction and 'pull' or positive motives relating to a belief in increased satisfaction being associated with the move. Pull motives included a special interest in the particular host country, increased promotion prospects, wider career opportunities or generally more favourable economic conditions. Torbiorn found some evidence for his thesis that positive rather than negative, and greater rather than lesser freedom in choosing the host country, was associated with higher levels of adaptation and satisfaction.

Motives of students and volunteer workers

Why do students go abroad to study? There is no dearth of opinion on this topic, but very little empirical evidence. As part of a major study in which sixty-nine returned students were interviewed in their homeland after the completion of their overseas sojourn, Bochner (1973) asked the respondents why they had accepted their respective scholarships and what they had hoped to get out of the experience. The subjects, all of whom had earned a higher degree in the United States, were 27 Thais, 16 Pakistanis and 26 Philippine respondents, and the interviews were conducted in Bangkok, Karachi and Manila, respectively. Several measures of motivation were used, some direct and others indirect. Of special interest in the present context were the responses to the question: What was your main reason for going abroad to study? The answers were coded into four categories: get a degree; gain academic or professional expertise; culture-learning; and personal development. Of the sixty-nine responses, sixty-four (93 per cent) fell into the first two categories. Only two of the students said that their main reason was culture-learning, and three (all from the Philippines) listed personal development (e.g. to gain insight, to become better people, to find themselves) as their main purpose. Other questions yielded a similar pattern. More recently, in a study of 2536 foreign students in ten different countries by Klineberg and Hull (1979), 71 per cent of the respondents said that obtaining a degree or diploma was important, and again the acquisition of qualifications and experience ranked as the single most important reason for going to a foreign university.

Thus there is no doubt that the overwhelming majority of foreign students are primarily interested in getting a degree and/or professional training rather than learning a second culture or achieving personal growth. Uppermost in their minds are concerns about the tangible pay-offs a sojourn might provide in the shape of career advancement, prestige and upward mobility. Indeed, it would be remarkable if this were not the case, given the amount of dislocation and hardship involved in an educational sojourn abroad.

However, as some observers have noted (Bochner, 1979; Bochner, Lin and McLeod, 1979), there is a discrepancy between the motives of the students participating in educational exchange, and the concerns of those persons and organizations which administer, fund and sponsor the participants. Although there are substantial numbers of private students in the system, a great many of the sojourners are sponsored by various governments, foundations and international agencies (Bochner and Wicks, 1972), and even the so-called private students do not fully pay their way, particularly in countries where tertiary students are not charged fees. Thus, since the taxpayer is deeply involved in contemporary international education, there arose a need to justify it to the public. To that end there has emerged a curious alliance between the idealists who see international education as a way of solving some if not all of the world's ills, and the pragmatic politicians who represent overseas-student programmes as being in the national interest, usually as an extension of foreign policy (Bochner and Wicks, 1972) and who use their advocacy for educational exchange to get themselves re-elected (e.g. Fulbright, 1976). Neither assumption is supported by a great deal of empirical evidence, that is sponsoring foreign students is not a very efficient way of solving the world's problems, nor of conducting foreign policy, but that has not deterred governments from continuing to commit extensive funds to international education; which is just as well, since otherwise a great many young people would have been denied access to higher learning. It is interesting to examine why there is almost unanimous support for educational exchange, despite its somewhat flimsy empirical foundations.

The idealists regard it as self-evident that educational exchange must lead to improved international relations. They take it for granted that cross-cultural contact, particularly among young people, creates mutual understanding, and when these students in the fullness of time assume positions of influence in their societies, this will be reflected in harmonious relations between their respective countries, and thus contribute to world peace. The evidence reviewed elsewhere in this book, both with regard to the contact hypothesis in general (Amir, 1969, 1976; Cook and Selltiz, 1955) as well as its application in the area of host–foreign student relationships, indicates that the connection between inter-group contact and inter-group attitudes is very complex, such that contact may either increase or reduce mutual tolerance and understanding, depending on a very large matrix of interacting variables. Indeed, as we saw, there have been instances where educational exchange has led to a worsening of cross-cultural attitudes (Tajfel and Dawson, 1965), a proposition that many people find difficult to accept and therefore tend to ignore.

The politicians likewise assume that foreign students will return home full of good-will for their erstwhile hosts, thus making them easier targets for subsequent influence. Often too, educational exchange is seen as a part of economic aid (Bochner and Wicks, 1972), the idea being that the skills that the students acquire abroad will be used to further the economic and technical development of their countries, thereby reducing hunger and poverty, creating markets and promoting stability in the regions concerned. Although, no doubt, these objectives have at times been achieved, such results are not inevitable or, for that matter, necessarily desirable (Bochner, 1979). Thus some foreign students return home with an abiding hatred for the country in which they sojourned (Tajfel and Dawson, 1965). Not all students return home, giving rise to the notion of a brain drain (Adams, 1968) or the tendency of the brightest students to emigrate, usually to the country where they had studied. Sometimes students return home so imbued with the notion of the superiority of the technology they acquired abroad that they set about applying these techniques, solutions and practices in an unthinking and inappropriate way, making no attempt to adapt what they have brought back with them to conform to local cultural requirements (Alatas, 1972, 1975), sometimes with disastrous results (Boxer, 1969; Mortimer, 1973). Sometimes, also, the students use their overseas qualifications to improve their own conditions at the expense of those who were not able to go abroad; to exploit their countrymen on behalf of foreign interests (Curle, 1970; Wade, 1975); and in extreme instances, perpetuate repressive social systems that lack humanity and equity. None of this should be taken to suggest that we in any way oppose international education. Study abroad can be justified on intrinsic grounds, as increasing humankind's sum total of furnished minds (although whether there are any votes in that idea is debatable). However, there is a need to evaluate the various programmes and describe their actual rather than their assumed or intended effects. Such research is almost non-existent, partly because of the enormous methodological and logistical problems involved, but also because, on the one hand, the benefits of educational exchange are seen to be self-evident and hence not in need of scrutiny and, on the other hand, because many educational exchange programmes have become identified with the conduct of a country's foreign policy, so that investigators in this area have to contend with an uncooperative or hostile establishment. After all, if educational exchange did not exist, governments would have to invent it. How else would they suitably commemorate a visit by a royal personage or a head of state, sweeten a trade treaty, show concern for the poor and disadvantaged of this world or signal an indication of good-will towards a previously ignored or maligned nation? There are literally thousands of fellowships and scholarships which have been conceived under such circumstances, and the authors as well as many people reading this book have or will at some time in the future travel to distant places under their auspices. It is highly unlikely that the motives of the sojourners will coincide fully with the objectives of those who established these schemes. Incidentally, this is another reason why evaluation in this area is so difficult, because the criterion variables shift according to whether the objectives are regarded from the perspective of the donor/sponsor, the incumbent, the recipient nation, the region or the global community. However, such complexities do not preclude making these various considerations explicit, examining their desirability and evaluating the extent to which the various goals are realized. We are not aware of any research which has tackled this problem in such a systematic way.

The motivation of Peace Corps Volunteers

An examination of the motives of Peace Corps Volunteers (PCVs) also reveals some complexities and contradictions. In a study of the first four groups of trainees (about 300 individuals) Guthrie (1966) reports that about 80 per cent evinced interests closely resembling those of the typical social worker. When interviewed, they freely acknowledged that they had joined the Peace Corps because they wanted to do something significant and because they had not found a satisfying career at home. At the same time, many of these individuals brought with them highly unrealistic notions as to what they could achieve, how quickly they could solve the problems of the region in which they served or what tangible results could be expected from their work.

Although it is customary to refer to the Peace Corps as if it were an entity, it really consisted of three sub-groups, each with its own particular aims, values and standards, not equally shared by each group. In addition to the PCVs in the field, there was the Peace Corps/Washington staff subculture, and the Overseas Representative staff subculture. The primary aim of the Washington organization was to gain and expand domestic political acceptance of the Peace Corps, to administer its day-to-day operations within the framework of a civil-service bureaucracy and to develop effective new overseas programmes. The officials in Washington saw themselves as accountable to the politicians from whom they derived their budgets, authority and power. In contrast, the volunteers in the field regarded themselves to be in the business of communicating and co-operating with the local people and striving for goals consistent with indigenous concerns. The success of the Volunteers was judged according to how well they were able to bridge the gap between their own culture and that of the people whom they were assisting. Finally, the job of the Local Representatives was to establish administrative and communication links between Washington and the Volunteers, and provide logistical and other support for the workers in the field. Local Representatives were in a particularly difficult position, because the standards which Washington used to gauge their per-formance were sometimes quite different from those employed by the Volunteers. In addition, staff members were usually older, had dis-tinguished themselves in their professions and enjoyed a relatively high income. In contrast, the Volunteers were young, received no salary (they were paid an allowance geared to the cost of living in the host country) and for many of them their transcultural experience was their first adult job. The Washington staffers differed from the Overseas Representatives in being more career orientated, who in turn were much more career orientated than the Volunteers. Nevertheless, according to Textor (1966), despite all these differences, the three subcultures all shared one overriding value, namely that the most important thing that one can do in one's job is to facilitate the success of the Volunteers in the field. Textor suggests that this unifying ethic was one of the major reasons for the success of the Peace Corps programmes. Nevertheless, the tensions in that organization parallel the discrepancies in motives that occur in overseas-student programmes.

The general conclusion to be drawn is that the motives and concerns of sojourners cannot be assumed to coincide with the motives and concerns of those who set up and direct these programmes. Although we have illustrated this proposition with reference to overseas students and PCVs (because there is direct evidence in these two areas to draw on) we suspect that the same tensions occur with respect to most categories of sojourners. Since such conflicts may impede the process of culture-learning and accommodation, this relatively neglected aspect of the sojourn process deserves more attention than is generally accorded to it, both in regard to research concerning its extent and effects, as well as in establishing procedures to contain its impact.

Motives for migration

The topic of migration has interested historians, geographers, sociologists and many others for a long time. Peterson (1958) has categorized types of migration, and these are given in Table 3.1.

Despite the voluminous literature in this area, there is little information regarding people's motives to migrate. Most studies have concentrated on the demographic, historical or structural variables of migration and from these have made certain assumptions about motives. Ghosts of economic determinism abound in this literature, yet study after study has shown that although economic factors are important, people are not simply economic maximizers (Lansing and Mueller, 1967).

Taylor (1966) has suggested that one needs to know a number of factors about an individual's *subjective perception* of his or her home place of residence in order to understand the motives for migration – that is, the degrees of structural 'conductiveness' or strain at the place of origin and the person's evaluation of it; the presence of long- or short-term aspirations; feelings of alienation and dislocation; objective feasibility of migration as a project; and trigger factors which spur a decision. Naamary (1971) has suggested that the predisposition to migrate is a function of the relative deprivation of full employment opportunities, educational facilities, health facilities, social and community ties, housing facilities and climate. Others have also put stress on the idea of place

Table 3.1 Peterson's general typology of migration

	Migratory force	Class of migration	Type of Migration	
			Conservative	*Innovating*
Nature and man	Ecological push	Primitive	Wandering Ranging	Flight from the land
State (or equivalent) and man	Migration policy	Forced Impelled	Displacement Flight	Slave trade Coolie trade
Man and his norms	Higher aspirations	Free	Group	Pioneer
Collective behaviour	Social momentum	Mass	Settlement	Urbanization

Source: W. Peterson, 'A general typology of migration', *American Sociological Review*, 23 (1958), 266.

utility – subjective evaluations of the composite utilities (goods, services, benefits) derived from alternative (i.e. home versus foreign) places (Wolpert, 1965; Brown and Holmes, 1971). That is, people rationally weigh up the advantages and disadvantages of different places before deciding whether to migrate.

Sociologists and anthropologists, on the other hand, have stressed the importance of kinship ties in migration.

In a critical review of the predominantly economic, geographic and sociological literature Shaw (1975) concluded that:

> just as it is important to consider the socio-demographic and socio-economic elements in questions concerning 'Who are the migrants?' and 'Why did they migrate?', it is important also to consider the influence of culture-systems components (including ideological commitments), personality systems (including the individual's aspirations, identity, integrity, role performance), social-system components (including socialization practices) and levels of stress in the system. (p. 116)

Various attempts have also been made by social psychologists over the years to study the motives of migrants in moving from one country to another. What is perhaps most disappointing about this literature is its simple-minded, a-theoretical nature. While it may be that early periods of migration were less complex motivationally than they are today, current studies on migrant motivation still remain too simplistically conceived and executed to capture the complexity of a migrant's motives.

Turner (1949) investigated the attitudes, motives and personal characteristics of migrants in a medium-sized American city. He found that his respondents gave essentially four sets of reasons for their migration: economic or job considerations; the influence of friends or relatives; standard-of-living considerations; and other, miscellaneous reasons, such as to retire.

A number of studies have been done on migration to Australasia (Brown, 1959, 1960; Richardson, 1974). Brown (1960) found immigrants to New Zealand provided five types of explanation for their decision to migrate: personal reasons (a new life, travel experience), the appeal of New Zealand, a dislike of England, job opportunities and other miscellaneous reasons. However, the author did notice some dissonance reduction: 'When a favourable attitude to the destination is formulated, other destinations are systematically undervalued' (p. 173). Richardson (1974) has done an extensive psycho-social study of British immigrants to Australia. He looked at people's decisions to emigrate as well as specific factors which he labelled 'opportunity', 'personality', 'precipitating' and 'bolstering'.

Whereas most studies have looked at the more common experience of migration from less to more developed countries (or between countries of equal development), there have also been studies of why people migrate from more to less developed countries. Berman (1979) followed up Antonovsky and Katz's (1979) study on why North Americans migrate to Israel, and found six major reasons: Zionism (identification as a Zionist); Jewishness (to lead a fuller Jewish religious life); attraction to life in Israel (interesting, less hectic, sense of community); family reasons (for raising children); dissatisfaction with North America (crime, anti-Semitism) and personal reasons. The typical migrants are thus in search of Jewishness and see Israel as a good rich environment for the expression of their and their children's Jewish identity.

Many writers have distinguished between factors that *push* and *pull* people to emigrate from one country and immigrate to another (Rossi, 1955). However, most researchers have commented on the problems of this simplified distinction. For instance, Brown (1960) wrote, 'It should be pointed out, however, that this model is an oversimplification because the relationship between pushes and pulls is complex, with each of these forces interacting and having both positive and negative components' (p. 168); and Berman (1979) said:

The difficulty of conceptually separating 'push' and 'pull' motives for migration has been acknowledged in the literature. Motives can reflect both 'push' and 'pull' elements. For example, if poor job opportunities in the country of origin were a reason to move, then better opportunities in the new country would likely to be a correlate. (p. 143)

Nearly all of the psychological studies of migration have been concerned with immigrants' reasons or motives for leaving one country (usually the country of their birth) and choosing another country. However, almost no research appears to have been done on the native inhabitants' beliefs about the immigration and emigration. This is surprising given the widespread social and political debate on immigration in Britain and other developed countries. And although immigration is a much discussed topic, emigration is practically ignored even though, for instance, as many people leave Britain as enter it. Thus, between 1961 and 1971 nearly 500,000 *more* people *left* Britain than entered, yet this topic has remained very little researched in that country (Sillitoe, 1973).

Furthermore, very little research has been done on the difference between natives' and immigrants' explanations for or beliefs about immigration. Studies from a social-attribution framework in other, but related, areas (Furnham, 1982) suggest that different social, cultural or political perspectives lead people to make different attributions for political or economic phenomena. Older people, and those from a more conservative background, are more likely to explain the motives of migrants in negative, selfish terms, while younger, less conservative natives would explain immigration in more positive terms.

Furnham (1986a) has attempted to apply attribution theory to a study of migrants' and non-migrants' explanations for immigration to and emigration from Britain. Not surprisingly, he found striking differences in the explanations native Britons offered for people leaving or coming to Britain as migrants (Table 3.2). People believed that the most important motives for *both* immigration and emigration were personal advancement and better job opportunities. Overall there seemed to be five factors or types of explanations for both immigration and emigration – four 'pull' factors (destination's culture and values, high standard of living, benefits of the welfare state and improved quality of life) and one 'push' factor (political and economic reasons). Furnham (1986a) has noted that the acceptance of immigrants may depend partly upon whether it is believed that they come for cultural or family reasons rather than to benefit from the welfare state. Thus the study of natives' perceptions of migrants' motives may be as important as the study of the migrants' motives themselves, for an understanding of how, when and why migrant groups do or do not adapt to the native culture.

In summary, research into the motives of migrants needs to take into account three issues. First, it must be recognized that there exist various types of migration, such as internal versus international; voluntary

Table 3.2 Means and F levels for the explanations for people either immigrating to or emigrating from Britain

Explanations	Immigration	Emigration	F levels
There are better job opportunities here/there.	2.24	1.67	23.62***
They want to join other members of their family already here/there.	2.27	2.94	23.02***
They were suffering from political oppression at home.	3.39	5.59	183.90***
Their previous living conditions were very poor.	2.48	4.18	115.57***
They believe that there is greater political freedom in —.	2.78	4.83	159.26***
They admire — values and culture.	4.81	3.50	59.95***
They believe that the prospects for personal advancement are better.	1.93	1.77	1.91
There are better educational and cultural opportunities here/there.	2.69	3.59	31.77***
They want to provide a more secure future for their family.	2.52	2.26	3.55
They want to benefit from our social-security system.	4.22	5.50	52.03***
They had poor access to places of interest/amusement at home.	5.02	5.00	0.02
They will have a much higher standard of living here/there.	2.93	2.00	45.67***
They believe that — has a better climate.	6.02	2.54	566.78***
They like the tolerant attitude of the — towards foreigners.	4.96	4.18	21.54***
Their ancestors come from — originally.	5.21	4.71	8.17**
They will get free education and health services here/there.	3.40	5.06	89.32***
They believe that life is more exciting in —.	4.93	2.61	233.33***
They prefer to live in less crowded countries.	5.32	3.59	99.85***
They have been encouraged by advertising to come here/there.	4.92	3.44	73.12***
They hope to marry someone from — and acquire citizenship.	4.66	5.35	14.90***

Notes: The numbers represent the mean score on a 7-point important–unimportant scale. The — refers to Britain in the case of immigration and 'another country' in the case of emigration. *** p < .001   ** p < .01   * p < .05
Source: A. Furnham, 'Explanations for immigration to and emigration from Britain', *New Community* (1986a)

versus forced; legal versus illegal; and permanent versus temporary. To talk of motives for migration in general is misleading as the motives vary with the type of migration. Second, economic determinism and a rational calculus will not suffice to explain motives for migration. People do not, indeed cannot, simply work out a balance sheet between positive and negative economic, political and life-style factors. People decide to migrate for a variety of reasons. For instance, they might be urged into working abroad by a domineering parent; they may feel the need to follow a close family member whose decision to migrate was highly whimsical; there may be powerful religious or political motives for migration which override all other considerations. Third, every country has an immigration policy which may inhibit or encourage particular types of migration. Immigration decisions and policies may be based on population requirements, economic and political considerations or humanitarian principles, all of which would encourage some migrants while making it practically impossible for others. Further, the official policy of government may be quite different from what is actually implemented. Consequently, the motives to migrate are often shaped by others both in the migrants' countries of origin and destination.

Motivation to migrate, therefore, should not be conceived of merely in individualistic terms. The decision to migrate is shaped by many people, including family, friends and employers, their access to information, and the various policies of the countries to which one might migrate.

Definitions and typologies

The title of this book – *Culture Shock* – warrants some discussion. This section sets out to look at how anthropologists, psychologists and sociologists have used the term 'culture shock'. Then the concept of 'mental health', as it appears in the migration and mental-health literature, will be briefly reviewed.

Culture shock: the shock of the new

The culture shock 'hypothesis' or 'concept' implies that the experience of a new culture is an unpleasant surprise or shock, partly because it is unexpected and partly because it may lead to a negative evaluation of one's own culture. Like the related concepts of 'jet-lag' and 'alienation', 'culture shock' is a term used by the lay person to explain, or at least label, some of the more unpleasant consequences of travel. However, like a lot of pseudo-psychological jargon (e.g. 'nervous breakdown'), it is more of a generic expression connoting much and signifying little – a term which in attempting to explain all, fails to explain a great deal.

The anthropologist Oberg (1960) is the first to have used the term. In a brief and largely anecdotal article, he mentions at least six aspects of culture shock:

1. *Strain* due to the effort required to make necessary psychological adaptations.
2. *A sense of loss* and *feelings of deprivation* in regard to friends, status, profession and possessions.
3. Being *rejected* by/and or rejecting members of the new culture.
4. *Confusion* in role, role expectations, values, feelings and self-identity.
5. *Surprise, anxiety*, even *disgust* and *indignation* after becoming aware of cultural differences.
6. *Feelings of impotence* due to not being able to cope with the new environment.

The flavour of Oberg's observations may be gathered from this quote:

Culture shock is precipitated by the anxiety that results from losing all our familiar signs and symbols of social intercourse. These signs or cues include the thousand and one ways in which we orient ourselves to the situations of daily life: when to shake hands and what to say when we meet people, when and how to give tips, how to give orders to servants, how to make purchases, when to accept and when to refuse invitations, when to take statements seriously and when not. Now these cues which may be words, gestures, facial expressions, customs, or norms are acquired by all of us in the course of growing up and are as much a part of our culture as the language we speak or the beliefs we accept. All of us depend for our peace of mind and our efficiency on hundreds of these cues, most of which we are not consciously aware. . . .

    Some of the symptoms of culture shock are: excessive washing of the hands; excessive concern over drinking water, food, dishes, and bedding; fear of physical contact with attendants or servants; the absent-minded, far-away stare (sometimes called 'the tropical stare'); a feeling of helplessness and a desire for dependence on long-term residents of one's own nationality; fits of anger over delays and other minor frustrations; delay and outright refusal to learn the language of the host country; excessive fear of being cheated, robbed, or injured; great concern over minor pains and irruptions of the skin; and finally, that terrible longing to be back home, to be able to have a good cup of coffee and a piece of apple pie, to walk into that corner drugstore, to visit one's relatives, and, in general, to talk to people who really make sense. (Oberg, 1960, p. 176)

Cleveland et al. (1960) offered a similar analysis relying heavily on the personal experience of travellers, especially those at two extremes of the adaptation continuum, individuals who act as if they had 'never left home' and those who immediately 'go native'. These two extremes are well described, but the various possible 'intermediate' reactions are not considered.

Researchers since Oberg have seen culture shock as a normal reaction, as part of the routine process of adaptation to cultural stress and the manifestation of a longing for a more predictable, stable and understandable environment.

Others have attempted to improve and extend Oberg's definition and concept of culture shock. Guthrie (1975) has used the term *culture fatigue*, Smalley (1963) *language shock*, Byrnes (1966) *role shock* and Ball-Rokeach (1973) *pervasive ambiguity*. In doing so, different researchers have simply placed the emphasis on slightly different problems – language, physical irritability, role ambiguity – rather than actually helping to specify how or why or when different people do or do not experience culture shock.

Bock (1970) has described culture shock as primarily an emotional reaction that follows from not being able to understand, control and predict another's behaviour. When customary categories of experience no longer seem relevant or applicable, people's usual behaviour changes to becoming 'unusual'. Lack of familiarity with both the physical setting (design of homes, shops, offices) as well as the social environment (etiquette, ritual) have this effect, as do the experiences with and use of time (Hall, 1959). This theme is reiterated by all the writers in the field (e.g. Lundstedt, 1963; Hays, 1972) – culture shock is a stress reaction where salient psychological and physical rewards are generally uncertain and hence difficult to control or predict. Thus a person is anxious, confused and apparently apathetic until he or she has had time to develop a new set of cognitive constructs to understand and enact the appropriate behaviour.

Writers about culture shock have often referred to individuals' lacking points of reference, social norms and rules to guide their actions and understand others' behaviour. This is very similar to the attributes studied under the heading of *alienation* and *anomie*, which include powerlessness, meaninglessness, normlessness, self- and social estrangement and social isolation (Seeman, 1959). There appears to be a connection between the concepts of culture shock, alienation and anomie.

In addition, ideas associated with *anxiety* pervade the culture-shock literature. Observers have pointed to a continuous general 'free-floating' anxiety which affects normal behaviour. Lack of self-confidence, distrust of others and mild psychosomatic complaints are also common (May, 1970). Furthermore, people appear to lose their inventiveness and spontaneity and become obsessively concerned with orderliness (Nash, 1967).

Central to the concept of shock are questions about how people adapt to it, and how they are changed by it. Hence there exists an extensive literature on the U-curve, the W-curve and the inverted U-curve (see

Ch. 5), referring to the adjustment of sojourners over time. Many (e.g. Torbiorn, 1982) are happy to interpret their data in terms of these curves, although there is a debate in the literature about the validity of this approach (Church, 1982).

Most of the investigations of culture shock have been descriptive, in that they have attempted to list the various difficulties that sojourners experience and their typical reactions. Less attention has been paid to explaining who will find the shock more or less intense (e.g. the old or the less educated); what determines which reaction a person is likely to experience; how long they remain in a period of shock, and so forth. The literature suggests that all people will suffer culture shock to some extent, which is always thought of as being unpleasant and stressful. This assumption needs to be empirically supported. In theory some people need not experience any negative aspects of shock; instead they may seek out these experiences for their enjoyment. Sensation-seekers, for instance, might be expected not to suffer any adverse effects but to enjoy the highly arousing stimuli of the unfamiliar (Zuckerman, 1981). However, it is likely that their numbers are very small.

For instance, Adler (1975) and David (1971) have stated that although culture shock is most often associated with negative consequences, it may, in mild doses, be important for self-development and personal growth. Culture shock is seen as a transitional experience which can result in the adoption of new values, attitudes and behaviour patterns:

> In the encounter with another culture the individual gains new experiential knowledge by coming to understand the roots of his or her own ethnocentrism and by gaining new perspectives and outlooks on the nature of culture. . . Paradoxically, the more one is capable of experiencing new and different dimensions of human diversity, the more one learns of oneself. (Adler, 1975, p. 22)

Thus, although different writers have put emphases on different aspects of culture shock, there is, by and large, agreement that exposure to new cultures is stressful. Fewer researchers have seen the positive side of culture shock either for those individuals who revel in exciting and different environments or for those whose initial discomfiture leads to personal growth.

Defining 'mental health' as it relates to migration

There are numerous problems both in the definition of mental health and in the definition of migration. Definitional problems are, however, not unique to the social sciences. For instance, studies may not be directly comparable if different definitions, nosologies or measures are used. These differences may account for the numerous contradictory findings in this intriguing but frustrating literature. Indeed, the different definitions may also give a clue as to why mental illness has come to be associated with migration, because sometimes the 'different' behaviour patterns (dress, non-verbal behaviour, food preferences, sense of time, etc.) of migrants compared with natives make them look as if they are mentally disturbed.

To consider the relationship between mental health and migration requires some agreement as to the meaning and measurement of mental health. There is a long-standing debate in psychiatry concerning the effect of culture on mental health and the definition of 'mental health'. On the one extreme are the absolutists who argue that mental illnesses, like physical illnesses, are found in all cultures, though possibly at slightly different rates. This group uses standard western nosologies and cites as evidence studies which have found a similar range and incidence of symptoms in rural Third World countries as in urban western countries (Kapur et al. 1974). On the other hand, there are the relativists who accuse the above of psychiatric imperialism and argue that some mental illnesses which are common in one culture (i.e. depression, schizophrenia) do not exist in the same form (symptoms, language) in others (Marsella, 1979). There is a rich and vigorous debate concerning the relationship between race, culture and mental disorder which cannot be considered here (Yap, 1951; Rack, 1982). This issue is discussed at length by Draguns (1980).

There is an equally extensive and complicated literature on the diagnosis of mental illness. Rack (1982) has considered in some depth the cultural pitfalls in the recognition (diagnosis and hospitalization) of depression and anxiety, mania, schizophrenia, paranoia and hysteria.

Table 3.3 presents a nosological diagram which attempts to spell out the type and regularity of the diagnoses made in Britain. The evidence suggests that the incidence, cause, diagnosis and treatment of mental health varies significantly across cultures. Hence the measurement of mental health in two different cultures may not be strictly comparable. It is well known, for instance, that the chances of being diagnosed schizophrenic in America are much higher than in Britain (Draguns, 1980).

A great deal of the mental health and migration literature relies on mental hospital admission statistics, which are notably weak. Cochrane (1983) has pointed out the various stages in becoming admitted to a mental hospital. Table 3.4 explains why a (possibly very large) number of people never get admitted to mental hospitals. There are many cross-cultural studies on different patterns of somaticization and help-seeking behaviour in different cultures (Cheung and Lan, 1982). The figures that are available may be misleading because inpatient statistics give no clue about the range, amount or type of outpatients; admission is largely dictated by the number of beds available; the data are aggregated and give no idea of degree of distress; many confounding variables are not reported, and so on. It is because of these difficulties that community

Table 3.3 Rack's nosological diagram for psychiatric diagnosis in Britain

	Depression	*Excitement*	*Schizophrenia*
ENDOGENOUS Biological, genetic factors. Stress not primary cause.	1 *'Endogenous depression'* (psychotic depression). Recognized in all cultures, but symptoms may differ.	3 *'Mania'*. Recognized in all cultures. Less common than depression.	5 *'Schizophrenia'*. Probably exists everywhere.
REACTIVE Response to stress, conflict, 'neurotic' rather than 'psychotic'.	2 *'Reactive depression'*. Common in Britain. In other cultures may be regarded as not being a 'medical' problem.	4 *'Reactive excitation'* ('reactive mania'). Rare among British but well known elsewhere. Psychogenic psychoses.	6 *'Acute schiz-ophreniform stress reaction'*
HYSTERICAL Motivated, attention-seeking.	7 (E.g. many cases of 'parasuicide'.) Common in Britain. Rare in some other cultures.	8 Varieties of *'Hysterical madness'* (hysterical pseudo-psychosis). Uncommon among British. More common in non-European cultures.	9

Source: P. Rack, *Race, Culture and Mental Disorder*, London, Tavistock, 1982.

surveys properly conducted with sensitive instruments and representative random samples present a better picture of the true rate of mental illness. Pope (1983) was particularly interested in the relation between migration and manic-depressive illnesses. His interest arose from the seemingly discrepant findings that pre- and actual schizophrenics migrate more often than others, and yet migration is a stressful and complicated

Table 3.4 Stages in becoming admitted to a mental hospital

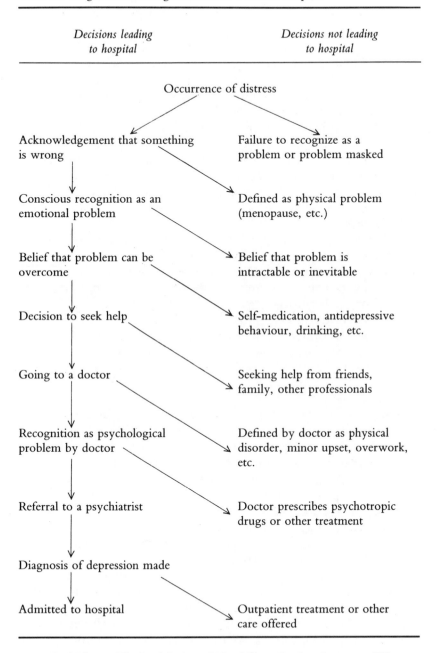

Decisions leading to hospital	*Decisions not leading to hospital*
Occurrence of distress	
Acknowledgement that something is wrong	Failure to recognize as a problem or problem masked
Conscious recognition as an emotional problem	Defined as physical problem (menopause, etc.)
Belief that problem can be overcome	Belief that problem is intractable or inevitable
Decision to seek help	Self-medication, antidepressive behaviour, drinking, etc.
Going to a doctor	Seeking help from friends, family, other professionals
Recognition as psychological problem by doctor	Defined by doctor as physical disorder, minor upset, overwork, etc.
Referral to a psychiatrist	Doctor prescribes psychotropic drugs or other treatment
Diagnosis of depression made	
Admitted to hospital	Outpatient treatment or other care offered

Source: R. Cochrane, *The Social Creation of Mental Illness*, London, Longman, 1983.

process likely to be avoided by schizophrenics. His conclusion, which was tested in Massachusetts, is that manic-depressives, rather than simple or other schizophrenics, are more likely to migrate. This is because hypomanic individuals may be more likely to migrate than the average individual and experience psychotic depression while in their new country. To test this hypothesis, hospital and other records were examined which showed manic patients were significantly more likely than schizophrenic patients to be foreign-born, and also that 30 per cent of the manics' parents were foreign-born compared to 9.5 per cent of the schizophrenics' and 18.2 per cent of the controls' parents. The birth places of the manics' parents compared to migrant controls showed that no one national or cultural group was more represented than others. It seems reasonable to accept the author's conclusion that earlier studies may have diagnosed as schizophrenic, individuals now considered to be manic-depressive.

Suffice to say that there are numerous difficulties in defining and measuring mental health. Crude, biased, confounded statistics are misleading as has already been established. The issue is made more complex by the political overtones of the research which may be seen to be racist or ethnocentric.

Good psychiatric epidemiological research takes time and care because of sampling difficulties and the specification of transcultural measures of distress. Certainly one reason for ambiguities in the literature may be the very different (and often unreliable) measures of mental health.

Typologies of migration

Migration occurs when people move within one community/area; from one community/area within the same country to another; or from one community in one country to another in another country. There are therefore two variables which, though often correlated, may also be oblique or orthogonal – that is *geographic distance* and *amount (quality)* of change. It is quite possible for people to move a comparatively short distance – in miles/kilometres – but to experience large socio-cultural, economic and political differences, while the opposite may also be true in that people may migrate very great distances to be in a community almost identical to the one they left.

Figure 3.1 illustrates some of these possible relationships. That one can experience great change by migrating comparatively short distances *within* a country has been pointed out. Whereas geographic distance is comparatively easy to quantify, quality or quantity of change is much more difficult. Change may range from variations in meteorological and dietary to socio-economic and religious conditions, some of which may be more disturbing than others. Furthermore, change may be experienced very subjectively, depending on the socio-economic status, age and education level of the migrant. Some attempt has been made to get an

Figure 3.1 A representation of possible patterns of migration based on
geographic distance and cultural difference

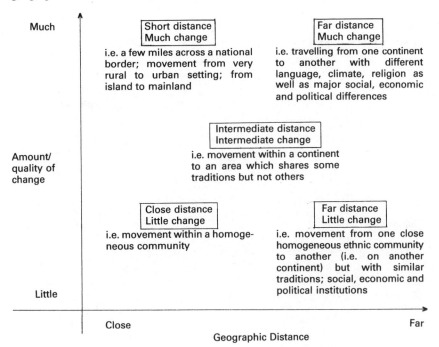

operational definition by factor-analytic studies, such as those done by
Cattell (Cattell et al., 1951, 1979). For instance, in a study of 82 variables
(social, economic, educational, behavioural) of 120 nations, Cattell et al.
(1979) found 21 clear factors, such as Cosmopolitan Muslim; Nordic-
Protestant Industriousness and East-Asian Buddhist. It may therefore be
possible to create various linear scales and measure the distance between
the country of departure and the country of arrival and then sum them
for a crude but objective measurement of change. This has been done
with various degrees of success (see Chs. 4, 5 and 8).

A second crucial definition for migration concerns the circumstances
or *motives* under which the change occurs, and the intended *length* of time
spent in the other country. Some immigrants are political refugees or
deported people who often involuntarily migrated, many with the hope
of eventual return, while others migrate happily with no thought of
return.

Figure 3.2 illustrates a possible relationship between these two
variables. Strictly speaking, not all of the categories in Figure 3.2 could
be described as migrants (e.g. tourists). However, if the length of stay is
for three years and over – which is fairly common for students and

Figure 3.2 A representation of possible patterns of migration based on proposed length of stay and motives for migration

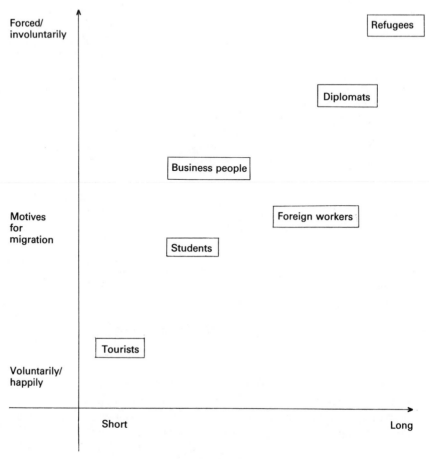

diplomats – the experience may have all the characteristics of migration. Again, the length of stay is relatively easy to operationalize, although time may not necessarily be experienced subjectively as linear. Yet, as has been noted, the motives for migration are difficult to specify. The dimension of voluntarily/happily is, of course, very crude, as it itself is of necessity a balance of positive and negative motives. For instance, a business person could always resign his job and in that sense is not forced to live abroad for a number of years. However, various other commitments mean that resignation, although voluntary, may be unwise. To this extent, therefore, the move abroad may be seen to be only partially voluntary.

The placing of the various groups in Figure 3.2 is hypothetical and not meant to suggest a positive correlation between the two axes. Indeed, many western developed societies impose severe restrictions to prevent potential immigrants from coming to their countries. What the figure is attempting to illustrate, however, is that migrants differ not only according to their country of origin (its distance from the chosen point of arrival and the difference between the two countries) but also according to their motives and their proposed length of stay.

Combining Figures 3.1 and 3.2 to yield four dimensions gives some indication of the complexity of the definition of migration. It should be pointed out that various other dimensions could be considered. For instance, the amount of difficulty/distress or the change required in adaptation may be a useful psychological dimension to understand reactions to geographic movement. Other typologies exist. Consider Gudykunst's (1983), which yields nine categories based on two rather different dimensions (Table 3.5).

Table 3.5 A typology of stranger–host relations

Host's reaction to stranger	Stranger's interest in host community		
	Visit	*Residence*	*Membership*
Friendly (leaning to positive)	Guest	Newly arrived	Newcomer
Ambivalent (indifference)	Sojourner	Simmel's stranger	Immigrant
Antagonistic (leaning to negative)	Intruder	Middle-man minority	Marginal persons
General area of research	Sociology of tourism	Intercultural adjustment	Acculturation/ assimilation

Source: W. B. Gudykunst, 'Toward a typology of stranger–host relationships', *International Journal of Intercultural Relations*, 7 (1983), 401–13.

There are therefore many ways to arrange and categorize travellers. The next section in this book considers four groups: migrants, sojourners, tourists and business people. These groups differ according to length of stay, motives for movement and amount of psychological/ behavioural adaptation required.

Chapter summary

This chapter set out to describe the reasons or motives for geographic movement. The motives of tourists were manifold, though these were classifiable into various groups, such as ego-enhancement and educational. The motives of students and volunteer workers seem more straight-forward – education, culture-learning and personal development – but there is often a discrepancy between the motives of students and those persons and organizations which administer, fund and sponsor the participants. Special mention was made of the motives of Peace Corps Volunteers, who were among the first group of sojourners to be studied by psychologists. The chapter also considered general motives for migration, but it was argued that there were various types of migration (each of which affects motives), that a simple economic calculus is insufficient to understand the complex motives for migration, and that various migration policies of different governments may inhibit or encourage various types of migration.

The chapter also examined the concepts of 'culture shock' and 'mental health' as they relate to migration. Although there are serious definitional problems in this area, various schemes or typologies were proposed based on two sets of two dimensions: geographic distance/amount of change, and motive for migration/amount of time spent in the other country. Various other typologies were also considered.

Part II
Varieties of culture travellers

Introduction

This section of the book offers a detailed and comprehensive description of four groups of culture travellers: migrants, sojourners, tourists and business people. The section is therefore organized sequentially in terms of the duration of the visit (and the sojourners' commitment to it).

Three things need to be said about this section, which is devoted primarily to a description of the diffuse and often equivocal empirical findings. The first is that the topic of each of the three chapters has tended in the past to be the prerogative of different disciplines: psychiatrists have been most interested in migration and mental health, psychologists in adaptation during a sojourn and sociologists in the motives for and types of tourism. Although there is a great deal of epistemological and empirical overlap between these different disciplines, there are clearly different emphases in theory and method. Hence many psychiatric epidemiological studies have relied on figures from mental-health admission records, while psychologists have preferred self-report methods. Similarly, there are differences in the level of analysis: sociologists prefer a societal or sub-group type of explanation, while psychologists and psychiatrists favour intrapersonal or interpersonal explanations. Thus the studies in the three chapters in this section tend to be rather different methodologically.

Second, as there are no grand – or even mini – theories guiding research in this general area, one is often left overwhelmed by a welter of unrelated research findings. These differ in quality, quantity, scope, and so on, as well as in general orientation. Although nearly all are in a hypothesis-testing tradition, the hypotheses are not derived from any one theoretical tradition. The findings are, as a result, difficult to integrate into a coherent pattern. Of course, there are various ways in which the studies may be classified or catalogued, such as by the country in which they were carried out, the travellers' country of origin, and so on. Thus each chapter will review a large number of relevant studies, while the conclusion will attempt to draw together the significance of these findings.

Third, the task is made all the more difficult by the fact that the results of numerous studies are equivocal or even contradictory. To have equivocal or contradictory findings in the social sciences is not unusual, and these may often be resolved by examining subtle differences in studies such as the subject population under study, the way in which dependent measures were operationalized, and so on. Thus, for instance, if one study found African migrants adapted well in Europe, while another found the complete opposite, this apparent contradiction may be due to the fact that the migrants came from or went to different African or European countries, respectively, or that completely different measures of adaptation were used. Only careful replications, which systematically alter one variable at a time, can determine whether the results are actually incompatible or simply a product of a sampling or methodological artefact. Alas, there are very few of these careful replications.

Despite the above problems, there is no shortage of studies in this area. This section aims to detail in the following three chapters four specific varieties of cultural travellers: migrants, sojourners, tourists and business people. Although some mention will be made of the explanation for these findings this section will be primarily descriptive while the next section will be primarily theoretical and explanatory.

4 Mental health and migration

Introduction and historical background

It is no accident that the terms *travel* and *travail* are etymologically linked, for in all cultural traditions there are tales about the stress and strain of travel and travellers. Furthermore, there are in many ancient writings accounts of migrants being mentally or physically ill. Although this may simply be a form of extravagant xenophobia, there has been a consistent interest in the topic of mental health and migration.

Essentially the work in this field is of two related kinds. First, it is necessary to establish whether migrants are more or less mentally ill than natives. This involves careful epidemiological research attempting to determine which factors (i.e. sex, age, education) associated with which migrant group (e.g. Indo-Chinese, Jewish war refugees) in which specific countries (e.g. North America, Australia) are associated with which illnesses (manic–depressive psychoses; psychosomatic illnesses, etc). This involves extensive archival as well as longitudinal research.

Second, and perhaps more importantly, if various differences are found, they need to be explained. Essentially, the causes of these differences may be attributed to one of three sources. The first explanation is that they arise from importation/selection/predispositional sources, which suggest that migrants are different from natives before the travel and hence import their illnesses which are in some sense predispositional. Second, the differences may be due to socialization/traumatic/travel or other reaction variables, which suggest that differences in mental-health patterns are a consequence of the migration experience itself and do not necessarily have anything to do with predispositional factors. The third explanation is that these findings are mythical/epiphenomenal/artefactual and the consequence of methodological problems rather than actual circumstances.

Of course, these three explanations are not mutually exclusive, and it is possible to use them simultaneously when considering a set of findings. Hence one may argue that a particular migrant group were more or less vulnerable to a particular illness due to some predispositional factor, and that a series of particular positive or negative experiences in their host country led to the particular record of illnesses, but that a section of the data should be disregarded because of artefactual findings.

After a brief description of the historical background in this area, this chapter will consider the research done in four main countries: Australia, Britain, Canada and the United States, as well as other countries. This arrangement has been chosen not only because it is convenient but because there are interesting and important historical differences in the type of migration to these different countries. Also, internal migration will be considered as the stress of migration is not exclusive to international migration. Finally, some attempt will be made to survey the 'explanations' for this phenomenon.

There is no shortage of books, pamphlets, official records and other materials published in the late-nineteenth and early twentieth centuries on the relationship between migration and insanity. The majority of these publications were, however, as short on data as they were on testable theories. This early literature has been reviewed and criticized by Ødegaard (1932) and Malzberg (1940), who were amongst the best of the early researchers in the field.

A lot of the early 'empirical' literature was partisan in that statistics on mental-health populations were cited to prove (or occasionally disprove) the high prevalence of various sorts of insanity among the foreign-born. The protagonists were under the influence of the then popular eugenics movement and were, therefore, neither sufficiently disinterested or dispassionate to do good research.

One of the first countries where the mental health of migrants was studied was the United States, where a census of all state mental hospitals was conducted in 1903. This established that immigrants were over-represented (70 per cent in mental hospitals versus 20 per cent in the population) in the hospitals, a finding that was replicated some seven years later. As a consequence it was decided to screen potential immigrants at Ellis Island in New York, where most immigrants landed. Later researchers were to point out how misleading these findings were, in that numerous confounding variables (age, sex, class, marital status) could have accounted for the results (Malzberg, 1962, 1964, 1968, 1969). For instance, Malzberg (1940) found that when the statistics were standardized for age and sex, the percentage of immigrants in mental hospitals dropped from 91 per cent to 19 per cent. In fact, the necessity of age controls had been pointed out as early as 1903 (Robertson, 1903) and discussed at length in the first decade of this century. Nevertheless, various government-sponsored committees in the United States ignored the need for taking these confounding variables into account.

Subsequently, a number of careful studies were carried out, up to the end of the Second World War (Tietze et al. 1942). Perhaps the two most influential were those of Ødegaard (1932, 1945) and Malzberg (1940).

Ødegaard (1932) based his study on a comparison between the mental-hospital admission rates of Norwegian-born immigrants and native Americans in Minnesota, as well as rates for the general population and those Norwegians who returned to Norway from 1889 to 1929. Ødegaard, using the technique of age–sex standardization, found that there was a 30 to 50 per cent higher mental-hospital admission rate for Norwegian-born than American-born equivalents. Furthermore, when compared to the admission rates of natives in Norway (and taking into consideration various national differences), Norwegian-born immigrants again had a higher incidence of mental illness. He believed these differences to be due to both the process of *selection* and to adaptation *difficulty*. He also found a higher incidence of insanity among returning emigrants than those who stayed in the United States, suggesting 'certain psychopathic tendencies in the constitution of those who emigrate' (p. 176). In regard to specific illnesses, there appeared to be much more schizophrenia but much less manic-depressive reactions among the Norwegian immigrants. Ødegaard believed that in a significant number of cases the difficulties of adaptation triggered off the outbreak of psychoses, which he assumed to be latent in many of the immigrants.

As well as studies of international migration, Ødegaard collected statistics on internal migration within Norway. He found that practically all over Norway migrants had considerably lower admission rates than those who remained in their country of birth. He believed that this was so because migrants who develop signs of mental illness are likely to be sent back to their home communities prior to hospitalization. Two competing explanations may account for Ødegaard's findings: the positive social selection of migrants; or the possibility that migrants may encounter more favourable economic or social conditions by migrating. Ødegaard believed selection to be responsible, but the data do not allow the alternative hypothesis to be ruled out.

Ødegaard has rightly been regarded as the first person to do good epidemiological work on the topic. However, he has been criticized by reviewers as being 'too predestinarian for many people, offering no real pointers towards prevention, ignoring illnesses other than the psychoses and ignoring also the obvious stresses of immigrant life at that time' (Murphy, 1977, p. 677).

Malzberg's pioneering studies on mental health and migration were also carefully conducted. They are very extensive: between 1928 and 1955 Malzberg was responsible for some twenty-seven publications (Malzberg and Lee, 1956).

In a major American study Malzberg (1936) looked at hospital first-admission rates of white American, foreign- and mixed-parentage patients during the years from 1929 to 1931. The raw rates showed that the foreign-born exceeded the native by almost 100 per cent, and that the rates for the mixed-parentage groups exceeded those for natives by 15 per cent and 30 per cent, respectively. However, when the results were standardized against the total population aged 15 years and over, the native–foreign differential was reduced to 19 per cent, showing age alone accounted for the greatest part of the difference. After standardization, the rates for foreign-born males and females exceeded those for the natives by only 16 per cent and 20 per cent, respectively; and the foreign-parentage and mixed-parentage excesses were 35 per cent and 60 per cent for males, and 32 per cent and 50 per cent for females.

Disregarding rates for those under 15 years of age and for those 75 years of age and over, Malzberg found that with but one exception (55–9 years old) for males, 'the rate of the foreign-born exceeded that of the natives in each interval . . . the maximum excess was not above 30 per cent (at ages 20–4 and 40–4), and in many cases the excess was less than 10 per cent (at 45–9 and intervals comprising ages 60–74).

With some exceptions, when looking at specific diagnoses the results revealed that admission rates were lowest for those of native parentage, intermediate for those of foreign parentage and highest for those of mixed parentage. However, when urban–rural *and* age differences were controlled Malzberg (1940) concluded that the available data indicate few, if any, differences in the relative incidence of mental disease among native and foreign whites in New York State that cannot be accounted for adequately on the basis of environmental and age differentials.

In other different studies Malzberg looked at racial differences in mental-health admissions and the effect of migration within the United States. On the basis of this work he concluded that migration is in itself and through its attendant circumstances an important contributory factor in the causation of mental disease (Malzberg, 1936, p. 109).

In a study of first admissions to mental hospitals in New York over the period from 1939 to 1941 Malzberg and Lee (1956) found the rates to be much higher for migrants than for non-migrants when age, sex and race were controlled – frequently 100 per cent higher. This was particularly true of psychoses, where migrants showed higher rates than non-migrants for non-functional as well as functional psychoses.

Although Malzberg and Lee (1956) were very careful about their analysis, they did not aim to test a specific theory for *why* rates of first admission were higher for migrants than for non-migrants. However, they tend to support two factors, selective migration and migration stresses (particularly selective migration) given the very high rates of first admission among recent migrants so soon after entry to the United States. But they were careful to qualify their findings:

First admissions may not be sufficiently adequate indices of mental disease, and the comparisons of migrant and non-migrant populations are affected to an unknown extent by differential ability or willingness to care for mentally ill persons at home. A higher proportion of non-migrants than of migrants live in rural areas where it is easier to maintain harmless but mentally disordered persons at home; in fact, such persons may retain high degrees of usefulness in the rural situation. It should also be noted that a much higher proportion of migrants than of non-migrants live as one-person households, often in boarding houses or hotels . . . .

A second qualification is that the rates of first admission of recent migrants may be unduly high because of the quick hospitalization of persons who would have been admitted at younger ages if the states from which they came had the same standards of admission as New York State. This would seem to be especially true for Negro migrants from the South. There is also the possibility that migrant and non-migrant rates are differentially affected by out-migration of the New York State born or of persons who had previously in-migrated. It is well known that some in-migrants leave the state soon after entry, and it may therefore be that the number of migrants at risk of first admission at some time during a given period is appreciably higher than the number present at any given date.

A third qualification centers around the point that the same factors that impel migration may also result in mental disease, or that the early stages of mental disease may often be accompanied by migration. The rates for non-migrants defined by place of birth may be relatively low because some of the worst risks have been eliminated by out-migration. Since many persons make more than one interstate move, even within a short period of time, such elimination may also take place within the migrant group as length of residence in New York State increases, thus accounting for part of the differences between recent and earlier migrants.

A fourth reservation about generalizing our findings is that New York State is decidedly atypical. It is highly urban and contains the nation's largest city. A large part of its population consists of racial, ethnic and religious minorities. For these and many other reasons assimilation may be more difficult than in most other states, especially for migrants from rural areas. Finally, it may be that the very atypicalness of New York State is in itself highly attractive to less stable individuals. (p. 123–4)

In the 1950s there seemed to be some researchers who were primarily interested in psychoses and favoured the social-selection hypotheses, while some were more concerned with the non-psychotic disorders and argued for the social causation or stress hypothesis. The 1960s saw an expansion of research on two fronts: looking at figures from other *countries* (not just the United States) and looking at a *range of symptoms* (not just psychoses). As Murphy (1977) has noted: 'Instead of asking *why* migrants have higher rates of mental disorder, it became necessary to ask *under what circumstances* do they have higher rates – something which brought new hope' (p. 678).

After the Second World War, social psychiatrists, psychologists and sociologists, as well as epidemiologists, became interested in the migration problems of particular countries. Some of the best research has been done in Australia, Britain and North America, though nearly every. country in the world that has received a sizable number of immigrants has a record of research in the area of mental health and migration.

Migration to Australia

Probably because, with the exception of the Aboriginals, all Australians are migrants, a great deal of research has been done there on the experience of immigration, assimilation and integration. Most of this research has occurred since the Second World War, during a period of high influx of non-British migrants. Table 4.1 shows the number of people from various countries who went to Australia between July 1947 and June 1970 with the intention of settling there.

Table 4.1 Number of immigrants to Australia from various countries, 1947–70

British Isles	1,086,500	Germany	121,300
Italy	337,700	Malta	68,400
Greece	200,000	Other East Europe	220,600
Netherlands	140,600	Others	334,100
Yugoslavia	136,800	*Total*	2,646,000

Source: Charles A. Price (ed.), *Australian Immigration, a Bibliography and Digest, No. 2*, Canberra, Australian National University, Department of Demography, 1970, p. A15.

The new migrants lived in the major cities, often forming substantial minorities and keeping alive their national language. They were mostly welcomed until the 1960s, when there were concerns about their effect on the nation's culture, traditions and economic structure (White and White, 1983). By the end of the late 1960s, if the children born to immigrants were added to the total number of immigrants, they exceeded a quarter of the population. Some immigrants were refugees and displaced persons who came mainly from Europe, and many were on 'assisted immigration' schemes.

Many studies have been performed in Australia on migrant assimilation (Taft, 1963, 1966, 1977), language acquisition (Krupinski and Stoller, 1971), patterns of marriage (Price, 1966), and interpersonal relations between immigrant families of different generations (Krupinski and Stoller, 1965). Researchers have tried to distinguish between different types of assimilation in Australia. These include total cultural versus behavioural assimilation or acculturation; structural assimilation versus institutional dispersion; marital assimilation; and identificational assimilation. For instance Taft (1966), who has done extensive and excellent work on immigration to Australia, specified five facets in the immigration process, each of which has its own dynamics, goals and ideal ecological conditions. The five facets are as follows: (1) cultural knowledge and skills, in which migrants learn the language, learn new roles and acquire knowledge of the history and culture of the host society; (2) social interaction, in which the migrant is socially accepted and interpersonal contacts occur; (3) membership identity, in which the migrant is granted formal membership in groups within the host society; (4) integration into new groups within the host society, in which the migrant assumes some status within the new society and is granted attendant roles, privileges and rights; and (5) conformity to group norms, in which the migrant adopts the values, frames of reference and role perceptions of the host society, performing roles according to its norms and conforming to its norms in appearance and expressive behaviour. .

No doubt because they are the largest group, British immigrants to Australasia have long been the focus of study, and a number of investigations have been done on their motives for migrating (Brown, 1959, 1960; Richardson, 1974). Clearly the reasons for immigration have important implications for adjustment. In an extensive psycho-social enquiry into British immigrants to Australia, Richardson (1974) studied their adaptation patterns. He found a U-curve pattern of elation (characterized by novelty, social freedom and self-justification), followed by depression (characterized by culture shock, sensory shock, nostalgia and reactive non-acceptance), followed by recovery, identification and acculturation. Richardson also looked at those migrants who planned to re-emigrate – an area of research rarely considered. Although comparatively few aspects of the study concern mental health, many of the issues are related to it. He found various correlates of assimilation, which are presented in Table 4.2.

Richardson suggested that potential immigrants and settlers undergo psychological screening and counselling to catch and educate those most likely to suffer from distress or mental illness. In addition to the British, studies have also been done on American (Bardo and Bardo, 1980), Dutch (Taft, 1961), Hungarian (Taft and Doczy, 1962) and Italian (Heiss, 1963) immigrants to Australia. Apart from looking at how well the various groups assimilated, some of these studies dealt with. the relationship between satisfaction, identification, integration and social mobility. The relationship between these factors is complex and non-linear; that is, satisfaction may relate to integration and identification,

Table 4.2 Correlates of assimilation scale

Year		Variable	56 Assimilation level (H)★	57 Assimilation level (W)★
1959	27	Association activity (H)	0.16†	0.12
	30	Association activity (W)	n.s.	0.13
1961	2	Working conditions (H)	0.13	n.s.
	4	Better off in Australia (H and W)	n.s.	0.15
	5	General satisfaction (H and W)	0.27	0.15
	7	Correct decision to emigrate (H and W)	0.23	0.19
	8	Spend rest of life in Australia (H and W)	0.18	n.s.
	9	Feels more Australian (H)	0.26	n.s.
	10	Support Australian team (H)	0.13	n.s.
	11	Passive vocabulary (H)	0.20	n.s.
	12	Active vocabulary (H)	0.46	0.13
	31	Feels more Australian (W)	0.18	0.20
	32	Support Australian team (W)	n.s.	n.s.
	33	Passive vocabulary (W)	n.s.	n.s.
	34	Active vocabulary (W)	0.25	0.38
	35	Assimilation level (H)	0.43	0.14
	36	Assimilation level (W)	0.22	0.29
1966	37	Housing satisfaction (H and W)	0.18	0.16
	38	District satisfaction (H and W)	0.15	0.25
	43	Better off in Australia (H and W)	0.16	0.15
	44	General satisfaction (H and W)	0.20	0.25
	46	Feels more Australian (H)	0.59	0.33
	47	Feels more Australian (W)	0.34	0.56
	48	Support Australian team (H)	0.18	n.s.
	49	Support Australian team (W)	0.15	0.15
	50	Correct decision to emigration (H and W)	0.26	0.20
	51	Spend rest of life in Australia (H and W)	0.26	0.23
	52	Passive vocabulary (H)	0.17	n.s.
	53	Active vocabulary (H)	0.70	0.26
	54	Passive vocabulary (W)	n.s.	0.14
	55	Active vocabulary (W)	0.20	0.57
	56	Assimilation level (H)	–	0.34
	57	Assimilation level (W)	0.34	–

★H = husband; W = wife;   †numbers represent correlations between the assimilation scale and the various self-report measures at three periods in time.
Source: A. Richardson, *British Immigrants and Australia: A Psycho-Social Inquiry*, Canberra, Australian National University Press, 1974.

which increase the chances of mobility, which in turn increases satisfaction. Other studies have looked at value differences between parents and children in immigrant and native groups (Feather, 1979), as well as ethnicity, adjustment and conflict in immigrant and nonimmigrant adolescents (Rosenthal et al. 1983; Rosenthal, 1984).

Studies on mental health and migration tend to be beset by several problems, including small samples, poorly kept mental-health admissions records, little differentiation as to origin of immigrants or specific diagnoses. Nevertheless, some of the oldest and most interesting Australian research has been done on mental health and migration. For instance, Chiu (1977a,b) traced the plight of the mentally ill in Victoria, Australia, from 1867 to 1879 and found 'the mentally ill Chinese, together with their "sane" compatriots, were misunderstood and discriminated against and provided a convenient scapegoat upon which the colonial racist society could project its frustration and anger' (p. 544). Research has also been done on suicides but, contrary to expectations, the results have not shown any difference between natives and migrants (Edwards and Whitlock, 1968).

Some of the most extensive and thorough research on migration and mental health in Australia has been done by Krupinski and his colleagues (Cade and Krupinski, 1962; Krupinski and Stoller, 1965; Stoller and Krupinski, 1973) who examined the health of migrants born outside Australia. They did not treat them as a homogeneous group, and analysed illness in terms of specific diagnostic categories. Stoller and Krupinski (1973) suggested that Australian immigrants can be classified into four main groups: British (the most numerous and mobile); those from western, northern and central Europe; those from southern Europe; and those from eastern Europe. Most of the data has been based on the first admissions to various hospitals and out-patient clinics in Victoria. They found that whereas such problems as mental retardation and senile brain disorders occur less frequently in the migrant populations, and alcoholism showed no link with migration, other mental illnesses tended to occur to a much higher degree with the migrant groups. In a longitudinal study of schizophrenia in the 1960s they found the incidence to be higher for all non-British immigrants than for the British and the Australian born, eastern European immigrants (often refugees or displaced people) being affected most. This trend was consistent over various years and was not related to age. Further, depressive states were found to be more common in some groups, especially the British and eastern European immigrants, and personality and behaviour disorders were noted to a greater degree in second generation immigrants. However, it was found that standardization according to age diminished the incidence of depressive states and of psycho-neuroses in migrants, compared to the native population.

As to the question of the direction of causation between mental health and migration, Schaechter (1965) found the shorter the time interval between the arrival in Australia and admission to a psychiatric hospital, the higher the percentage of patients with previous psychiatric histories – 45.5 per cent of those admitted within three years compared to 17.5 per cent of those in Australia after eight or more years. In a study of 100 non-British migrant patients she found twenty-seven definite and ten probable cases where patients had an established previous history of mental illness. Further, the results looking at specific diagnoses (depression, personality disorders, neuroses, psychoses) suggested that depressive states were more likely the result of the stresses of migration than personality disorders before migration.

Krupinski, Schaechter and Cade (1965) found a fairly normal curve when plotting the incidence of psychiatric disorders in male and female migrants according to age on arrival in Australia. The peak was between 25 and 40 years old, but there were some sex differences. The incidence in males was highest one to two years after arrival in Australia, whilst the peak in females occurred seven to fifteen years after arrival.

Stoller and Krupinski (1973) have argued that language attainment is the most important aspect in migration integration. Inability to speak the language usually limits upward social mobility, encourages exclusive living in ghettos and tends to cause disruption between parents and their children. Detailed studies of psychiatric disorders of eastern European (socialist countries) patients showed the importance of experiences prior to immigration. Krupinski et al. (1973) compared three groups of east European migrants, distinguished in terms of the severity of their war experiences. Jews, who had suffered from the most severe persecutions, had lower rates of schizophrenia than the other refugee groups, yet showed more signs of neurotic rather than psychotic illness, probably due to genocidal selection during the war and a further selection on migration. Instead of these psychiatric disturbances hindering socio-economic development, the persecuted Jews showed considerable upward mobility, even compared to Jews who had migrated before the war. Poles, Russians and Ukrainians came from and tended to remain in unskilled and semi-skilled occupations, while middle-class immigrants from the Baltic countries tended to show downward mobility, and their high psychiatric disturbance rates were associated with loss of social status and the effects of stresses connected with migration. Other noteworthy findings were that neither family support nor degree of assimilation seemed to have any protective influence on the refugees' mental health. Finally, over a quarter of the children of refugees had some sort of psychiatric illness, which suggests that they are a psychiatrically vulnerable group.

One area of research which has only become possible as immigrant numbers increased was the relationship between the incidence of psychiatric disorders in immigrants and the numerical size of the ethnic community of which they form a part. Kraus (1969) found a highly significant negative correlation between the rate of schizophrenia and the size of the particular immigrant group. The correlations were -0.67 for males and -0.82 for females, suggesting that where individuals are isolated in the host community their breakdown rates go up dramatically, and *vice versa*. The same issue was tested in a more rigorous fashion by Krupinski (1975), who examined the incidence of various psychiatric illnesses (depression, schizophrenia, alcoholism and personality disorders) among British, Dutch, German-speaking, Italian, Greek and Yugoslav populations as a function of the size of their ethnic groups. The relationship between decline in the incidence of psychiatric disorders and the growth of a particular ethnic group was found only in the Yugoslav population. In order to explore the possible beneficial influence of ethnic concentration, Krupinski looked at the ages of patients on admission to mental hospitals as well as their age on arrival in Australia. Most of his conclusions are in the form of questions rather than answers but very effectively describe his findings and provide possible hypotheses:

Why were Dutch immigrants, in terms of psychiatric morbidity, more like the British- than the German-born? Was it because they were, as Banchevska suggested, the most assimilated ethnic group with the least attachment to their old nationality? If so, why were those of their children who arrived in this country under the age of 10, as also with German migrants, the most vulnerable group in their population, especially in terms of personality disorders? And why, against expectations, was it not the non-English speaking Greeks, Italians or Yugoslavs who arrived here between their tenth and fifteenth birthday but their British counterparts who proved to be more vulnerable to personality and behaviour disorders? Was this due . . . to the discrepancy between the high expectations of British immigrants and the situation with which they were confronted, whilst the southern European immigrants did not suffer from such disillusion due to their low expectations? But if so, why did such disillusions affect children more than adults?

Why have only the Yugoslav-born shown an association between the numerical size of their ethnic group and psychiatric morbidity? Was it so because there is some critical numerical size of an ethnic group which is required to ensure the necessary support to its members? Can one assume that, after reaching this size, further growth of the ethnic community does not have any bearing on its mental health?

Why, except for Greek females in 1965–67, was no difference found between psychiatric morbidity inside and outside ethnic concentrations? Can one assume that, with the availability of the car, it does not matter whether you live close to or far from your compatriots, as long as you can reach them with a certain ease? But, if so, why did the Greek females show significant differences in the first triennium? Was this related to the lower proportion living outside ethnic concentration in the first triennium (1.3 per cent) as compared with the second triennium (1.8 per cent) and with the Italian in both triennia (3 per cent)? Would this suggest that, after reaching some critical size, immigrants create small ethnic pockets in areas of low ethnic concentration, which give them similar support? But, if this is so, why did we not find differences between the ethnicity of the immediate surroundings of psychiatric general hospital patients?

Why was there no association between the level of education and psychiatric morbidity in Greek and Italian migrants, such as noted in the Australian-born and in other immigrant groups? And why, in Greek females, were professional and clerical workers more vulnerable than were those engaged in menial tasks and home duties, a reverse trend to the one noted in the Australian born and other migrant groups? (p. 57)

Essentially, what all studies on mental health and migration have attempted to do is to specify which *factors* are related to which *mental illnesses* in which *immigrant groups*. That is, what most researchers have wanted to know is which are the major risk factors. However, there is not a very high amount of agreement between studies either on the factors isolated for study or the results. For instance, Krupinski, Schaechter and Cade (1965) looked at the influence of nine factors on the mental illnesses of migrants: age on arrival and duration of residence, family, social class, income and employment, housing conditions, wartime experiences, assimilation and integration, difficulties with people at work and at home, and drinking habits. Age on arrival and duration of residence, number of family present, housing conditions, wartime experiences, amount of assimilation and integration, and difficulties at home and work – but not class, income or employment conditions – appeared to be related to mental illness. However, because of the way in which the analysis was conducted, it was impossible to determine the relative importance of the various factors.

Bardo and Bardo (1980) did a stepwise multiple regression study of socio-demographic determinants of adjustment in a sample of American migrants to Australia. Four adjustment/attitude measures served as the dependent variables, one of which – the general satisfaction scale – was divided into six factors. The demographic variable which most consistently predicted any dimension of adjustment was the length of residence in a metropolitan area.

Sex of respondent was found to significantly predict two adjustment dimensions, Missing Family and Friends, and Attitudes toward Crime (males tended to score higher than females), while nationality of one's spouse was most closely associated with Cultural Expectations (i.e. respondents with Australian spouses tended to score higher on this index than did those with American spouses). Social class, as measured by occupational status, was able only to discriminate on one adjustment dimension – Anomia – while marital status predicted both Alienation and Attitude toward Crime. Yet the most complex set of predictors was found for the Index of Alienation. Type of housing, marital status and length of residence all were significant in this equation. In this case, people who lived in single-family housing tended to be less alienated than those who resided in attached housing or apartments. There was also a tendency for married respondents to be less alienated than single and for those who had resided in the metropolitan area longer to be less alienated than those who had lived there for shorter periods. (p. 258)

What is required is not only a list of risk factors, such as those presented in Table 4.3, but some idea of their relative importance. Table 4.3 leaves out a number of potentially important factors, such as motives for migration, culture distance, the relative economic situation of the two countries, and so forth.

Table 4.3 Factors relating to risk of psychological disturbance among immigrants

1. *War experiences*	– particularly in eastern European refugees.
2. *Housewives*	– particularly middle-aged, non-assimilated southern Europeans whose families had been assimilated via work or school.
3. *Single men*	– particularly those with a pre-emigration history of psychological problems.
4. *Adolescents*	– particularly those caught between the culture (language, traditions, values) of their parents and their Australian peers.
5. *Professionals*	– who dropped in status because of the non-recognition of their qualifications.

Source: Based on J. Krupinski, 'Psychological maladaptation in ethnic concentrations in Victoria, Australia', in I. Pilowsky (ed.), *Cultures in Collision*, Adelaide, Australian National Association of Mental Health, 1975.

There are a number of complications with any definitive list of risk factors; for instance, that they might be differentially rank-ordered for different groups or that they may change over time. Nevertheless, both from a theoretical and a counselling perspective it seems important that such a table be provided.

Scott and Stumpf (1984) compared fifty-six immigrant families before and after emigration to Australia on adaptation measures including job, school, friends, possessions and home, self-esteem and wealth. Degree of personal satisfaction was positively correlated with all of the measures of adaptation and correlated with the respondents' self-esteem. Furthermore, the importance accorded to a particular aspect of adaptation tended to correlate positively with the satisfaction derived from it. Overall it appeared that the migrants' success in economic, interpersonal and familial fields was correlated with the person's level of cultural skill (linguistic, numerical and informational).

More recently there have appeared some major reviews of the migration and mental health literature in Australia. Krupinski (1984) has examined the changing patterns of Australian migration and their influence on migrant health. Physical health and illness differences were related to 'imported diseases' due to changes in the environment or in dietary habits, while psychiatric disorders were associated with traumatic experiences prior to migration and the stresses of migration and adjustment in the new culture. Of the many contributory factors to the migrants' adjustment and mental health, Krupinski's review appears to stress the *working conditions* of migrants, the *patterns of settlement* with associated social support, their *psychological experiences and stability prior* to migration and their *length of residence*. An understanding of these variables will, it is argued, help health-service planners to apportion help rationally.

Taft (1985), whose research in the area of adjustment and adaptation of migrants in Australia has spanned nearly thirty years, has recently reviewed the literature in this field. He has proposed a conceptual framework for studying immigrants through their various stages, which includes their adjustment, national and ethnic identification, cultural competence and role acculturation. Taft argues that because of the number and complexity of the different salient variables relating to adjustment and adaptation, a multidimensional, demographic approach is necessary. He suggests that there are a number of immediate needs for research in this area: the use of *standardized scales* so that comparisons can be made between groups and over time; the focusing on *specific aspects* of adaptation such as the self concept, coping strategies, expectations; and the *compilation of case studies* of immigrants and their families.

Certainly the Australian research remains innovative and well executed, partly because it appears to be well supported by various agencies.

Migration to Britain

Britain, a country which has had Dutch, French, German and Scottish, as well as English monarchs, has a long history of immigration (and emigration). There has been a constant stream of immigrants to Britain since the Middle Ages, but it is only in the past twenty-five years that the topic has become politically controversial (Walvin, 1984). Indeed, it is probably because of increased public debate and awareness that there has been an increase in research on the psychological status of immigrants

(Littlewood and Lipsedge, 1982). The literature on migration to Britain, however, goes back a long way. Frost (1938) looked at the relationship between homesickness and immigrant psychoses in Austrian and German domestic servants working in Britain before the war. He found that homesickness combined with loneliness and exhaustion comprised the principal aetiological factors producing mild psychoses, which had, however, a good prognosis.

Most but not all of this research has been concerned with the mental health of immigrants to Britain, though there is also a diverse and largely unempirical literature of educational, housing, language and other problems, nearly all of which are interrelated (Watson, 1977). For instance, Bagley (1969) analysed 11,000 letters in Urdu or Hindi sent to a BBC programme 'Make Yourself at Home'. There were 602 letters requesting specific help with a problem, and these were analysed in detail. Nearly 40 per cent concerned problems relating to immigration and the division of families; 27 per cent to education, training and careers; and 12 per cent to legal, taxation and insurance problems.

During the 1960s, which saw a fairly large-scale, particularly non-white, immigration into Britain, a number of studies compared mental-hospital admission rates for immigrants as opposed to natives (Kiev, 1965); Hashmi, 1968; Bagley, 1968). Most of these studies were confined to relatively small samples in large cities such as London, Bradford and Birmingham. For instance, Hemsi (1967) examined all the case records of patients admitted to all of the seven mental hospitals in the south London boroughs of Camberwell and Lambeth. All patients with a previous history of psychiatric hospital admissions were excluded, as were those born outside Britain or the West Indies. The admission rates were much higher for West Indians than for the native population (per 10,000 of the population, 31.8 versus 9.5 for men and 30.4 versus 12.2 for women). The diagnostic distribution showed that schizophrenia (30 per cent West Indian, 22.5 per cent British), affective disorders (45 per cent West Indian, 35.5 per cent British) and character disorders (25 per cent West Indian, 34.4 per cent British) accounted for most of the difference. Looking at only forty West Indians, the author tried to determine the timing of migration in relation to mental illness. Of these, 27 per cent showed some signs of illness on arrival or very soon thereafter, 25 per cent became ill within two years, but 47 per cent showed no sign of any illness until two or more years had elapsed after migration. Hemsi (1967) readily admitted the limitations of this study – the possibility that native Britons and West Indians use psychiatric services differently; the restricted sample in terms of size and area – but he noted the similarity in findings between this and other such studies.

Bagley and Greer (1972) compared twenty-five 'black' with twenty-five 'white' cases of attempted suicide by looking at the relationship between various social and clinical variables and the suicide attempt.

They found black suicide was significantly associated with younger age; diagnosis of acute situational stress; and being discharged by hospital authorities without psychiatric referral. Most were fairly recent migrants with multiple social and family problems.

Burke (1977) did a comparative study of immigrant West Indian and British patients in Birmingham. Important predisposing factors such as an unhappy childhood and a family history of mental disorder were associated with psychiatric illness but not ethnic origin. Interpersonal conflicts within the family were asserted to have more importance in the aetiology of mental illness among West Indian immigrants than non-migrants, though no attempt was made to check for the possibility of innumerable confounding variables. Bagley (1971) studied the rates and patterns of mental illness of various ethnic groups aged 15 to 64 having contact with Camberwell (London) psychiatric services from 1966 to 1971. There were very low contact rates for immigrants from Cyprus and Malta, and very high rates for immigrants from Africa and, to a lesser extent, Ireland. Indians and Pakistanis had higher rates than the British themselves, but Caribbean immigrants had much the same. Irish patients displayed a marked lack of schizophrenia and a marked excess of alcoholism while Caribbean–African patients showed an excess of schizophrenia conditions but few signs of tension, depression and anxiety states. Furthermore, Bagley attempted to specify those factors which affect the illness rates (see Table 4.4). This is an interesting and imaginative attempt to describe (and explain) the relationship between migration and mental health. However, this study, like many others using hospital statistics, failed to take into account the already-mentioned numerous confounding factors that are known to be related to mental illness in all cultures (e.g. sex, age, class). Therefore, if a migrant population differs from the native population on any (or all) of these, one cannot be sure whether it is the demographic variables *and/or* the experience of migration which accounts for different mental hospital admission rates.

Other problems include the meaning and appropriateness of diagnoses such as 'paranoid schizophrenia', which has been found to be much higher among Asians, African and West Indians (Carpenter and Brockington, 1980) and eastern Europeans (Hitch and Rack, 1980) than among native Britons.

However, fairly reliable data have recently come to hand. In a large nation-wide sample, Cochrane (1977) looked at mental hospital admission statistics for the big immigrant groups. The unstandardized figures show crude admission rates of natives at 265 per 100,000 while for immigrants it was 495. However, once age–sex standardization was done, a different, clearer pattern emerged. Whereas the Irish (1110) and the West Indians (539) showed *higher* rates than native Britons (494), Indians (403) and Pakistanis (336) showed *lower* admission rates. These figures are then

Table 4.4 The combination of factors affecting illness rates

Ethnic group	(1) Lack of community integration	(2) Status isolation	(3) Experience of discrimination	(4) Selective migration	(5) Under-reporting of illness	Combination of weights ★	Rank of weight	Rank of illness rates
British-born	No	No	No	No	No	0	7.5	7
Irish	Yes	No	No	Yes	No	2	3.5	4
Old Common-wealth	Yes	No	No	Yes	Yes	2	3.5	2
India and Pakistan	No	Yes	Yes	No	Yes	2	3.5	3
Caribbean	Yes	No	Yes	No	Yes	2	3.5	6
Cyprus and Malta	No	No	No	No	Yes?	0	7.5	8
Africa	Yes	Yes	Yes	Yes	Yes	3	1.0	1
Other foreign	No	No	No	Yes	No	1	6.0	5

★*Note:* 'Combination of weights' is based on assigning a weight of one to each 'Yes' in columns (1)–(4), and a weight of zero to each 'No', and adding the total. Rank-order correlation between rank of weights and rank of illness rates is 0.85, which is significant at the 5% level.
Source: C. Bagley, 'Mental illness in immigrant minorities in London', *Journal of Biosocial Science*, 3 (1971), 449–59.

Table 4.5 Rates of mental hospital admission per 100,000 population over fifteen years in England and Wales (1971) by diagnosis and country of birth

Country of birth	Schizophrenia, schizo-affective paranoia	Affective disorders	Senile and pre-senile psychoses	Alcoholism, alcohol psychoses	Neuroses	Drug dependence	Personality and behaviour disorders	Others
A. Males								
England and Wales	87	45	19	28	48	6	43	140
Scotland	90	42	18	218	56	10	100	178
N. Ireland	153	78	22	349	121	15	201	341
Irish Republic	183	69	27	265	88	20	139	265
West Indies	290	30	1	14	19	3	27	100
India	141	31	4	34	33	7	36	101
Pakistan	158	22	1	10	36	2	18	105
Germany	99	35	3	23	41	9	58	102
Italy	71	35	11	4	22	0	30	62
Poland	189	63	17	33	42	1	27	137
USA	76	32	0	49	30	7	54	79

B. Females

England and Wales	87	92	37	8	88	3	41	202
Scotland	97	99	37	46	111	4	67	227
N. Ireland	160	147	38	69	172	21	111	373
Irish Republic	254	174	40	54	165	9	114	395
West Indies	323	91	3	7	67	3	46	186
India	140	57	8	9	64	3	29	147
Pakistan	103	38	0	14	103	0	55	175
Germany	130	59	12	3	98	5	48	142
Italy	127	61	10	2	67	4	33	136
Poland	301	119	26	9	139	6	40	241
USA	133	122	12	38	78	12	98	124

Notes: England and Wales, Scotland, N. Ireland and Irish Republic rates include reallocated patients for whom country of birth was not available. 'Other' includes other psychotic disorders, depression not specified as neurotic or psychotic, other psychiatric conditions, epilepsy, undiagnosed cases and admissions for other than psychiatric disorders.
Source: R. Cochrane, 'Mental illness in immigrants to England and Wales: an analysis of mental hospital admission, 1971', Social Psychiatry, 12 (1977), 25–35.

Table 4.6 Estimated suicides in England and Wales by country of birth for males and females aged 20 years and over, 1970–2

Country of birth	Standardized mortality ratio	
	Males	Females
All countries	100	100
Scotland	138	145
Ireland (all parts)	154	149
West Indies	85	60
India and Pakistan	100	122
Germany	177	239
Poland	221	207
USA	98	198

Note: Estimated suicides include official suicides, undetermined deaths and accidental poisoning.
Source: R. Cochrane, 'Mental illness in immigrants to England and Wales: an analysis of mental hospital admission, 1971', *Social Psychiatry*, 12 (1977), 25–35.

further broken down according to the various diagnoses (Table 4.5). Cochrane (1977) also recorded suicide rates for the native-born and immigrants (Table 4.6).

As Table 4.6 indicates, all immigrants, except West Indians, have elevated rates of suicide, though the exact pattern is not clear. Cochrane (1977) concluded that migrants from within the British Isles (Scotland, Ireland) have higher rates of mental illness (particularly alcoholism, drug dependence, personality and behaviour disorders) than native-born English and Welsh people. There is also evidence that Scottish migrants to England have higher rates of mental illness than those Scots who remain in Scotland. Overseas immigrants, on the other hand, have varied rates of mental illness, some of which are lower than those of the native born, but overall rates of mental-hospital admission for schizophrenia are higher for foreign-born than native-born. A tentative thesis for these findings is suggested in terms of differential self-selection for migration, depending upon economic conditions in the country of origin and the relative difficulty of migration.

Cochrane and his colleagues have carried out a series of well-conducted and carefully analysed studies on the four main immigrant groups to Britain: the Irish, West Indian, Indian and Pakistani. Cochrane and Stopes-Roe (1979) investigated the mental health of England's largest immigrant group by doing a community survey of Irish emigrants to England which they compared with native English people and native residents of the Irish Republic. They predicted, but did not find, that Irish emigrants to England would show higher levels of psychological disturbance. Indeed, they found the opposite and conclude that the high rate of mental-hospital admissions among Irish immigrants is attributable to a small separate group of 'deteriorated' (alcoholic, schizophrenic) individuals rather than reflecting high levels of psychopathology throughout the community. Because hospital-admission studies reveal a high incidence of Irishmen (Cochrane, 1977) yet community surveys show a low incidence of mental disturbance, it is likely there exists a dual Irish immigration phenomenon. Some well-motivated, ambitious, psychologically stable individuals escape various religious and economic pressures and rapidly adjust and settle happily, while others, who are less well motivated and adjusted, emigrate to find jobs they cannot hold down and then turn to alcoholism.

Cochrane (1980) found very similar results when studying the Scots' rates of admission to mental hospitals, which were higher in Scotland than in England. Yet Scottish migrants to England had a higher rate of readmission than either group. Yet if the number of admissions is considered, it seems Scots living in England were less likely to be mental patients than Scots at home but that once they do achieve this status they are very much more likely to be subsequently readmitted. Once again Cochrane floats the idea of two distinct migrant groups from the same culture – stable, economically motivated people who move south for definite employment-related reasons and those with established or potential problems who move more in hope than in expectation.

Cochrane and his colleagues have done most research on Asian (Indian and Pakistani) immigrants to Britain. Having established the suitability of various self-report measures (Cochrane et al., 1977), Cochrane and Stopes-Roe (1977) set out, in a community survey, to investigate the psychological and social adjustment of Indian and Pakistani immigrants. Using a battery of measures (psychological symptoms, negative life-events, employment, housing, life satisfaction), they found the Asians *better* adjusted than the British. Within the Asian community there were some interesting age, sex, class and nationality differences: experiencing disruptive life-events was most important for Pakistani females (and the British controls), crowding correlated with symptoms for Indian and Pakistani females (but not males), and length of residence in Britain was negatively related to symptom level for Indian males. In another study Cochrane and Stopes-Roe (1980) found Indian immigrants better adjusted than Pakistani immigrants (though both better adjusted than the British controls). The difference between the two Asian groups is attributed to the Pakistanis being less committed to living in Britain and less likely to be middle class. In a more detailed study of Indian immigrants Cochrane and Stopes-Roe (1981a) found that stable psychological adjustment was related to being young at migration, acculturated to life in England and socially integrated. However, there were numerous sex differences which indicated that higher-status, upwardly mobile females had higher levels of mental illness than the equivalent males. They note:

> The pattern of relationships between social status and employment variables, on the one hand, and symptom levels, on the other, within the female immigrant group is also important. Indian women are more responsive to the employment status of their husbands than English women, but having employment of their own does not offer the same protection from psychological problems as it does for their English counterparts. On the contrary, employed Indian women have higher symptom levels. At the same time the positive correlation between upward social mobility and symptom levels reinforces the picture already suggested of strain being placed upon certain Indian women who are becoming materially successful in the role of worker. This appears to be true also of the unmarried Indian woman who is increasingly fending for herself (and being successful in so doing) but who, it may be assumed, is experiencing considerable value conflicts. In all these discussions, however, it must be borne in mind that even those Indian women most at risk have symptom scores no higher than the average for all English women. It could also be the case that the L22 Scale [Langner 22 Scale] is better at detecting the distress of one group (higher status) than another (lower status) which may exhibit distress in different ways. (p. 326–7)

Cochrane and Stopes-Roe (1981b) also looked at the role of social class in Asian immigration to Britain. However, they found no evidence for the hypothesis that social class was significantly related to psychological disturbance.

Not all of Cochrane's work has been replicated. Brewin (1980) compared the consultation rates in a GP's surgery of natives and Asian immigrants and found no difference at all, which casts doubt on the thesis that Asians are in better psychological health. However, it may be that less frequent psychiatric treatment for Asians is a function of different referral practices on the part of general practitioners. That is, because of different models or explanations for illness, different taboos regarding revealing symptoms or disclosing personal facts, Asians are not as frequently referred for psychiatric treatment as native Britons, thus accounting for their low mental hospital admission records.

The possibility that there might be a difference in the referral patterns of different ethnic groups who are subsequently admitted as in-patients to psychiatric hospitals was investigated by Hitch and Clegg (1980). As source of referral they had five groups: GP, hospital emergency, social worker, police and other, and they paid particular attention to the diagnostic categories – schizophrenia/paranoia and affective disorders. Their results showed that New Commonwealth (black) patients are much more likely to reach hospital via the police and mental welfare officers and less likely through a general hospital ward than the native-born. The results also suggested that New Commonwealth schizophrenics were more overtly disturbed than the native-born, which may have accounted for the high amount of police involvement. Furthermore, police officers often act as social workers and it could be that due to cultural stigma attached to mental illness among the population, relatives who call the police prefer to look at the provoking behaviour in terms of *legal* rather than psychological deviance. General practitioners often call social workers when admitting cultural minorities to mental hospitals.

Although there still remains some doubt about the actual findings concerning the mental health of migrants to Britain, Cochrane (1983) has tried to specify the extent to which the various major immigrant groups are assimilated, and also to offer explanations for these findings. This may be useful in explaining the relationship between mental health and migration in general (Table 4.7).

Various studies have attempted to assess the adjustment of the children of immigrants (Ballard, 1971). Studies in the area of delinquency have revealed that West Indian and Asian youths have high delinquency rates compared to natives (Wallis and Maliphant, 1972). However, there remains a good deal of debate as to the accuracy of these figures, due to biases in official data and the necessity of separating out different kinds of delinquent acts (Bottoms, 1967). Batta et al. (1975) looked at juvenile delinquency amongst Asians and 'half-Asians' in a comparative study in a northern town. Despite the acknowledged problems with official statistics, the authors found that the 'half-Asian' group had the highest rates of juvenile delinquency – almost five times the rates for the Asian groups and double the rates for the remainder of the population. Both Indian and Pakistani children appeared to be, on the whole, less delinquent than the British control group:

> Clearly, on the evidence available, the Asian juveniles would appear to be much more law-abiding than the other groups studied, but, of course, we have already suggested that delinquent propensities may be controlled or contained by their ethnic group or may be diverted into other symptoms. In so far as half-Asians are concerned, we have seen, yet again, that in terms of indices of social or psychological malaise, they are very much a 'high risk' group. (p. 41)

This result was confirmed by Cochrane (1979) who compared children of West Indian and Asian parents with native British children on the Rutter Teachers' Questionnaire. Compared to the British controls, Asian children have lower rates of behavioural deviance and mental-hospital admissions, but although West Indian children show no more behavioural

Table 4.7 Extent of assimilation and explanations for different mental-health patterns of the four immigrant groups

Group	Approximate population in 1976	Assimilation								Mental Illness	Explanations for differential mental illness rates
		Cultural	Structural	Economic	Marital	Identifi-cational	Attitudinal	Behaviour	Civic		
Irish	700,000	x	x	(x)	(x)			x	(x)	*Higher than natives*	1. Late age of marriage, censorious view of sex, large celibate adult population living in the parental home. 2. Lack of emotional closeness between male members of the family which extends to a basic distrust of all other members. 3. Ambivalent relationship between mothers and sons with a concomitant, emotionally blackmailing mother being associated with alcoholism and schizophrenia.
West Indian	365,000	x	x				(x)	(x)	x	*Higher than natives*	1. Direct and indirect prejudice and discrimination in the occupational and social sphere. 2. Alienation and frustration due to high hopes of material success not being fulfilled.
Indian	?			(x)					x	*Lower than natives*	1. Highly selected migration of the successful, upwardly mobile, ambitious, psychologically stable. 2. Relatively supporting community and family life with an extended family and active participation in the cultural and religious life. 3. Flexibility in the culture of origin which often shows considerable ingenuity and adaptability in their adjustment.
Pakistani	?								x	*Lower than natives*	1. Highly selective migration as above. 2. Relatively supportive social network. 3. Worse adjustment than Indians due to a less flexible culture, stronger ties with Pakistan and the view that migration is temporary to acquire wealth before eventual return.

Source: Based on R. Cochrane, *The Social Creation of Mental Illness*, London, Longman, 1983.

involvement with formal agencies of social control. This process may also have involved different segments of the Chinese communities, such as the aged or foreign-born who possessed fewer skills or resources to cope with their changed social conditions or who stood out more conspicuously as being less integrated into American culture. Conversely, Chinese women, largely remaining in the home, were less visible, therefore not so conspicuously less integrated. (Berk and Hirata, 1973, p. 165)

In a rather more sophisticated study, Kuo (1976) tested four mental-health and migration theses about Chinese Americans. The four different theories ran thus:

1. *Social isolation.* Migration involved not only physical separation but separation from one's orientating set of mutual rights, obligations and networks of social interaction, which is profoundly disturbing.
2. *Culture shock.* Shock is caused by immigrants' feelings of personal inefficacy, normlessness, role instability and role displacement.
3. *Goal-striving stress.* The discrepancy – usually fairly large – between an immigrant's aspirations and actual achievement.
4. *Cultural change.* Adoption of American core cultural values involves a fundamental and uncomfortable shift in cognitive, affective and evaluative models.

Although clearly related, these four theories emphasize different features. For instance:

while three of the theories suggest higher mental illness rates for immigrants, the theory of goal-striving stress contends that immigration and mental health problems are inversely related; it is speculated that the major intervening variable in this theory is the goal-striving stress itself, i.e. the magnitude of discrepancy between achievement and aspiration. Second, the theory of cultural change assumes that acculturation varies directly with psychological stress, and the cultural shock theory predicts an inverse relationship. Third, each of the four theories focuses on a particular aspect of the immigrant's adjustment of life change and contends that the aspect of life change so identified exerts the greatest influence on the immigrant's mental health. (Kuo, 1976, p. 299)

Interviewed were 107 Chinese-Americans, and comparisons were made between foreign-born and Chinese-born. Results showed that the foreign-born Chinese were less mobile, had more Chinese as best friends, occupied lower socio-economic status, were less Americanized and were relatively less well adjusted than American-born Chinese. Using regressional, correlational and path analysis, the various theories were compared and contrasted. The author found:

(1) The Chinese-American's mental health varies positively with his

social status. (2) Although the Chinese-American's adjustment problems in American society usually co-vary with social class, the stresses of adjusting and adapting alone exert substantial negative effects on mental health. The independent effect due to adjustment problems suggest that within each social stratum, the individual's severity of adjustment is a good predictor of mental health. (3) Geographical mobility as measured by frequency of inter-city mobility correlates with poor mental health. It appears that anonymity, social isolation, and tensions among Chinese-American family members to adjust to new places increase the propensity toward mental distress. (4) Goal-striving stress tends to increase symptomatology of psychiatric distress, and its adverse effects are more severe among the American-born than the foreign-born. (5) Acculturation or 'Americanization' seems to improve the foreign-born Chinese-American's mental health, but its impact is too small to warrant a definite conclusion. (p. 305)

Overall Kuo believed his evidence favoured the social-isolation and culture-shock hypothesis better than the goal-striving stress or cultural change hypothesis. However, some predictions were not confirmed, indeed were contradicted, suggesting the limited explanatory value of all of the hypotheses.

Yao (1979) has looked at the assimilation of contemporary Chinese immigrants to America, paying particular attention to *intrinsic* cultural traits (religious beliefs, ethnic values, cultural heritage) and *extrinsic* cultural traits (dress, manners, life-style, patterns of emotional experience, mastery of English). Predictably the immigrants showed less change in the intrinsic traits (value systems, use of mother tongue) than the extrinsic traits, such as integrated residences, membership of professional organizations, social acceptance and economic position. The author believed that these results fitted well into various theoretical expositions of the process of assimilation.

Studies have also been done on Indo-Chinese refugees to America. Nicassio (1983) has argued that relative to other migrants, refugees experience high levels of unpredictability, stress and powerlessness leading to higher incidences of depression, anxiety and psycho-somatic complaints. As part of a study on the psycho-social correlates of alienation, he interviewed 460 Indo-Chinese heads of households. He found that alienation was negatively related to socio-economic status, language proficiency, number of American acquaintances and friends, and self-perceptions; and positively correlated with the degree of perceived difference between refugees and Americans. It was also established that Laotian and Vietnamese refugees showed evidence of a more favourable adjustment than Hmong and Cambodian refugees, which is consistent with the finding of better English proficiency, higher socio-economic status and more positive self-perception. As a result of this study, Nicassio maintained 'that alienation may serve as a benchmark for psychological adjustment in refugees is both theoretically stimulating and practically significant' (1983, p. 349).

More recently, Nicassio and Pate (1984) looked at the various problems of adjustment of over 1500 Indo-Chinese refugees in the United States. They found that refugees who were more advanced in age, who had less education and income, who were unemployed and who were comparatively recent arrivals reported more adjustment difficulty on a range of dimensions. Socio-economic level as defined by education, income and employment status seemed the most important determinants of the various dimensions of adjustment problems. Interestingly, separation from their family, a bad war and memories of flight from Indo-China were viewed as more serious problems than the day-to-day practical problems such as learning English and getting a job. As in other studies, the authors stress the importance of social support and hence the preserving of the family unit and the natural development of ethnic enclaves in rural and urban areas.

In a detailed study of Hmong refugees' mental health in Minnesota, Westermeyer et al. (1984) used a self-report general-symptom index to look at the adjustment of people 1.5 and 3.5 years following migration. The results showed an improvement over the period which confirms theories that migration serves as a psychopathological agent only in the early years of migration. Essentially, the increase in mental health was associated with more time spent in America, more job training, more English-language training and an increase in living standard.

Along with the Chinese immigrants, *Mexican* (or Chicano) immigrants to America have been fairly extensively studied, no doubt because they are one of the largest minority groups in America. Some studies have been concerned with the effects of fatalism on Mexicans' psychological adjustment (Ross and Mirowsky, 1984), while others have studied their assimilation (Wallendorf and Reilly, 1983). It is often assumed that the prevalence of social and environmental stresses (underemployment or unemployment, poor housing, undereducation, poor English) accounts for the behavioural problems among the Mexicans, though actual evidence of the prevalence of Mexican-American psychological distress is scarce. Numerous studies have been done on mental-hospital admission records in various parts of the south-western United States, but the results are fairly equivocal in that some find an underrepresentation of Mexican-Americans, some no difference and a few overrepresentation. Although some concluded from underrepresentation figures that the Mexicans were better adjusted than the natives, others have pointed out the perhaps more plausible hypothesis that underutilization is a function of the various barriers between Mexicans and the mental health services (Trevino et al., 1977).

Roberts (1980) conducted two large-scale surveys comparing various indices of psychological distress among black Americans, Mexican-Americans, and Anglo-Americans. In contrast to previous studies Roberts found few differences between the three groups, though on some specific measures the Mexicans were intermediate between the black Americans and Anglo-Americans. When the effects of age, sex, education, income, marital status and physical health were controlled for, the results did not change much, and in no case was the rate of psychological distress for the Mexicans lower than that of the Anglo-Americans. Strictly speaking, however, this study was not about migrants, as it contained migrants as well as first, second and later native-born generations. Nevertheless, it represented an important attempt to assess the prevalence of psychological distress among a large migrant group in America.

Puerto-Rican immigrants to America have also been studied. Krause and Carr (1976) interviewed a random sample of 219 Puerto-Ricans living in a mid-western industrial community. Five predictions were made based on previous literature: native Puerto-Ricans would have higher symptomatology scores than American Puerto-Ricans; high anomie scores would be associated with high symptomatology scores; women would have higher symptomatology scores than men; age would be positively related with symptomatology, and education would be inversely related. However, all five hypotheses received only partial support, probably due to a strong response set bias operating. Although these sorts of studies seem preferable to studies using only mental-hospital admission records, they too have their limitations.

There are also some excellent studies done in Canada (Murphy, 1973, 1977). For instance, Danziger (1974) looked at the acculturation of Italian immigrant girls in Canada and found evidence of the immigrant female's greater salience in maintaining traditional family culture, which is perceived as being threatened by migration to North America.

Some work has also been done on *African* migrants to Canada. Using a self-report psychiatric-symptom checklist, Lasry (1977) tested 480 North African immigrants living in Montreal, Canada, stratified according to their length of residence in the country. The results were compared with six other large-scale studies using the Langner scale in countries such as the United States, Canada, Mexico, Belgium and France. Although the subjects had higher scores than Americans, their scores were comparable with (and not significantly different from) native French-speaking Montrealers. However, when the subscale scores (e.g. anxiety, depression, psychosomatic illnesses) were considered, it was apparent that the African immigrants' depression scores are lower, and the psycho-somatic symptomatology and the anxiety rate are higher than the natives', though depression gradually diminishes over the years to reach the native population level.

It should not be thought that all the studies on mental health and migration to Canada were simply concerned with studying one group or another. Various specific phenomena have been investigated, such as the evidence for and causes of the underutilization of mental-health facilities by migrants.

In one of the most thorough investigations of the underutilization of mental-health facilities, Morgan and Andrushko (1977) surveyed 2,867 admissions in Toronto hospitals for non-toxic, non-organic psychiatric diagnoses. The most interesting results are given in Table 4.8.

Table 4.8 Native-born and foreign-born admission rates for diagnoses, by sex

Birthplace	Schizophrenia		Affective		Neurosis		Personality disorder	
	M	F	M	F	M	F	M	F
NB	197	205	48	87	189	387	139	87
FB	171	146	34	61	80	178	34	40
FB %NB	0.87	0.71	0.71	0.70	0.42	0.46	0.24	0.46

Notes: Admission rates are per 100,000 p.a. 1971. FB rates are adjusted to Canadian population by direct method.
Source: H. M. B. Murphy 'Migration, culture and mental health', *Psychological Medicine*, 7, 677–84.

Results showed immigrants' rates for psychosis to be 84 per cent and 79 per cent of the native-born, for males and females, respectively, while for the non-psychotic disorders the rates were 35 per cent and 46 per cent. When looking specifically at the immigrant's country of origin it was found that the admission rates for the non-psychotic disorders were lowest in groups most culturally distant from Canadian society. The authors attempt two explanations for these findings: the first is essentially the social-support hypothesis, which suggests that an immigrant's immediate family and friends act as a buffer against stress and disease; the second is that cultural access to care may be limited by cultural differences. However, these explanations are interrelated, and it is believed that while structural and institutional assimilation is minimal, the utilization of mental-health facilities will also be minimal.

These results are interesting for two reasons: first they cast further doubt on the use of mental-hospital admission figures but, second, they suggest that assimilation is not necessarily (immediately) beneficial.

As in the studies done in other countries (i.e. Krupinski in Australia) the relationship between cultural isolation and admission to mental hospitals has been looked at. Using the 1970 American census and 1970 psychiatric hospitalization rates for persons born in Ireland, Germany, Poland, Austria, Hungary, Russia and Italy, Muhlin (1979) tested the hypothesis that there is an inverse relationship between the density of an ethnic group in a community and the rate of mental illness among that group. His results strongly confirm the hypothesis – the correlations for first- and second-generation Irish were −0.33, German −0.46, Polish −0.34, Austrian −0.41, Russian −0.29 and Italian −0.40, all of which were highly significant. Because correlations do not allow one to infer cause, isolation from fellow co-nationals may well be a consequence rather than a cause of mental illness.

Table 4.9 presents the results of a study by Murphy (1973). From these figures Murphy suggests that immigrants should be encouraged to settle in large groups, as this appears to protect them from schizophrenia. It also provides companionship which acts as a protection against other stress related diseases.

Table 4.9 Ratios of immigrant to local-born rates of first admission to mental hospital in nine Canadian subcultures; standardized for age, sex, education and provincial distribution; with separate ratios for schizophrenia and correlation coefficients relating ratios to population sizes.

Cultural 'origins' in order of population size	Ratios of immigrant to native-born rates of first admission	
	Schizophrenia	*All disorders*
British	0.75	0.99
French	0.66	0.89
German	0.86	0.76
Russian and Ukrainian	1.51	0.78
Scandinavian	1.31	0.63
Dutch	2.13	1.31
Polish	1.08	1.26
Italian	1.21	0.71
Asian	(1.13)	1.37
	0.43	0.41

Source: H. M. B. Murphy, 'Migration and the major mental disorders: a reappraisal', in M. B. Kantor (ed.), *Mobility and Mental Health*, Springfield, Ill., C. C. Thomas, 1973.
Note: Ratios were calculated after rates had been adjusted for four age groups, three educational groups, the seven provinces and the two sexes. All data refer to the Atlantic and Prairie provinces only.

Of course, there are dangers in creating cultural ghettos as well as benefits. It may be that actual migrants may be better served by living initially in large co-national groups but that after a period they or their children should be encouraged to integrate socially, politically, and geographically more with the natives.

Many of the aspects of mental health and migration research have important, politically sensitive, social-policy implications. The contributions of social science to policy-making is to be welcomed as long as the results are valid and reliable, and are the consequence of disinterested and impartial research. The North American literature on mental health and migration remains among the most empirically sound and conceptually thoughtful. Over 100 years ago the US census (1880) noted the very high ratio of insanity among foreign-born migrants, and American researchers have been trying ever since to describe and explain the relationship between mental health and migration (Burvill, 1984).

Studies from other countries

It is probably the case that the amount of research in any one country on mental health and migration is directly related to the number of recently arrived migrants in that country.

Hence there is an extensive literature all around the world. For instance, some work has been done in West Germany. Following the economic miracle of the 1950s and Germany's expansion, a large number of *gastarbeiters* from southern and south-eastern Europe were recruited to work there (Boker, 1981). Not unnaturally they occupied the lowest socio-economic rung in society, but they were also the victims of discrimination and prejudice. This was particularly true of the Turkish workers, who numbered well over half a million. Suzuki (1981) looked at the psychological problems of Turkish migrants in West Germany, though he believes the problems are not unique to the Turks. He found from participant observation that lack of jobs and the breakdown of the family structure have led to the youth feeling isolated, deprived, rejected and alienated and hence becoming delinquent. Although women and the aged also have disproportionately more problems than natives, it is the adult males who suffer most. As a consequence of vocational, sexual and social frustration the Turks appear to have a large number of psycho-somatic symptoms such as gastritis, ulcers, sweat paroxysms and anxiety attacks. Further, returning migrants are distrusted by their co-nationals, their skills are underutilized, and they are forced to conform to pressures which are no longer familiar.

Apart from studies already reported, there are a host of others – of widely varying quality. For instance, there has been a great deal of research on migration to Israel (Bar-Yosef, 1969; Engel, 1970; Penalosa 1971). Not all of the studies have simply been concerned with psychopathology but also with issues related to it. Berman (1981) looked at the effect of job satisfaction on the general adjustment of some North

American immigrants to Israel. Results indicated a close positive relationship between high satisfaction at work and life adjustment. Closer inspection showed that job satisfaction contributes significantly to life adjustment except where commitment to work is missing or there exists a relatively strong religious commitment. Similarly, Krau (1982) tested a career-stage model for immigrants in Israel which could be related to their mental health and adjustment. Others have looked at the advantages and disadvantages of using immigrants as therapists (Basker and Dominguez, 1984).

The list of other studies in other countries is long. Suffice it to say that although studies on migration and mental health in Australia, Britain and North America have been highlighted, many others exist.

Refugees: the psychology of forced population movements

Another major category of culture travellers are those individuals and their families who have been forced to flee from their homelands to avoid real or imagined religious or political persecution; to escape from natural disasters such as floods or droughts; or to avoid the ravages of war (Eichenbaum, 1975). The common denominator among all these culture travellers is the involuntary nature of their migration and a degree of hardship and suffering associated with it. The term 'refugee' has been used to capture the essential aspects of the dislocation caused by migrating under these circumstances.

Refugees are by no means a modern phenomenon, probably having been a fact of international life since the emergence of city- or nation-states. History records many instances of refugee movements. For example, the Pilgrim Fathers who sailed to New England in the Mayflower in the seventeenth century, and others who followed them (Trevelyan, 1947), would certainly fit our definition of refugees. More recently, the Second World War created vast numbers of what were called 'displaced persons', as did the partition of the Indian subcontinent, which resulted in a veritable two-way flood of persons fleeing actual or anticipated religious persecution in those respective sectors where they constituted a minority. These are only some of the examples of involuntary migration that could be listed. It has been estimated (e.g. Harding and Looney, 1977) that between 1945 and 1969, 45 million people left their homelands in this way. It is clearly outside the province of this book to provide a comprehensive account of refugee movements. What we propose to do is to concentrate on one, very recent refugee problem, namely the still-ongoing mass departure of Indo-Chinese people to avoid alleged persecution because of their support for the previous, now defeated, regimes in that region. We have selected this particular movement for two reasons: first, it is of great magnitude, involving large numbers of people, spanning vast geographic and cultural distances; second, a reasonable amount of *psychological* research has been conducted in this area, something which is not the case with many of the other refugee groups.

The movement of Indo-Chinese refugees began in 1975 (Liem, 1980). In response to political and social upheaval in Indo-China, over 500,000 refugees have subsequently fled Laos, Cambodia and Vietnam, according to the most recent figures available (Nicassio, 1985). The majority have made the United States their final destination, although there are significant concentrations of South-East Asian refugees in other countries, mainly in Australia, France and Canada. However, the bulk of research deals with the adjustment of those who have settled in the United States. This literature in some ways is more notable for what it does not find than for its positive results.

There is unanimous agreement that for most refugees the circumstances under which they left their homeland were very stressful, if not traumatic (Nicassio and Pate, 1984). Many observers also make the point that there are large and significant differences between the culture of origin and the cultures of the receiving countries. For instance, in a study that compared Indo-Chinese refugees with a random sample of American controls, Smither and Rodriguez-Giegling (1979) found that the Indo-Chinese scored significantly higher on scales of marginality and anxiety, and lower on a test of modernity, all measures used to gauge cultural distance from the mainstream of American society. Another measure of distance or separation between refugee and American cultures has been social alienation. Based on data collected from 460 Indo-Chinese heads of households, Nicassio (1983) found alienation, as measured by a ten-item scale regarding the degree of separation from the socio-cultural environment, to be negatively related to a variety of indices of adjustment, such as socio-economic status, English language proficiency, media usage, number of American friends and acquaintances, and self-esteem. There is also an indication that refugees encounter some prejudice and hostility in their new countries.

These factors in combination should predict that Indo-Chinese refugees as a group would have particular difficulty in adjusting to their new circumstances. However, although problems are not absent in accounts of refugee adjustment, by and large one gets the impression from the literature that for most of these people the transition has not been as difficult as the theories would imply – a puzzle in its own right. The rest of this section is an elaboration of this issue.

The traumatic nature of the refugee experience
South-East Asians as a group are involuntary migrants who emigrated out of fear rather than from a rationally arrived at decision to settle elsewhere. They were therefore pushed rather than pulled, which

distinguishes them from voluntary migrants, whose decision to migrate is usually based on a desire to improve their economic status or to be reunited with family members (Eichenbaum, 1975).

In most cases, these people left hurriedly and there was little time to prepare for the separation from loved ones and familiar surroundings. Many spent days in small, unseaworthy boats without proper food or shelter, and were attacked by pirates, and many fellow-refugees lost their lives while fleeing in this way. For instance, Liem (1980) has estimated that more than half the boats never reached port. Those who made it spent periods of up to two years in refugee camps in Thailand, Hong Kong, the Philippines, Malaysia, Wake Island, Guam and elsewhere, under adverse conditions while waiting for final settlement – in an atmosphere of uncertainty about the future and in almost complete ignorance of what had happened to the families most of them had left behind. Furthermore, they had experienced a profound loss, not just in terms of status and material goods but also in the sense of seeing their native land transformed politically and culturally. There was also the loss associated with being separated from members of their family and other social support networks. In combination, these influences constituted a stressful, if not traumatic experience, further exacerbated by its prolonged duration for many of the participants.

Cultural differences

There is considerable disparity between the core values and behavioural norms of western and Indo-Chinese cultures. One of the more original accounts of these differences is that of Liem (1980), who shows how the subjective culture (Triandis et al., 1972) of the Vietnamese is based on a harmonious amalgamation of Buddhism, Taoism and Confucianism. From Buddhism they derive the concept of 'karma', or a fatalistic belief in the inevitability of suffering caused by desire – desire for life, happiness, riches or power. This explains why some Vietnamese refugees do not strive for success or try to make the most of their new life. Since renouncement is hardly a core value in American society, the apparent passivity of the Vietnamese is often misunderstood by westerners, and in a clinical setting may be misdiagnosed as depression.

From Confucianism, the Vietnamese derive the cult of ancestors, which places the spirits of dead relatives at the centre of each household. In order to care for their ancestors' tombs, successive generations try to remain in their native villages, which explains the strong attachment of the Vietnamese to their place of birth. In their homes the altars of their ancestors occupy the place of honour and that is where the whole, extended family also gathers on important occasions, particularly when decisions are made that affect its members. A literal dialogue with the ancestors is maintained, since they are consulted on any major matter through prayer. All these rituals are difficult to sustain in western countries and tend to be misunderstood when they are carried out. Ancestor worship also leads to conflict within the family, since parents fear that their children, raised in a western environment, will not worship them after death, an idea that too may appear strange to an American observer.

Confucianism also provides a model for social relations, based on the doctrine of Tam Cuong, which prescribes how three, all-important sets of interactions are to be conducted: those between ruler and subject, father and son, and husband and wife. The first leads Vietnamese employees to regard their employer as someone who is to be obeyed without question. At the same time, the Vietnamese expects the employer to be paternalistic, kind and soft-spoken. The scope for mutual misunderstanding here is clearly enormous, with American employers seen as rude and uncouth, and Vietnamese employees as passive, insincere and stupid. The enigmatic Vietnamese smile, which may signify politely not wishing to contradict a higher-status person, or merely a lack of understanding about what is being said, is a further source of cross-cultural friction.

Second, Confucianism teaches that sons are required to give their fathers total obedience. This is a major source of conflict for those Vietnamese who have fled to countries where family relationships are less formal and restrictive. Typically, the father adapts more slowly, if at all, to this aspect of the new culture. Third, Confucianism teaches that women should conform to the three obediences: obedience to her father until she is married, obedience to her husband after she leaves her father's house, and obedience to her eldest son should she be widowed. In most cases, whether due to economic or other pressures, Vietnamese women are unable or unwilling to maintain their traditional role, causing further tensions within the home.

From Taoism, Vietnamese derive the principle of Yin and Yang, or the constant duality of nature. Taoists refrain from disturbing the natural order of things. Taking initiative is considered to be vain, the active life is disdained and passivity is valued. These doctrines are summed up in the Taoist maxim: 'Do nothing and everything will be accomplished spontaneously'. This may lead to a defeatist attitude, particularly when faced with apparently insurmountable difficulties such as those associated with being a refugee.

This rather brief account of Indo-Chinese cultural influences can only hint at the complexity of the Vietnamese character. Nevertheless, it should be apparent that for the Vietnamese most western societies represent a very alien cultural landscape, one into which they have been abruptly propelled with very little preparation.

Finally, there is considerable evidence, both in the United States and elsewhere, in other receiving countries, that Vietnamese refugees encounter active hostility and prejudice from certain sections of these host societies (Bochner and Harris, 1984; Kinzie, 1981; Liem, 1980; Nicassio, 1985). A further difficulty is that in dealing with refugees, American professional helpers may lack sufficient cultural sensitivity to respond adequately to the problems of their 'unusual' and 'exotic' clients (Kinzie, 1981; Kinzie, Tran, Breckenridge and Bloom, 1980).

Psycho-social adaptation

The received wisdom in this area, based on past research in Norway, Australia and the United States, is that the refugee status is associated with an increase in psychotic behaviour (e.g., Harding and Looney, 1977; Kinzie, Tran, Breckenridge and Bloom, 1980; Lin, Tazuma and Masuda, 1979; Nicassio and Pate, 1984; Westermeyer, Neider and Vang, 1984; Westermeyer, Vang and Neider, 1983; Williams and Westermeyer, 1983). This assumption has coloured much of the research into this topic, at least in the United States. Most of the workers are psychiatrists or clinical psychologists working within a medical setting. We have elsewhere in this book questioned the appropriateness of applying the medical model to the coping strategies of sojourners, on the grounds that it implies adapting to, rather than learning, the skills of a new society, and thus the erosion of the culture of origin; and that the medical model stigmatizes those who fail to assimilate, by regarding their difficulties in psychiatric rather than social–skills–deficit terms. Nowhere is this more apparent than in the literature on the psycho-social adjustment of Vietnamese refugees in the United States. For instance, Harding and Looney (1977) categorically state that refugees have an increased incidence of mental disorders, that refugees lead isolated lives because of language barriers and that because of this isolation they develop feelings of insecurity and anxiety comparable to those experienced by the deaf, accounting for their frequently observed paranoid reactions. If refugees were not feeling paranoid previously, they would certainly do so after reading this description of themselves.

Since this view is typical of the orientation of many of the workers, it is not surprising that a great deal of psychopathology has been found in Vietnamese refugees. However, most of the studies do not contain adequate control or comparison groups, and therefore the results are often difficult to evaluate. For instance, Harding and Looney (1977) and Williams and Westermeyer (1983) studied groups of 'unaccompanied' children, that is refugee children who had become separated from or temporarily abandoned by their parents, and found these to be disturbed and depressed. No attempt was made to relate these findings to the incidence of disturbance in non-refugee waifs.

In a more systematic study, Rahe et al. (1978) selected a random sample of 200 refugees from a large camp in California and gave them a battery of tests, including life-change inventories, a version of the

Cornell Medical Index Health Questionnaire, and the Cantril Self-Anchoring Scale. The data were separately examined for males and females, and by age; the results are quite revealing, mainly for what they did not find. Although some of the groups scored above average on some of the scales, there were significant exceptions across the whole spectrum of subject x test categories, and again no comparisons were made with appropriate non-refugee controls. Indeed, contrary to the conclusions drawn by the authors of this study, it would be quite reasonable to say, on the basis of the data they present, that there was a surprisingly low incidence of psychiatric disturbance in the refugee camp under investigation.

In a longitudinal study, Lin, Tazuma and Masuda (1979) and Masuda, Lin and Tazuma (1980) administered the Cornell Medical Index (CMI), the Social Readjustment Rating Questionnaire (SRRQ) and the Schedule of Recent Experience (SRE) to a non-random sample of refugees, some of whom were subsequently followed up a year later. This study did confirm that the CMI scores, on both occasions, were significantly above norms established for this test in the general population, with about half of the Vietnamese being regarded as having emotional difficulties. However, as the authors themselves acknowledge, there are problems with comparing norms developed for one culture with data emanating from other cultures. Again, there were significant differences between age, sex and other demographic variables on the CMI, with some groups coping much better than others. Nevertheless, the results do indicate that the elevated CMI scores in some of the groups could in part be attributed to the refugee status of these people. Analysis of the life-change data as measured by the SRRQ and SRE showed a fourfold increase in post-evacuation units relative to the consistently low pre-evacuation units, and almost a year after arrival their life-changes remained high, indicating ongoing stress and instability in their lives. The significance of this finding is that a large body of literature, summarized in Masuda et al. (1980), and also referred to in Chapter 8 of this book, has found a positive correlation between the number and severity of life-changes, on the one hand, and physical and mental illness, on the other. The authors report that there was a positive and significant correlation between life-change and CMI scores but do not provide us with the actual figure. Once again, the results of this study, as distinct from the conclusions drawn by its authors, could be used to highlight the resilience of the Vietnamese in coping with their undoubted difficulties, particularly since quite high life-event occurrences were associated with only moderately elevated CMI scores. A positive contribution of this study is that the life-unit approach can identify those particular areas in which people experience difficulties. For instance, in this study the most frequent life-events mentioned by the Vietnamese included problems with finances, work, spouse relations, law and schooling. Such information can then be used in the construction of remedial programmes aimed at resolving these specific difficulties.

Westermeyer, Vang, and Neider (1983) administered a questionnaire to ninety-seven Hmong refugees in Minneapolis. The aim was to do a prospective study that would distinguish between those who during the subsequent twelve months became psychiatric patients and those who did not. The results showed that a number of pre- and post-migration variables did in fact differ significantly between the patients and non-patients. However, only tentative conclusions can be drawn from these data, because the analysis consisted of multiple t, X^2 and Fisher exact tests between highly unequal Ns, a method that is bound to produce a certain number of significant differences irrespective of whether these exist in nature. What is of interest, though, is the ratio of non-patients to patients. Ninety-seven subjects participated in the study. Of these, seventeen (or 16 per cent) became psychiatric patients – not really a very high figure, given the undoubted hardships these people had suffered. Of the seventeen patients, fifteen suffered from depression, which again is not a surprising pattern in the circumstances. Finally, the Vietnamese character traits of passivity and fatalism can quite easily be mistaken for depression by western psychiatrists unfamiliar with Vietnamese customs.

Westermeyer, Neider and Vang (1984) gave a scale of depression and a symptom checklist to a group of Indo-Chinese refugees. The tests were administered twice, separated by an interval of about two years. Approximately ninety subjects participated in this study. Although there were no changes in the socio-economic status of the refugees during this period, significant improvements occurred on all of the indices of psychopathology, including depression, somatization of symptoms, anxiety and obsessive-compulsive behaviours. This study suggests that even if psychopathology and migration are positively associated, the relationship may only hold in the early post-migration phase. Consequently, much care must be taken not to overgeneralize the results of the literature on refugee mental health, since a great deal depends on when in the post-migratory phase the data are collected. In the present context, Westermeyer, Neider and Vang's (1984) study provides further evidence for the resilience of the Indo-Chinese in coping with their refugee status, once the initial shock of entry has passed.

In another study which explicitly took into account the passage of time, Vignes and Hall (1979) administered several questionnaires and also interviewed fifty randomly selected Vietnamese families totalling 114 individuals. On the basis of their data, these authors conclude that after an initial period of anger and disappointment lasting about a year, Vietnamese adjust well in the United States, and that their treated incidence and prevalence of major psychiatric disorders is no higher than for the population at large. To the extent that problems did arise, they were associated with loss of status and professional identity. Unemployment and underemployment were also a problem, as was local prejudice against the refugees.

Sudden natural death that cannot be attributed to a particular, specific cause is a relatively rare occurrence in adult Americans. Among South-East Asian refugees, however, sudden unexplained deaths appear to occur with disturbing frequency. According to Baron et al. (1983), between 1977 and 1982, fifty-one unexplained, sudden deaths among Laotian, Kampuchean, and Vietnamese refugees had been reported from fifteen states. All the deceased had been relatively young, previously healthy adults in whom a post mortem examination did not disclose the cause of death. The authors interviewed the families of the victims in order to tease out those physical and psycho-social variables that might be associated with the syndrome, but after an exhaustive inquiry were unable to identify any particular antecedent conditions that might account for the sudden deaths. The pattern, though, was quite distinctive. Of the fifty-one unexplained deaths, all except one were males. Each of the deaths occurrred at night while the subjects were in bed, and death usually came very quickly after the onset of the seizure-like episode. The refugee status of the victims seems to have had very little to do with the syndrome, and the authors speculate that, as a group, South-East Asian males may have a congenital predisposition to sudden death. Whether the additional stresses of being a refugee heighten that susceptibility, if indeed it exists, is impossible to say. This study, like some of the previous reports reviewed in this section, by virtue of its negative findings, once again underlines the danger of jumping to preconceived conclusions about the noxious effects of the refugee status. Although being a refugee is certainly not a pleasant experience, it does not in and of itself appear to lead to the sorts of dire results some claim for it. Nor does it account for phenomena such as the sudden-death syndrome, where the explanation is much more complex than simply attributing these deaths to the process of dislocation.

One of the few large-scale surveys dealing with how the refugees themselves regard their situation was conducted by Nicassio and Pate (1984). They administered questionnaires and interviewed 1638 Indo-Chinese refugees in Illinois. The respondents were presented with a list of thirty-two potentially problematic social situations. The subjects then rated these on the seriousness that each problem posed for them personally in their daily lives. The refugees also responded to a ten-item measure of alienation, covering topics such as feelings of social isolation, cultural estrangement, and powerlessness. The data were analysed by rank-ordering the thirty-two adjustment problems according to their severity. The items rated as most serious were separation from family members, painful memories of war and departure, homesickness, communication with their native country, learning to speak English, finances, job skills and medical care. These data provide empirical support that refugee migration is a relatively traumatic experience. The data also reflect the post-migration survival needs of the refugees, particularly in regard to money, jobs and social services. Of interest, also, are the problems that were rated as least serious; the items in ranks 29 to 32 were, respectively, family conflict, marital conflict, difficulty in obtaining Indo-Chinese food, and alcohol/drug abuse, confirming the views of observers such as Liem (1980) that the main source of strength in Vietnamese culture is the mutual support provided by its family structure, greatly contributing to their ability to cope with the stresses of adjusting to a new environment.

Other analyses, including the results of the alienation index, found that socio-economic status was negatively related to the social adjustment of the refugees. Finally, the authors make the valid point that problems of family separation and painful memories from the past were viewed by the respondents as more serious than the numerous practical obstacles to resettlement and suggest that the associated unresolved grief and anxiety may predispose the refugees to depression and other psychiatric disorders. However, no direct evidence linking emigration stress to psychiatric disturbance is presented to support this quite plausible hypothesis.

Certain conclusions can be drawn from the literature. The clinical data indicate that the most frequent psychiatric condition found in those refugees *who have become patients* is depression. Somatization is also very prevalent in this group, probably because mental illness is regarded as a stigma in South-East Asian cultures and consequently emotional problems tend to be expressed in more socially acceptable, physical and bodily terms. However, a careful reading of the literature does not warrant the conclusion so often drawn that there is a higher incidence of mental illness among Indo-Chinese refugees than in the general population. This conclusion does not follow from the literature for three reasons: first, many of the studies do not have an appropriate control group; second, culturally insensitive western clinicians may mistake the passivity of the Vietnamese character for depression, leading to inflated rates of *diagnosed* (as distinct from actual) psychopathology; and third, many studies confound or do not control elapsed time since migration. The few studies that are explicitly longitudinal in their design tend to find a significant reduction in both clinical and psycho-social indices for adaptation.

Studies that have concentrated on quantifying the amount of socio-cultural difficulty experienced by Indo-Chinese refugees have consistently shown that they face a variety of major problems. Refugees have higher rates of life-change units than controls, they are alienated in the sense of being culturally distant from the mainstream of the host society, they face prejudice from the local population and they experience status loss and marginality. Where the literature has erred is, first, in treating the undoubted stresses of forced migration as the independent variable responsible for the psychiatric disturbances found in some of the refugees. However, as we have seen, refugee status cannot by itself account for mental illness in these patients. Second, there has been a tendency to then extrapolate the supposed link between migration stress and mental illness, to include all forms of psycho-social maladaptation, itself a natural consequence of adopting a medical model in this area. In fact, the Vietnamese refugees as a group have coped surprisingly well, given the immense amounts of stress they have been exposed to. It seems to us that the most interesting question in this area has so far been neglected, namely what are those specific aspects of Vietnamese culture which act as buffers to stress and which provide the refugees with the resources and hardiness to cope as well as they have. We suspect it has something to do with the three dominant cultural themes referred to earlier in this section, but we are not aware of any studies dealing with the determinants of positive mental health in refugees. This area would greatly benefit in shifting from its gloomy clinical perspective to a consideration of less spectacular but, in the long run, more theoretically interesting questions about the determinants of personal growth and self-actualization under conditions of forced or involuntary migration.

Internal migration

The 'culture shock' or migration-stress hypothesis suggests that the greater the socio-cultural difference between the country of origin and the country of migration, the more pronounced will be the stress and the resulting mental illness (Malzberg, 1955; Parker et al., 1969). Yet studies done on migration *within* one country – usually from rural to urban environments – show that even people from rural districts moving to a large town within the same country suffer from mental illness. Indeed, Parker et al. (1969) demonstrated that urban migrants within America showed higher rates of mental illness than rural migrants.

Another study concerned with within-country migration was done from the perspective of adaptation-level theory (Helson, 1964), which relates the individual's frame of reference established in the environment of origin to a subsequently experienced one. Wohlwill and Kohn (1973) found modest support for the hypothesis that a group moving from an environment characterized by relatively high levels of stimulation should experience an intermediate one as less intense or severe than would a group that has moved to the same environment from one characterized by low levels of stimulation.

There is an extensive literature on urban–rural migration in numerous countries. For instance, Benyoussef et al. (1974) looked at the health effects of urban–rural migration in Senegal. Their study showed that certain groups (e.g. young single women) were more likely to contract physical illnesses. They also found various physical correlates of rural migrants' adaptation in the city, that is blood pressure and transamines are negatively correlated with adaptation while serum protein was positively correlated with adaptation.

Cochrane (1983) has noted that until comparatively recently it remained the unquestioned and romantic wisdom within the social sciences that city dwellers experience greater levels of stress and consequently psychological disturbance than do country dwellers. However, studies done in the 1970s (e.g. Dohrenwend and Dohrenwend, 1974) found that although urban dwellers showed higher incidences of neurosis and personality disorders, more serious psychiatric disorders – particularly depression – were more frequently found in rural areas. Indeed, Cochrane (1983) has noted that in most societies the physical health (and presumably the mental health) of urban residents is better than rural residents.

Thus to suggest that the most common form of rural–urban migration (i.e. from rural to urban) is necessarily associated with mental illness, may be wrong. Indeed, as studies have shown, the opposite is more likely to be true. But as with all studies of migration there are many confounding variables that are extremely difficult to tease apart.

Explaining the relationship

The wealth and variety of studies in this area has, however, not led to any agreement as to the mechanism explaining the relationship between mental health and migration. Although most attention has been paid to the finding that migrants have *higher* rates of mental illness than natives, a number of studies done in various countries have shown that migrants have a significantly *lower* rate of mental illness, including internal migrants in Norway, America (Parker and Kleiner, 1966), Israel (Murphy, 1961), Singapore (Murphy, 1961) and Canada (Murphy, 1965). The above studies were mainly concerned with the psychoses but also included studies looking at minor psychiatric illness (neuroses) (Morgan and Andrushko, 1977).

Various authors have listed variables related to the mental health of migrants. For instance Morrison (1973) has listed ten:

Variables operating prior to migration:
1. Personality of migrant
2. Life experiences
3. Cultural background
4. Reasons for leaving old environment
5. Reasons for moving to new location

Variables operating during migration:
  6. Stress of moving

Variables operating after migration:
  7. Attitude of environment to migrant
       State policy
       Pressure to acculturate
       Economic opportunity
  8. Homogeneity of immediate environment
  9. Fulfilment of expectations and aspirations
  10. Personality of migrant

Morrison (1973) attempted to explain not whether migration is a factor in the aetiology of mental illness, but why it affects different groups in different ways, that is to describe how, which and why various conditions affect different groups in different ways. Murphy (1977) has argued that only misleading and unhelpful 'we/they' attitudes can result from generalizations without specifying the migrants' culture of origin; conditions, motives and feelings associated with migration; and the classification of illness. Furthermore, he argues that one should not focus exclusively on the individual but should also look at the experience which the person may have had in common with identifiable others.

As early as 1956 Malzberg and Lee noted that studies on mental health and migration 'have been based on scanty or otherwise inadequate data, and even the fact of higher incidence of mental disease among migrants is not firmly established, much less the theories as to cause' (p. 43).

One may conclude a review of the mental health and migration literature in a number of ways. One could argue that the studies tend to suggest that immigrants (of all types) are at greater risk of mental illness than non-migrants but that there are numerous exceptions and inconsistencies and further careful replicative work needs to be done. Alternatively, one could point out the number and complexity of the intervening and confounding variables and conclude that no one simple theory or explanation would suffice to explain this important and complex relationship.

Third, one may attempt to list and weigh those (universal) factors which appear to affect migrant adjustment or lack of it. There may be many ways of subdividing these factors into groups: one could do it according to whether or not they are 'psychological', or whether they relate to adjustment before, during or after migration. Some observers, less sympathetic to psychological/psychiatric research and theorizing, may be tempted to dismiss psychological factors completely in discussing the relationship between mental health and migration. For instance, an argument between a social scientist and a sceptic unsympathetic to psychological or sociological research may follow the pattern set out in Table 4.10. This is not to suggest that psychological researchers ignore, down-play or dismiss non-psychological factors in explaining the relationship between mental health and migration, but rather that these variables do not seem sufficient to explain the complex relationship.

Perhaps the most useful way of attempting *an* or *some* explanations for the relationship is to point out some of the more important distinctions in both the types *of migrants* and the *criteria of adaptation*. For instance, many of the studies reviewed in this chapter have used simple unidimensional self-report measures of minor psychiatric morbidity as the only dependent measure. Many other criteria of adjustment may be

Table 4.10 Psychological and non-psychological explanations for migrant–native differences in mental health

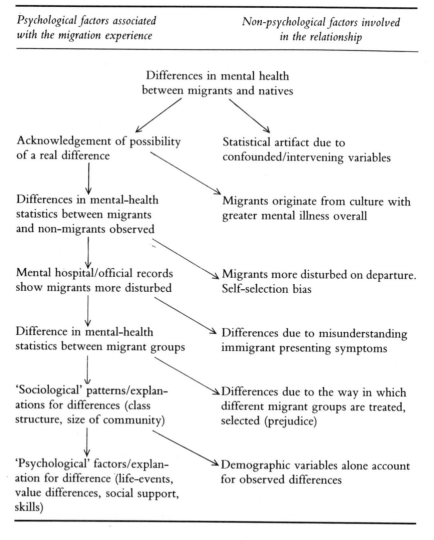

Psychological factors associated with the migration experience	Non-psychological factors involved in the relationship

Differences in mental health between migrants and natives

Acknowledgement of possibility of a real difference

Statistical artifact due to confounded/intervening variables

Differences in mental-health statistics between migrants and non-migrants observed

Migrants originate from culture with greater mental illness overall

Mental hospital/official records show migrants more disturbed

Migrants more disturbed on departure. Self-selection bias

Difference in mental-health statistics between migrant groups

Differences due to misunderstanding immigrant presenting symptoms

'Sociological' patterns/explanations for differences (class structure, size of community)

Differences due to the way in which different migrant groups are treated, selected (prejudice)

'Psychological' factors/explanation for difference (life-events, value differences, social support, skills)

Demographic variables alone account for observed differences used, for instance physical health, economic and social dependence on the community, acquisition of the new culture, socio-economic mobility and self-reported happiness and satisfaction. Though it is probable that many of these factors are intercorrelated, they may have different determinants. The first point, then, is that different criteria of mental health would lead to a different set of, or at least differently weighted, psychological and demographic migrant variables. There are other factors which need to be considered. For instance, whether the migrants are legal or illegal, voluntary or forced, semi-permanent or temporary, migrating alone or in groups – all make a difference to the relationship between migration and mental health. As has been pointed out in Chapter 3, motives for migration (economic, political, hedonistic) may also make a difference. Indeed, the admitting countries' explicit and implicit bases for selection is also an important factor in understanding the relationship between mental health and migration.

One way of looking at this problem is to categorize the major determinants of migration and adaptation in terms of the factors at *origin* (migrants' country of departure) and *destination* (migrants' country of arrival). Factors at origin include the migrants' mental health, education, age, intelligence, motives, social support and religion, while those at destination include the locals' prejudice, the economy, the prevailing values and the screening mechanisms.

Suffice it to say that no one grand theory or explanation could be put forward to account for all the findings reviewed. What is much more realistic is to try to understand why there is a particular association between certain specific groups of immigrants and certain aspects of their adjustments. Some relationships – such as the association between age and adjustment, or social support and mental health – may hold across various migrant groups while others may not. Work by Cochrane in Britain and Krupinski in Australia appears to have moved closest to offering general and specific explanations for this complex, elusive and intriguing relationship.

Chapter summary

Since research on mental health and migration began, over 100 years ago, a considerable amount of data has been collected in a wide variety of countries. Despite not inconsiderable problems of data collection – such as the use of mental-health admission record figures for comparative purposes without appropriate standardization for age, sex, class, and so on – enough reliable and valid data have been collected to examine mental-health statistics of different migrant groups compared to their host nationals.

Although some early research examined the mental health of migrants *before* they migrated, and even the mental health of those people who *re-*

migrated to their original destination, these highly desirable features have been missing from later studies. Instead, researchers have been content to compare specific migrant groups with host nationals. For historical, geographic and economic reasons, different countries have had very different migrant groups. In Australia the primary migrant groups have come from Britain, southern Europe, eastern Europe and western/ northern/central Europe, while migrants to Britain have fallen into four rather different groups: the Irish, West Indians, Pakistanis and Indians. American research has concentrated particularly on Chinese and European migrants as well as those coming from places such as Puerto Rico, and so on.

No matter where the studies have been conducted, two major findings emerge. First, it appears that frequently, but not always, migrants experience more mental illness than host nationals. There are important (and seemingly explicable) exceptions to this rule, but overall the findings seem pretty well consistent. Second, there are important differences between migrant groups both as regards the extent and type of illnesses they suffer from. For instance, the British in Australia tend to suffer from a relatively high incidence of alcoholism (compared to the natives), while the West Indians in Britain have an abnormally high incidence of schizophrenia. Although there are enormous problems of diagnosing illness in people from other cultures (e.g. the inaccuracy of official records, and a variety of data-collection methods such as general population surveys and the use of unobtrusive measures), these results have confirmed previously established findings. Furthermore, this pattern is equally true of internal migrants, that is those who migrate but not across national boundaries. Finally, some studies have concentrated on the adaptation or assimilation process attempting to trace the various stages migrants (and their children) pass through as they adjust to their new culture.

Many descriptive researchers have not been able to resist the temptation of speculating as to the origin of these differences. As has been noted, while some prefer predispositional explanations – in terms of demographic, cultural or personality factors – others opt for adaptation, reaction explanations, believing the stress of change to be the primary cause of this mental illness. Many of these explanations seem plausible but are unable to account for all the observed differences. Clearly there are universal, general factors, specific historical subcultural and individual difference factors – all of which operate together to produce or inoculate against mental illness.

Various 'traditional' explanations keep recurring, and these will be examined in Chapter 7. More recently, different types of explanation or factors have been put forward to account for these differences and these will be reviewed in Chapters 8 and 9.

The chapter also highlighted some of the more recent work on refugees. Many of these studies have been done on South-East Asian Chinese refugees in America. The results show a fairly high incidence of depression in these people but also that they tend to cope remarkably well under very difficult circumstances. However, this literature – often out of necessity rather than simply through poor planning – has a number of serious methodological faults which makes the whole business of interpretation very difficult indeed.

5 *Psychology of the extended sojourn: students and voluntary workers*

Introduction

A 'sojourn' is defined as a 'temporary stay at a new place'. The word 'sojourner' has usually been used to denote a traveller, and a 'sojourn' is most often thought to be an unspecified amount of time spent in a new and unfamiliar environment. The precise length of stay and the motive for travel are not specified.

As has been noted before, there are many types of sojourners: business people, diplomats, the armed forces, students, voluntary workers, missionaries, and so on, who often spend six months to over five years in 'other countries' in order to do business; represent their country; protect others or instruct other armed forces; study; teach or advise locals; convert and proselytize, respectively. It is obviously important that these sojourners adapt to the new culture rapidly in order that they may operate effectively. However, there are wide individual differences in how much and how quickly these sojourners adapt to new conditions, which may be very costly to their personal mental and physical health as well as being very expensive to the organizations they work for.

Despite the fact that people have sojourned since time immemorial, it is not until comparatively recently that systematic research has been done on this topic. Furthermore, it has been undertaken by researchers from a variety of academic backgrounds such as psychologists, psychiatrists, social workers and others. The research in this area has been primarily confined to two groups which often have a lot in common: students and voluntary workers. Although some work has been done on the adaptation of sojourning businessmen (see later in this chapter) and missionaries (see Ch. 10), the only extensive and intensive research has been done on foreign students and voluntary (especially Peace Corps) workers.

Students and Peace Corps workers have numerous features in common. They tend to be young (e.g. twenties), well educated, highly motivated and adaptable. However, whereas the former often originate in underdeveloped Third World countries and sojourn in the developed industrialized world, the opposite is true of the latter.

Nevertheless, psychological studies on sojourning students and voluntary workers have provided particularly interesting insights into various aspects of culture shock, such as a more careful definition of the components of culture shock, some idea of the more important predictor variables, stage-wise theories of adaptation, and so on. This chapter will review some of this work, attempting to highlight the substantial findings.

Although the practice of students travelling from one country to another has been established for centuries, particularly in Europe, it is not until comparatively recently that they have become the focus of study. One reason for increased interest in the psycho-social problems of students from abroad is simply their large numbers – estimated by Zwingmann and Gunn (1983) to exceed one million. The flow of these populations, as estimated by a UNESCO project in 1975, is shown in Table 5.1. Indeed, there is now a journal dedicated almost exclusively to the health of students: the *Journal of the American College Health Association*. Furthermore, there are various books exclusively on foreign students (Bochner and Wicks, 1972; Klineberg and Hull, 1979; Jenkins et al., 1983). It should be noted that not all this work has been done on students who go abroad to study, but also those of student age who go to foreign countries as volunteers of one sort or another (Di Marco, 1974; Smith, 1966). Traditionally both have become known as sojourners as their stay is usually temporary rather than permanent, although such 'temporary' visits can sometimes last up to five or six years.

Table 5.1 Flow of student population (UNESCO 1975)

1. From Asia	:	to N. America	111,206
		to Europe and USSR	86,000
2. From Africa	:	to Europe and USSR	61,315
3. From N. America	:	to Europe and USSR	26,648
4. From S. America	:	to N. America	17,141
		to Europe and USSR	14,822
5. From Arab States	:	to Europe and USSR	47,413
		to Asia	20,517
6. From Europe	:	to N. America	29,634
		to other European states and USSR	104,853

Source: C. A. A. Zwingmann and D. A. G. Gunn (1983) 'Uprooting and health: psycho-social problems of students from abroad', Geneva, World Health Organisation, Division of Mental Health.

In Chapter 2 we briefly described the development of this literature and placed it into its historical context. What follows is an elaboration of that discussion. In the 1950s, international education was regarded as very much a part of the post-war reconstruction effort. Later, as the Cold War increasingly cast its shadow on the world, student exchanges became linked to the foreign policy and diplomatic interests of the large donor countries (Bochner and Wicks, 1972), that is countries that provided the university places and often the scholarships that went with them. For instance, programmes such as the Australian Colombo Plan or the American Fulbright Scheme quite openly acknowledged that their aim was to boost the economies of the recipient countries, incidentally creating markets for their own export industries; to stem the tide of communism by improving the standard of living in Third World regions; and to make influential friends and allies who would support the donor countries in military and diplomatic initiatives and in world forums such as the United Nations.

The criteria by which international education was judged reflected these aims. Consequently, the focus of much of the research was on the attitudes that foreign students formed during their sojourn towards their hosts and towards western ideas and practices. This concern produced countless surveys, mostly a-theoretical in nature, and of rather limited value. Since an explicit aim of the officially sponsored programmes was the so-called diffusion of innovations, which in practice meant exporting western technical know-how to the Third World, there was also an interest in the pass rates of foreign students and how these might be improved, in turn leading to a consideration of their mental health, likewise a dubious enterprise. Later, the tendency of the brighter students to either not return to their country of origin after completing their studies or to emigrate soon after returning from abroad, became an issue. This process was called the 'brain drain' (Adams, 1968; Klineberg, 1981), and caused a good deal of concern because it negated the very principles on which many of the schemes rested. Numerous studies were conducted to shed light on the determinants of the brain drain and how it might be reversed.

The world in the 1980s presents a different picture. Many of the countries that were the recipients of technical and educational aid in the post-war era are now highly industrialized and have economies with growth rates that are the envy of their erstwhile donor nations. Technical assistance in the form of training students from the less-developed countries is no longer the pressing concern it once was. But the Cold War, or its current equivalent, is still with us, and governments of all persuasions are still concerned with influencing the hearts and minds of young people from other countries, particularly those that are 'non-aligned'. However, the foreign-policy objectives of international education are being de-emphasized, or possibly its political aspects are being handled with more subtlety and sophistication nowadays.

Current research into student exchanges reflects this move away from considerations of economic progress, the diffusion of innovations, the development of mutual understanding and friendly attitudes, and the mental health of foreign students. The dependent variables that are now increasingly appearing in studies deal with culture-learning and its effect on the ethnic identity of foreign students – very much a concern of the 1980s. There is also an increasing interest in the social networks of foreign students, both while on sojourn and after returning home. Studies have also looked at the cross-national networks that some of these individuals join as a result of having studied abroad, and at the mediating function that these individuals and their networks fulfil in bridging the various cultures that they have acquired. Current research is also much more theory-orientated. The better studies explicitly try to derive the actions of foreign students from a set of general principles of behaviour, particularly those constructs that have been found to be useful in social psychology. Another welcome development is that many of the studies now employ a quasi-experimental design, a far cry from the shot-gun surveys of the early days.

What follows is a brief, selective review of some of the empirical work that has been conducted in this field, illustrating the historical development of the substantive concerns, methods and approaches described in the preceding pages.

Empirical studies of student exchanges

Most of the early studies were concerned with such things as the relationship between student mental health and academic performance (Kelvin et al., 1965; Lucas et al., 1966) without any special reference to the particular problems of foreign students. Some of the earliest studies concerned the suicide of university students (Rook, 1954; Gunn, 1979) though there is some debate as to the extent of this (Schwartz, 1980). Some have argued that parasuicide and suicide attempts have reached epidemic proportions (Gunn, 1979), others have noted that suicide accounts for 50 per cent of all causes of student death (Norman, 1974). However, these studies have not separated foreign (overseas) from native (home) students, nor have they been able to overcome the problems associated with all suicide statistics (error, differential registration procedures of death, religious sanctioning).

The literature on the experience and, particularly, the difficulties of being a foreign student, dates back to just after the Second World War. Much of the earliest literature was non-empirical and impressionistic but rich in detail. Carey (1956) looked at the adaptation of then 'colonial' students, considering them in different groups one at a time, and also considered British reactions. Consistent themes running though Carey's book include the excessively optimistic (and subsequently disillusioned) expectations that the students had about their life in Britain and, second, the importance of British beliefs and attitudes. Carey noted:

> Both favourable and unfavourable stereotypes exist in relation to Asians and Africans: thus Asians are 'highly civilised', 'very brainy', philosophers who often perform truly astounding feats of memory; but they are also 'treacherous', cunning and cruel: 'you can't trust any of them'. Africans, on the other hand, are either 'savage' and 'primitive', with enormous sexual powers, or alternatively kind, loyal darkies, childlike and grateful for any kindness bestowed on them. But it is significant that of the stereotypes about Asians, some at least are unqualifiedly favourable; while those about Africans are favourable only in a highly patronising way, and hence unacceptable to African students. There is little doubt that this is at least partly connected with political status: some Asian countries have an unbroken tradition of independence, while most Londoners have by now at least some idea of post-war political developments in that part of the world. Africans, however, are closely associated in the public mind with the idea of dependent, colonial status, and it is only very recently that people have become aware of their political progress. Asia, moreover, is linked with vague notions about strange but elaborate religions and philosophies; while to many British people Africa before the coming of Europeans still is a place of primeval chaos and unrelieved night. (1956, p. 145)

In his analysis, Carey paid particular attention to student expectations and the difficulties associated with university life in Britain, and to the reactions of the host nationals. Because of their excessively optimistic expectations, often based on colonial education, students frequently became very depressed. This was exacerbated by accommodation problems and British prejudice:

> To a great extent, colonial students in London find that their contacts with British people are restricted to relationships of a 'formal' kind. Various organisations tried to introduce them to Londoners, but with relatively little success. In the formal context of official introductions both groups tend to regard the other as stereotypes, and the relationships that ensue are generally not what the students desire. (Carey, 1956, p. 164)

Carey stresses that because host nationals only make the roughest of distinctions between the various groups of colonial students, the variants of social adaptation are explained in terms of differences of social and cultural background.

In a similar report based on essays of 'disappointed guests' – overseas students – Tajfel and Dawson (1965) found much the same reactions:

initial optimism, surprise at the class system and evidence of prejudice and discrimination. There were six times as many unfavourable comments about the British (ignorant of the students' countries, reserved, patronizing, superior, conservative, hypocritical) as favourable (friendly, helpful, co-operative). The African students were most unfavourable and the West Indians most favourable, but overall their impressions were poor. These essays and the content analysis were mostly about racial prejudice and personal unhappiness. The authors did not go into any detail concerning how students attempted to cope with their problems and which strategies were least and most effective.

Others have attempted systematic observations and interviews with a limited number of specific students. For instance Schild (1962) studied fifty-nine Jewish-American students on a one-year trip to Israel. He was particularly interested in the foreign student as a stranger learning the norms of the host culture. He argued that though participation and explicit communication may be very effective for culture-learning, they depend on the willingness of the hosts to allow the stranger to participate or communicate, whereas opportunities for *observation* exist independently of the hosts' readiness to co-operate. The results showed that attitude change was primarily a function of participation, then observation and finally communication, in that order of importance.

A number of studies at various university health services in the 1950s and 1960s were published, though again not all looked specifically at foreign students. For instance, Hopkins et al. (1957) looked at non-intellectual correlates of success and failure of students at London University. Some of the more interesting results indicated that, as opposed to successful students (passed all their courses), failed students (academically failed or abandoned course) had significantly fewer opposite-sex friends, were less likely to marry at college and had fewer close friends. This latter finding was particularly striking and is shown below:

		Particular friend	No particular friend
Failed students	(N=176)	54 (31.6%)	122 (68.4%)
Successful students	(N=212)	133 (62.7%)	79 (37.3%)

The importance of friendship networks which was uncovered by this study has been extensively reviewed and will be discussed elsewhere.

Similarly, Rust (1960) at Yale University looked at the epidemiology of student mental health. Over a third of the students complained of nervousness, a quarter of loneliness and a tenth of insomnia, all of which appeared to interfere with their studies, friendship, sex life, and so on. Although Rust developed a simple discriminating scale to assess student mental health, the study did not and could not say very much about the aetiology of the students' problems. A recent Australian study (Cole et al., 1980), however, failed to find any evidence that foreign students are more prone than native-born students to visit university health centres. The study – conducted at the two universities in Hong Kong, the University of Singapore, and Monash University, Australia – did, however, yield interesting findings. First, foreign (ethnic Chinese) students consulted less in Australia than their counterparts at home. This result was explained in two ways: foreign students are highly motivated to do well and prepared for the experience, and most students were middle class. However, the authors believe that the contradiction between their and others' findings may be due to western physicians labelling as pathological the normal behaviour of members of another culture (see Ch. 4).

Other reports have looked specifically at the incidence of foreign overseas students using university health facilities. In a largely impressionistic paper, Eldridge (1960) reported on some of the difficulties of overseas students at Leicester University. He also explored some of the reactions of British students to their foreign peers. Many British students reported finding it difficult to express anything negative to foreign students and complained that if they expressed interest or friendship, they were perceived as patronizing, and if not, prejudiced. Little work appears to have been done on native student reactions and attitudes to foreign students, which are clearly important for the adjustment of the foreigners.

Still (1961) at Leeds University attempted a much more empirical study by looking at the incidence of different types of reaction in overseas students from various countries, as compared to British students. On average 14 per cent of the British students showed evidence of psychological problems, while with foreign students the percentage was always higher: Egypt (22.5 per cent), Nigeria (28.1 per cent), Turkey (21.0 per cent), Iraq (28.2 per cent), Iran (29.7 per cent), India (17.6 per cent) and Pakistan (18.7 per cent). Nearly half of the cases were hypochondriacal:

> Characteristically, the hypochondriacal overseas student almost continuously finds some source of discomfort in this or that part of his body. Usually the physical signs of disease that can be found by the examining physician are extremely trivial or non-existent – but not so the symptoms of which the patient complains. He feels extremely weak, he is very nervous, he cannot sleep, he has a cough and cold, he has no appetite, he has indigestion, he has first constipation then diarrhoea, his stomach feels heavy, he has constant nausea, his head feels heavy, he has pain in his chest, in his limbs, he has palpitations, his heart feels weak, he feels numbness, he is depressed, he is anxious about his sexual functions, he cannot concentrate on his work, his mind is not clear any more, he is afraid that he must have serious disease of the lungs, of the heart, of the stomach, of the intestines, of

the head, of the sexual organs, that he has some infection which is constantly spreading from one part of the body to another. Every other week, during the whole of his time in Leeds, he is attending the doctor for this or for that, rarely with any but trivial signs of illness, but always most concerned and anxious about the state of his health. (Still, 1961, p. 61)

One of the most influential papers in this area was that of Ward (1967), who argued for the existence of a 'foreign-student syndrome' which is characterized by vague, non-specific physical complaints, a passive, withdrawn interaction style and a dishevelled, unkempt appearance. His thesis, which was to influence a lot of subsequent work, was that depressed and 'culture shocked' overseas students tend to somatize their problems so as to avoid losing face, thus providing them with the justification to attend clinics for medical, as opposed to psychological help. Hence it is to be expected that foreign students would be overrepresented in student health services (Willmuth et al., 1975). Indeed, Gunn (1970) found a higher incidence of digestive, dermatological and sexual problems in overseas as opposed to home students.

Other studies have looked at the help-seeking behaviour of psychologically disturbed students (Mechanic and Greenley, 1976; Padesky and Hammen, 1981). More recently O'Neil et al. (1984) compared a sample of depressed Canadian students visiting a university psychiatric clinic with a group *not* attending the clinic. The severity of depression and being female were among the most important determinants of clinic use. After controlling for these two variables the discriminating factors showed that help-seekers were likely to be older, graduate students, living away from their family and used to visiting an ordinary doctor. Having a close confiding friend was not related to help-seeking, which suggests that the presence of a confidant may be preventive but does not necessarily decrease the need for professional help. Thus the study showed that a depressed student's decision to seek help is probably best predicted by the severity of the problem, past general help-seeking behaviour, the availability of other resources and the university health service in particular.

Often the most interesting and detailed studies are of particular student groups. For instance, in Britain there have been detailed studies of African students by Lambo (1960) and Noudehou (1982). Anumonye (1970) has tabulated the most common causes of difficulty for African students in Britain. He interviewed 150 African students and found a number of common experiences of distress (Table 5.2).

Similarly Singh (1963) interviewed 300 students in Britain in great detail and found that many experienced unanticipated difficulties.

1. *Emotional problems.* Nearly half of the sample experienced difficulties which they had not anticipated. These related mainly to loneliness,

Table 5.2 Common causes of psychological stress for African students in Britain

Inevitable problems	
British peculiarities	Sexual problems
Racial discrimination	Career-choice restrictions
Accommodation difficulties	Study-method discrepancies
Separation reactions	Dietary difficulties
Age-determined problems	Personality problems
Language and adjustment	British climate

Avoidable problems	
Financial stress	Over-identification
Misunderstanding and mistrust	Academic inadequacy
Teacher–student difficulties	Ethnocentrism
Vocational guidance	Disillusionment
Loneliness	Employment difficulties
Married-student difficulties	Inadequate embassy support

Source: C. A. A. Zwingmann and A. D. G. Gunn (1983), 'Uprooting and health; psycho-social problems of students from abroad', Geneva, World Health Organisation, Division of Mental Health.

homesickness, lack of training in looking after oneself, food difficulties and worries about domestic problems back at home. Upper-class students had less difficulty than middle-class students, and younger students – under 26 – were better adjusted than older students. Emotional strain was significantly associated with adjustment.

2. *Academic problems.* Nearly half the students had academic problems, mainly as a function of three factors: language problems, particularly in oral expressions; the higher standard of British universities; and difficulties in teacher–student relationships, particularly regarding status. Academic difficulties were significantly negatively correlated with adjustment.

3. *Adjustment.* Adjustment was related to place of residence (students had more difficulty at Oxbridge than provincial universities), social class (upper-class students were better adjusted than middle-class students), duration of stay (there is a U-shaped curve up to three years with least adjustment in the middle period), social skill (there was a positive correlation between social skill and adjustment).

Singh concluded:

the survey had shown that it may be misleading to consider the Indian students as an undifferentiated group. Their problems of adjustment to different spheres of life – social, personal and academic – depended on various factors such as social class, age, personality traits, levels of study, type of university and duration of stay in this country. It is important to emphasize this point since most of the previous studies of foreign students have overlooked the differences between them. (p. 117)

Bourne (1975) reviewed the history of Chinese students in the United States, and the particular problems they face. Over a four-year period he interviewed twenty-four Chinese students who presented themselves as patients, and a control group of twenty-four non-patients; he looked at the recurrent themes emerging from the interviews of patients and non-patients alike. He found parental, personal and other demands for excellence, which meant that Chinese students worked harder and for longer hours than most other students. Males tended to be unassertive, shy and have few friends, while females tended to be less isolated but felt guilty about dating non-orientals. He concludes:

In earlier years there was no conflict for the Chinese student in the American University environment. . . Now the demands are mixed and conflicting and too often, as in the case of the socially passive male, the Chinese student is ill equipped to deal with the Caucasian campus population. At the same time there are no longer the same rewards if he or she remains totally adherent to Chinese cultural values, as after graduation few professional opportunities exist any longer for the person who cannot deal effectively with the entire American population. (p. 276)

Earlier, Veroff (1963) studied the problems of African students in the United States. He found, not surprisingly, that African students became more tolerant of American informality and yet more intolerant of what they perceived to be insincere outgoingness. They also tended to change in their views of Africa, becoming more nationalistic, and to be more achievement-orientated than prior to their arrival. It would be most interesting to replicate this study in view of the many changes that have occurred in Africa and in America with regard to more civil rights and ethnic consciousness.

Researchers have introduced the concept of *culture-distance* to account for the amount of distress experienced by a student from one culture, studying in another. Babiker et al. (1980) hypothesized that the degree of alienation, estrangement and concomitant psychological distress was a function of the distance between the students' own culture and the host culture. They devised a culture-distance index (CDI) which they hoped would provide a fairly objective assessment of disparity between the two cultures uncontaminated by the subjects' own perception of these differences or feelings about them. Items included variables such as climate, clothes, religion, food, and family structure. The instrument was then used on 121 'foreign' students at Edinburgh University to investigate the possible association between culture-distance and medical consultations, and symptoms and academic success in examinations. Correlational analysis showed that culture distance was significantly related to anxiety during the Easter term and the total number of medical consultations during the year but not to examination success (Table 5.3). The authors argue that the relationship between the CDI and medical consultations may mean that culturally distant students perceived the health service as an approachable safe haven, or that they do suffer more physical illness, or that the opportunity of free and expert medical check-ups is being utilized. Clearly their study was unable to tease these variables apart, yet, as they note, perhaps the most important aspect of their study was the development of the CDI, which seems a useful instrument.

Table 5.3 Significant correlations (p.<0.05) between CDI items, symptoms, consultations and examination performance

CDI item	Anxiety	Tiredness	Headache	Consultations	Exam success
1. Climate	+0.18				
2. Clothes					−0.24[a]
3. Language					
4. Educational level				+0.27[b]	−0.21
5. Food	+0.32[c]			+0.30[b]	−0.20
6. Religion	+0.30[c]				
7. Material comfort		+0.25[b]			+0.20
8. Leisure				+0.24	
9. Family structure					−0.25[b]
10. Courtship/marriage			+0.19	+0.27[b]	−0.20
CDI	+0.23[a]			+0.26[b]	

Source: I. E. Babiker et al., 'The measure of culture distance', *Social Psychiatry*, 15 (1980), 109–16.
Notes: [a]p<0.02   [b]p<0.01   [c]p<0.001

Furnham and Bochner (1982) conducted a similar study and found, as predicted, that the degree of difficulty experienced by sojourners in negotiating everyday encounters is directly related to the disparity (or culture distance) between the sojourners' culture and the host society. They argued that the stress experienced by foreign students is due largely to their lacking the requisite social skills with which to negotiate specific social situations. However, they are aware that the distancing between foreign students and the host culture may be a two–way process, as they found that many of the foreign students did not seek out host-culture friends, through whom they might have been better able to learn the appropriate social skills necessary for a satisfying sojourn.

It is perhaps because different methods have been used that sometimes very different results have been found. The conflicting results are particularly noticeable when looking at sex differences. Davey (1957)

found that British women students at Cambridge had poorer mental health than men, yet Malleson (1954), who worked with British students at London University, found no sex differences. On the other hand Kidd (1965) who worked at Edinburgh University, found British women to have better mental health than men. Anumonye (1970) found that male African students studying in Britain showed better adjustment and less emotional distress, but he found no sex differences with regard to academic stress.

Studies purporting to show differences in the mental health of native and overseas students by using medical consultation rates must be interpreted with caution. Overseas students may have no other source of help, and their beliefs about illness may differ from those prevalent in the host country. For instance, diseases seen as trivial by one society may not be seen as such by members of another culture, so that newly encountered, if relatively minor, infections could lead to a greater proportion of foreign students seeking medical advice than native borns familiar with the problems. This might explain the larger number of overseas students supposedly with hypochondriacal symptoms. Of course, an above-average consulting rate for any group (native or foreign) may arise from very frequent visits from a small sub-group of its members prone to visiting doctors. Hence the average number of visits per individual has to be considered and if the distribution is badly skewed, appropriate corrective statistics used.

Other studies have failed to include a control group of native students who have migrated from their home communities and may also experience some of the same problems as foreign students. Indeed, no studies appear to have distinguished students in their first year, who are presumably more vulnerable to stress, from second- and third-year students who would have had more opportunities to adapt to the student 'culture'. Furthermore, many of the studies have not collected information in a systematic way, which makes any form of empirical analysis impossible. Finally, some studies on foreign students have concentrated on only one nationality (e.g. Indian) while others have haphazardly collected and confused a wide range of foreign nationals who might experience quite different problems.

Some studies have been conducted in a more rigorous manner. For instance, Furnham and Trezise (1981) compared four groups of foreign students in Britain (Africans, Europeans, Middle Easterners and Malaysians) with two British control groups (first-years and second/third-years) on a reliable and valid self-report measure of mental health. As predicted, the overseas students as a whole showed evidence of significantly more psychological disturbance than either of the British groups, though there was no sex difference. Further, with the exception of the Malaysian students, the British students were significantly more satisfied with their social lives than the other groups.

A study that stands head and shoulders above most of the work in this area is the recent investigation by Klineberg and Hull (1979), in which 2536 foreign students from 139 nations, studying in eleven countries, were surveyed. A notable feature of this study is that indigenous researchers participated on an equal-status basis with the principal investigators. The research strategy was determined at a meeting attended by fifteen scholars from the various countries. This group designed the questionnaire to ensure its relevance in all the nations and to establish its conceptual equivalence across the various cultural settings. Moreover, the items were chosen to enable testing certain hypotheses of interest to all the researchers and to verify the existence of certain interrelationships among variables known from previous research to affect the academic sojourn. For instance, the design permitted an explicit test of the importance of friendly social contact with host members and of whether adjustment follows a U-curve – both major theoretical issues in the field. Klineberg has written extensively on the foreign sojourn as a miniature life-history, and to test that idea a sub-sample were interviewed three times during their sojourn to trace the coping process over time. Only one or two other studies have employed such a longitudinal design. Another sub-group were asked to give a retrospective assessment fifteen years after the completion of their sojourn.

Substantively, four major themes were investigated: the sources of satisfaction, the difficulties encountered, changes in attitude and possible ways the sojourn experience might be improved. The data were analysed in the United States.

The findings cover many topics and are sometimes complex, and only those results relevant to the discussion in this chapter can be summarized here. Klineberg and his colleagues found that previous travel on the part of the respondents was associated with better coping skills, fewer difficulties and more contact with local people during their sojourn. Those students who had made satisfactory social contact and established relationships with local people during their sojourn, reported broader and more general satisfaction with their academic as well as their non-academic experiences. However, as other research has also shown (see the subsequent review of this area), a majority of the respondents failed to establish intimate relations with host members and associated mainly with fellow nationals or other foreign students. No support was found for the U-curve hypothesis of adjustment (an issue that will be discussed later). Almost a third of the respondents reported that they had been the object of discrimination, and a quarter said that personal depression was a problem for them. About 15 per cent of the respondents expressed a preference to remain in the sojourn country, evidence that the 'brain drain' is still something of a problem despite the big improvement in the economies of the sending countries in recent times.

The sheer size of this study and its methodological rigour add greatly to the robustness of the findings. Overall, the two most important factors implicated in the coping process of students at a foreign university were found to be social contact with local people and prior foreign experience. Both of these findings are compatible with and support a culture-learning/social-skills interpretation of the coping process, ideas that are discussed later in this chapter as well as elsewhere in this book (see Ch. 9).

Furnham and Bochner (1982) have argued that foreign students face four sorts of problems, two of which are exclusive to them (as opposed to native students). First, there are the problems that confront anybody living in a foreign culture, such as racial discrimination, language problems, accommodation difficulties, separation reactions, dietary restrictions, financial stress, misunderstandings and loneliness. Second, there are the difficulties that face all late adolescents and young adults, whether they are studying at home or abroad, in becoming emotionally independent, self-supporting, productive and a responsible member of society. Third, there are academic stresses when students are expected to work very hard, often under poor conditions, with complex material. Fourth, the national or ethnic role of overseas students is often prominent in their interactions with host members. In a sense, foreign students are being continually thrust into the role of ambassadors or representatives of their nation, often by well meaning people politely inquiring about their home customs and national origins, but sometimes by prejudiced individuals who may denigrate the policies or achievements of the student's country of origin. In shops there may be a tendency to speak slowly and clearly on the assumption that the foreigner's English is poor, and motherly ladies on buses will want to know if the student is feeling homesick. All this can be amusing, annoying or infuriating, depending on the circumstances, and is a burden that all foreigners must occasionally bear. However, studies of heightened national role salience (reviewed by Bochner, 1972) have shown that under some conditions this can lead to misunderstandings and hostility between foreign students and host members.

It is therefore not surprising that many foreign students suffer from poorer health than the natives, as they often face additional stresses. But the point needs to be made that not all of their difficulties can be attributed to their foreignness. Some of the problems are shared universally by all young adults pursuing a higher education.

Many attempts have been made to identify the most common areas of difficulty. Huang (1977) identified four:

1. *Communication barriers*, arising from unfamiliar and complex linguistic and paralinguistic features.
2. *Shifting cultural gears* as the student is forced to move between new

and old cultural values, identity, and so forth.

3. *Replacing a social network* of family, neighbours and friends at a time when they are regarded as a stranger and even an intruder.
4. *Multiple accountability,* to family, government or other sponsor, academic advisors and immigration officials.

More recently, Zwingmann and Gunn (1983) have attempted to understand the process of *uprooting* and its effect on the mental health of students (Fig. 5.1). The process is seen as the partial severance of individuals from their primary milieu and disruption of the habitual patterns of gratification. The authors distinguish between various types of conditions (Fig 5.1). The 'uprooting disorder' is related to both constitutional factors and also learned or conditioned factors. The latter are divided into various categories: the degree of psychological and socio-affective maturity; ideological and ethical differentiation; the extent and quality of motivation; previous exposure to other people from other systems or experience of living in other systems; and aspects of behaviour and linguistic ability. The authors point out that the following conditions also contribute to the uprooting disorder: climatic and topological dissimilarity; linguistic dissimilarity; politico-economic and social dissimilarity; ideological dissimilarity; general cultural dissimilarities in customs, rhythm of life, housing, nutritional habits, courtship patterns, religious beliefs, and so forth; racial dissimilarity and discrimination.

> Perfectly open systems are utopian. The majority of existing systems tend to be at least more closed than open. 'Closed' and 'open' are thus to be understood as relative notions. A system may, for instance, be relatively 'open' with respect to the equality and freedom of displacement (travelling), to express opinions, to choose pleasure, etc., but relatively 'closed' with respect to the existence of racial discrimination, the impossibility of transgressing caste-lines, social conventions or the necessity to be extremely competitive and consequently inconsiderate toward fellow men or women. A student from abroad may find his university or college is an 'open' system, yet the town or the country of temporary adoption 'closed'. However, in theory, according to national constitutions (e.g. declarations of independence, freedom, human rights, etc.), most western systems adopt the stance of being 'open'. (p. 20).

Low risk	*High risk*
– The individual who goes from one open system to another: (after correction for unfamiliar conditions: ethnic, climate, etc.).	– The individual who goes from one closed system to another closed one: meets accommodation problems, unfamiliar rules and contradictions of previous experience.

Low risk
- The individual who goes initially from an open system to a closed (after adaptation) because of social and communication skills that have been developed.
- The individual who goes from a closed to an open system: who benefits thus from hospitality.

High risk
- The individual who returns to a closed system after enjoying the life-style of an open one.

- The individual who experiences both open and closed systems at the same time and in the same country.

(Zwingmann and Gunn, 1983)

Zwingmann and Gunn also mention other factors, such as financial support and degree of volition and motivation, in the move abroad. Over two-thirds of their report concerns practical prevention and

Figure 5.1 (a) Parameter of uprooting and reaction modalities and (b) sample of possible reaction patterns

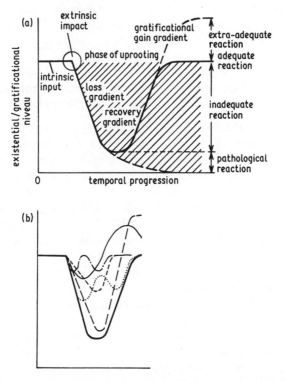

Source: C. A. A. Zwingmann and A. D. G. Gunn (1983) 'Uprooting and health: psychosocial problems of students from abroad', Geneva, World Health Organisation, Division of Mental Health.

remedial matters by which they hope to prevent student breakdown. It is, however, unclear from their work what might be the most important factors in predicting sojourner adjustment.

One area of research that is theoretically important is the work on foreign student friendship networks (Duck, 1977; Duck and Craig, 1978; Duck and Spencer, 1972; Klineberg and Hull, 1979). Recently, Bochner and his co-workers (Bochner, Buker and McLeod, 1976; Bochner, McLeod and Lin, 1977; Bochner and Orr, 1979; Furnham and Bochner, 1982) have shown some interesting trends in the friendship networks of overseas students. In a study of foreign students in Hawaii, Bochner et al. (1977) developed a *functional* model of overseas students' friendship patterns, stating that the sojourners belong to three distinct social networks. These are:

1. A *primary, monocultural* network consisting of close friendships with other sojourning compatriots. The main function of the co-national network is to provide a setting in which ethnic and cultural values can be rehearsed and expressed.
2. A *secondary, bicultural* network, consisting of bonds between sojourners and significant host nationals such as academics, students, advisors and government officials. The main function of this network is to instrumentally facilitate the academic and professional aspirations of the sojourner.
3. A *third, multicultural* network of friends and acquaintances. The main function of this network is to provide companionship for recreational, 'non-cultural' and non-task-orientated activities.

Although Bochner did not interpret his findings within a social-network framework, others have found that the degree of social interaction between the host national and the sojourner is related to the latter's adjustment. For example, Sewell and Davidsen (1961) reported a significant relationship between the social interaction of Scandinavian students with Americans and their satisfaction with their sojourn. Similarly, Antler (1970) in a study of 170 foreign postgraduate medical students found that those who reported more frequent personal contacts with their American hosts were least distant from them culturally and socio-economically. Richardson (1974) also noted a difference in the friendship patterns of satisfied as opposed to dissatisfied British migrants to Australia, the latter having more compatriot and fewer host-national friends. Selltiz and Cook (1962) found that sojourners who had at least one close host-national friend experienced fewer problems than sojourners with no close national friends. Based on the findings of a study in Australia, Au (1969) reported that the degree of personal contact between Chinese-Malaysian students and host nationals positively related to the student's attitude towards Australia.

The social-support hypothesis places more importance on the *quality* and *quantity* of support than the nature or *source* of that support. Thus it is the amount of social support that is seen as crucial rather than who provides it.

Others, however, (Bochner, 1982) place more emphasis on the *source* of support and its function. Thus help from a host-national network is important because through it foreign students can learn the social skills of their culture of sojourn. Help from the co-national network is important because through it foreign students can maintain their culture of origin. The theory predicts that the well-being of foreign students depends on them having access to both types of networks. However, the evidence suggests that most foreign students do not belong to a viable host-national network. Recently, Furnham and Alibhai (1985) replicated and extended some of the earlier studies done by Bochner and his co-workers. They used 140 students from thirty-five different countries, which were roughly categorized into nine groups: Asian, African, Oriental, European, Middle Eastern, North American, South American, West Indian and British. Overall the data were strikingly similar to those of Bochner et al. (1977). For instance, North Americans nominate a fairly large number of Europeans and British people as friends, which no doubt reflects cultural similarities (Furnham and Bochner, 1982) as do South Americans and Europeans presumably because they share the same religion and language. However, only about a quarter of the foreign students nominated a British person as a best friend. Indeed, 56 per cent of all the foreign students had no British friends at all. This tends to confirm the view that foreign students have limited contact with host nationals and may explain why many overseas students return home disgruntled with the society in which they studied. As Bochner et al. (1977) have noted:

> Thus monocultural [co-national] bonds are of vital importance to foreign students, and should therefore not be administratively interfered with, regulated against, obstructed, or sneered at. On the contrary, such bonds should be encouraged and, if possible, shaped to become more open to bi- and multi-cultural influences. In particular, mediating individuals who function as links between different cultural networks, should be identified and supported. Bi-cultural (foreign student/host national) bonds should be expanded to reach beyond their initial task-orientated and instrumental function. This often happens spontaneously, and ways and means should be found to capitalize on this tendency. Multi-cultural associations (bonds between non-compatriot foreign students) could likewise be expanded beyond their recreation-orientated function towards the non-superficial learning of each other's cultures. (p. 122)

Table 5.4 Adler's five-stage theory of culture-shock development

Stage	Perception	Emotional range	Behaviour	Interpretation
Contact	Differences are intriguing. Perceptions are screened and selected	Excitement Stimulation Euphoria Playfulness Discovery	Curiosity Interest Assured Impression-istic	The individual is insulated by his or her own culture. Differences as well as similarities provide rationalization for continuing confirmation of status, role, and identity.
Disintegration	Differences are impactful. Contrasted cultural reality cannot be screened out	Confusion Disorientation Loss Apathy Isolation Loneliness Inadequacy	Depression Withdrawal	Cultural differences begin to intrude. Growing awareness of being different leads to loss of self-esteem. Individual experiences loss of cultural support ties and misreads new cultural cues.
Reintegration	Differences are rejected	Anger Rage Nervousness Anxiety Frustration	Rebellion Suspicion Rejection Hostility Exclusive Opinionated	Rejection of second culture causes preoccu-pation with likes and dislikes; differences are projected. Negative behaviour, how-ever, is a form of self-assertion and growing self-esteem.
Autonomy	Differences and similarities are legitimized	Self-assured Relaxed Warm Empathic	Assured Controlled Independent 'Old hand' Confident	The individual is socially and linguistically capable of negotiating most new and different situations: he or she is assured of ability to survive new experiences.
Independence	Differences and similarities are valued and significant	Trust Humour Love Full range of previous emotions	Expressive Creative Actualizing	Social, psychological and cultural differ-ences are accepted and enjoyed. The individual is capable of exercising choice and responsibility and able to *create* meaning for situations.

Source: P. S. Adler, 'The transitional experience: an alternative view of culture shock', Journal of Humanistic Psychology, 15 (1975), 13–23. Copyright © 1975 by A. S. Adler. Reprinted by permission of Sage Publications, Inc.

Stage-wise theories: the shape of curves

Since Oberg (1960) it has been fashionable to describe the 'disease' of culture shock in terms of a number of stages (Smalley, 1963). These attempts have all been descriptive and tend to overlap.

Oberg (1960) listed four stages of shock:

1. *Honeymoon stage.* An initial reaction of enchantment, fascination, enthusiasm, admiration and cordial, friendly, superficial relationships with hosts.
2. *Crisis.* Initial differences in language, concepts, values, familiar signs and symbols lead to feelings of inadequacy, frustration, anxiety and anger.
3. *Recovery.* The crisis is resolved by a number of methods such that the person ends up learning the language and culture of the host country.
4. *Adjustment.* The sojourner begins to work in and enjoy the new culture, though there may be occasional instances of anxiety and strain.

Adler (1975) has proposed five stages in the development of culture shock. His stage-wise theory is set out in Table 5.4. Others have proposed a nine-stage sequence (Jacobson, 1963) and some a three-stage sequence (Garza-Guerrero, 1974; Lesser and Peter, 1957). But as Church (1982) has noted, there are numerous problems with these simple descriptive studies:

> Is the order of stages invariant? Must all stages be passed through or can some be skipped by some individuals? In order to classify individuals, key indicators of each stage are needed, indicators that may vary with the culture of origin or be indicative of more than one stage, reflecting superficial adjustment in an early stage but a true 'coming to terms' with the new culture in a later stage. (p. 542)

One of the more interesting consequences of these stage-wise theories is the debate on the U- or W-curve. The idea of the U-curve has been attributed to Lysgaard (1955). He concluded from his study of over 200 Norwegian Fulbright scholars in the United States that people go through three phases: initial adjustment, crisis and regained adjustment. Nowhere in the paper does Lysgaard describe the shape of the U, though he did imply that the period of adjustment took about twenty months with some point between six and eighteen months being the bottom of the U. The idea is quite simple: if one traces the sojourners' level of adjustment, adaptation and well-being over time, a U-shape occurs such that satisfaction and well-being gradually decline but then increase again. The W-curve is an extension by Gullahorn and Gullahorn (1963), who found that once sojourners return to their home country they often undergo a similar re-acculturation process, again in the shape of a U, hence the double U, that is W.

It is partly the appealing nature of the thesis but also the vagueness in the initial description that has led so many researchers to do studies on this particular topic. One problem has been the dependent variable (i.e. which aspect of adjustment is considered). Klineberg and Hull (1979) listed variables such as depression, loneliness and homesickness, while Torbiorn (1982) even included attitudes to the climate, sports and open-air facilities and knowledge of current affairs.

A second problem involves definition – when is a U not a U? Consider Figures 5.2 and 5.3 showing graphs by Torbiorn (1982) which depict ratings on a 9-point scale (1 = very good; 9 = very poor) of living conditions relating to food and perceptions of orderliness in the host country over time. According to Torbiorn (1982, p. 112), 'The characteristic U-curve appears with regard to food and orderliness, i.e. evaluations become less positive during the first year after which they "revive"'. It could hardly be argued that the above graphs constitute clear proof for the existence of a U-curve!

In a review of the U-curve literature, Church (1982) reports seven studies that found some evidence for the hypothesis but a similar number that did not. He concluded that support for the U-curve hypothesis is weak, inconclusive and overgeneralized. For instance, not all sojourners start off in the phase of supposed adjustment, elation and optimism – some are unhappy, depressed and anxious right from (if not before) the beginning. Second, some never become depressed or anxious, enjoying the experience and adjusting to the culture right from the start. Third, where there are U-curves, they are of dramatically different shape – some are flat, others tall and all are fairly irregular.

Few studies have tested the hypothesis longitudinally rather than cross-sectionally on a range of adjustment behaviours. Clearly what is required is a careful extensive longitudinal study aimed at determining which sojourner aspects interact with which aspects of the visited culture to produce which patterns of adjustment. At the present stage of its development, the U-curve hypothesis is too vague and too generalized to be of much use in predicting or understanding sojourner adjustment. Furthermore, it is not so much a theory as a *post hoc* description that has focused too much on single-outcome variables rather than on the dynamics or process of adjustment. There may be something salvageable in the U-curve hypothesis, but more sensitive, complex, longitudinal research will need to be done to determine either its existence or usefulness, and this work will need to be placed more firmly within a general theoretical framework.

These considerations led Bochner, Lin and McLeod (1980) to develop a model in which the dependent variable is interpersonal rather than intraphysic. Instead of construing adjustment as something that occurs

Figure 5.2 View of *food* in the host country (rated on a 9-point scale) as a function of time spent there.

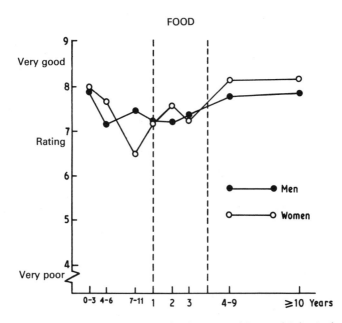

FOOD

inside the person, Bochner and his colleagues argued that so-called adjustment entails the acquisition, over time, of behaviours, skills and norms that are appropriate to the social roles that foreign students are required to enact. In particular, this involves entering into new relationships with significant people in the host country and resuming relationships with significant people after re-entry home. The sojourn U-shape can be derived from the distinction between observing a new culture and participating in it. When the sojourner's role as an observer shifts to that of a participant, a transition that is inevitable, the initial fascination with the new culture similarly shifts to now having to cope with it, which in Bochner's terms means learning its salient features. Some sojourners never learn the new culture nor develop reciprocal role relationships with their hosts. Other sojourners do acquire the social skills of the new society and develop genuine contacts with their hosts. Others again stand somewhere between these two extremes. Thus the rate of culture-learning is not uniform across sojourners but depends on all the contact variables discussed elsewhere in this book. This may explain why the U-curve is not supported in some studies, since some individuals may not experience it, such as sophisticated culture travellers who

Figure 5.3 View of *orderliness* in the host country (rated on a 9-point scale) as a function of time spent there.

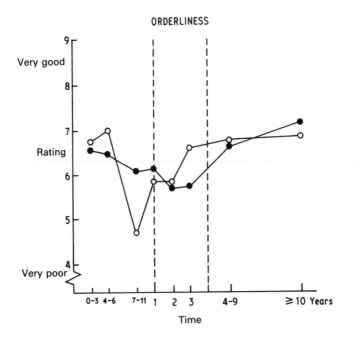

Source: See Fig. 5.2.

immediately become full participants and hence their curve never drops. Likewise, there are some very poor culture-learners who fail to ever participate in their new society, and their curve of satisfaction would therefore never rise. We are not aware of any empirical studies that have deliberately set out to test these hypothesized determinants of sojourn 'adjustment' over time.

The re-entry U-curve can be derived from the notion of contradictory role demands. Bochner, Lin and McLeod (1980) have shown that returning students anticipate that they will be subjected to contradictory social expectations. In particular, they think that there will be some ambivalence in the treatment they will receive from their professional, peer and family groups. For instance, the students feared that their stay-at-home friends would view them differently, that their parents may think them to have become too westernized and that in their occupation they may not be able to apply the knowledge they had gained overseas. Again, the rate of resolving these role conflicts may vary with a number of circumstances and could account for the absence of a W-curve in some studies.

The advantage of the social psychological model of temporal adjustment is that it can predict and explain different 'adjustment'

Figure 5.4 Different adjustment profiles of culture learners and travellers.

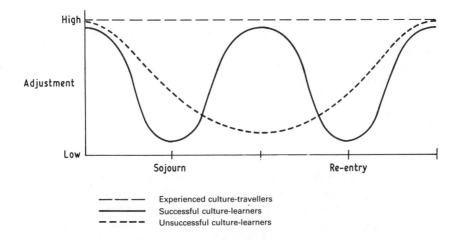

Experienced culture-travellers
Successful culture-learners
Unsuccessful culture-learners

profiles as a function of quite specific determinants. Thus the successful culture-learner should exhibit a typical U-curve and, after re-entry, a W-curve. Experienced culture travellers should show a flat 'curve' and unsuccessful ones a declining curve during sojourn and a rising one after re-entry. Figure 5.4 shows some of these possible relationships, all of which can be put to an empirical test. The other advantage of this model is that it is not restricted to the adjustment patterns of sojourners but has general implications. The model predicts that all persons entering into new relationships or social situations can be expected to develop sequential feelings of satisfaction or dissatisfaction. The shape of these curves will depend on how well the persons acquire the relevant behaviours, to what extent they can clarify their new roles, avoid role ambiguity and resolve any contradictory role demands in their relationships with significant persons in these new situations. Thus the model has application in areas such as entering into marriage, assuming a new job, becoming a parent for the first time or moving into a new neighbourhood. The model states that coping successfully with any life-event changes that have an interpersonal aspect (and most do) depends on processes similar to those involved in learning a new culture and may explain why some people cope with change better than others. Again, these assertions can be translated into specific predictions and tested empirically. The model also has clear-cut implications for remedial action.

Although not explicitly couched in the above terms, the work of Torbiorn (1982) is consistent with the model. His subjects were Swedish expatriate businesspersons working abroad. He plotted the adjustment pattern, over time, of two groups of these sojourners: those whose companions were predominantly fellow nationals, and those who spent their time mostly in the company of locals or third-country nationals. Both graphs followed a U-curve, but the pattern differed. Those with local friends went through a deeper adjustment trough than those whose companions were mainly co-nationals, but their level of satisfaction after six months was higher and the curve continued to rise. After three years the satisfaction level of those whose friends were mainly host members remained significantly higher than the amount of satisfaction reported by those who associated only with fellow nationals. These findings are consistent with a culture-learning interpretation of coping.

Voluntary workers

Another major category of persons who embark on extended sojourns abroad are voluntary workers. These are individuals who of their own volition choose to work in foreign countries, not for profit or to gain qualifications, but in order to provide services to people regarded as being in need of assistance. Thus, what sets voluntary workers apart, ostensibly at any rate, is that they tend to be motivated by altruistic or at least idealistic considerations, and it is of some theoretical interest whether this orientation towards service has any implications for coping with culture stress. Typically, the contact takes place on the home territory of the host people, usually in villages or small towns, with the voluntary workers deliberately setting out to reduce the social distance between themselves and their 'clients'. In practice this means attempting to adopt the life-style of the indigenous society where the actual sojourn is taking place, such as being housed in local accommodation, eating the food of the region and having an income that reflects the local economy. The kinds of services that have been provided include education, language-teaching, sanitation, technical and agricultural advice, health, nutrition and, in the case of missionaries, spiritual guidance.

The largest, systematically organized voluntary programme to be mounted in modern times must surely be the United States government-sponsored Peace Corps, which since 1960 has sent out tens of thousands of volunteers to most parts of the less-developed world. We have already referred to this scheme elsewhere in this book (see Ch. 2). The Peace Corps is of special interest to social scientists because in addition to the sheer size of the sample of sojourners who participated in the programme, it has the unique distinction of having been monitored, evaluated and partially guided by a large team of psychologists almost from its inception. Consequently, a good deal of empirical data are available about the adjustment patterns, problems and coping processes of this group of sojourners. There is a voluminous literature, which cannot be summarized here. Excellent summaries and overviews can be found in the writings of Guthrie (1975, 1981); Guthrie and Zektick

(1967); Harris (1973); Smith (1966); and in a book edited by Textor (1966). Our aim here is to select from this vast literature material that is relevant to the theme of the present chapter. From this perspective, two major items of interest emerge: the high attrition rates of the sojourners, and the recognition of the importance of situational determinants of adjustment in the field as distinct from selection procedures aimed at choosing the right individuals for the job. These issues will now be briefly discussed.

Attrition rates

Because the Peace Corps kept fairly good records, there was a unique opportunity to establish the rate at which volunteers did not complete their assignments, and the stage at which they dropped out. No such precise information exists with regard to foreign students or indeed any other category of sojourner. Consequently, the Peace Corps data provide a valuable guide to the extent to which the stresses of living in an unfamiliar culture become so acute that a sojourner withdraws from the programme despite having expressly volunteered to join the scheme in the first place.

The attrition information for the decade from 1961 to 1971 appears in Harris (1973). For each of the years Harris lists the number of applications, the number who registered for training, the number who terminated during training, the number who terminated early in the field (i.e. were repatriated before their tour of duty had ended) and the total attrition rate, made up of those who terminated either in training or in the field. The justification for combining these two figures into a single index is that much of the training occurred in simulated or real, in-country field sites and therefore exposed the trainees to second-culture influences. The figures are quite startling. The world-wide attrition rate exceeded 40 per cent in seven of the years listed, and even Harris, who has an obvious emotional attachment to the programme, admits in the text that an overall figure of 50 per cent probably reflects the real situation. Given that the participants were volunteers, mostly young and imbued with a spirit of idealism, these data provide clear evidence that culture travelling was not meant to be easy.

Personality versus situational determinants of coping

The high attrition rate gave rise to a lively debate about what might lie at the heart of the problem. Gradually it was acknowledged that the selection techniques, in which the Peace Corps had deployed most of its social-science resources, were unable to predict success in the field. It became clear that one could not go from a few indicators or self-reports to predicting remote outcomes far removed ecologically, psychologically and culturally from the original samples of behaviour on which the predictions were based. This in turn led to a general reassessment of the concept of personality and, in particular, of the usefulness of regarding enduring traits or dispositions as major determinants of behaviour. These theoretical developments are outside the scope of the present book and cannot be pursued here in any detail. Suffice to say that Mischel, who has been one of the leaders in the movement away from a simple trait model of behaviour (e.g. Mischel, 1973), in a recent retrospective review of his career (Mischel, 1984) wrote that his own failure in 1965 to predict success for Peace Corps teachers in Nigeria caused him much concern. Ultimately this led him to a reconceptualization of personality in terms of an interaction between the person and the situation, an idea that has had far-reaching consequences in general psychology, well beyond the confines of the Peace Corps predicament (for a review of this area, see Argyle, Furnham and Graham, 1981).

Of all the psychologists working with the Peace Corps at the time, Guthrie and his colleagues were the most explicit in rejecting the selection approach as a means of reducing culture stress (Guthrie, 1975, 1981; Guthrie and Zektick, 1967). Guthrie became convinced that in unfamiliar cultural settings situational determinants assume far greater significance than they do when one moves to a new assignment in a relatively familiar environment. He argued that during the first few weeks in a strange place, the volunteers would develop confidence or despair due to the experiences they encountered and over which they had little control. These experiences far outweighed whatever attributes of character or personality the volunteers might have brought with them to the new culture. In other words, technically Guthrie concluded that most of the variance in performance in the field could be attributed to situational influences, and only a relatively small amount of the variance could be accounted for by the enduring personality structure of the volunteers. Guthrie's solution, which is consistent with the position taken elsewhere in this chapter, was to emphasize training and social support during the early stages of life in the second country, based on the premise that external (i.e. environmental and situational determinants of behaviour) are more important than internal ones in coping with second-culture stress. Besides, it is easier to systematically manipulate the social and situational variables that impinge on a sojourner, rather than trying to modify the person's character or personality. The evidence reviewed in the present chapter suggests that the most important situational variables affecting the extended sojourn are the socio-cultural skills and information that a culture traveller requires in order to participate successfully in the new society, and the social-support systems that enable these skills to be acquired, rehearsed and deployed.

Chapter summary

This chapter concentrated primarily on the adjustment of foreign students, though voluntary workers were also briefly considered. Though research on foreign students has focused on different topics, most workers have attempted to specify which factors in the student's personality or previous experience and which factors in the host society in combination lead to healthy adjustment. Many studies – such as those looking at the incidence of using student health-service facilities – have come up with equivocal results, probably for methodological reasons. In fact, a surprising variety of dependent variables have been used in this research, ranging from suicide attempts and psycho-somatic illnesses to self-reports of unhappiness and academic failure. It is no doubt because of the enormous differences in the student groups studied (i.e. Chinese students in Australia, Americans in Israel, Africans in Britain), as well as the different dependent measures used, that the results have been so equivocal.

However, despite these contradictory findings, various patterns in the literature have begun to emerge. For instance, foreign students do appear to experience more physical and mental ill-health as well as more academic problems than native students. Although there are no grand theories attempting to explain this phenomenon, various concepts have been put forward to predict the quality, quantity and chronicity of sojourner distress. One such concept is the *culture-distance concept*, which states simply that the absolute amount of difference or distance (defined both objectively and subjectively) between a sojourner's own and the host culture is directly proportionally related to the amount of stress or difficulty experienced. Another concept relates to social support (see Ch. 8) and has been described as the *functional friendship model* which suggests that various friendship networks (host, bicultural and multicultural) serve important psychological functions, which in turn help a sojourner over numerous difficulties.

Considerable research effort has gone into trying to describe the various stages that sojourners go through in attempting to adapt to a new culture. There is as much doubt as to the number of identifiable stages as there is to the shape of the curves (with time plotted on the x axis and difficulty on the y axis). There appears to be weak support for the well-known U-shape hypothesis, though some reviewers believe the evidence inconclusive and overgeneralized. A major problem for the stage-wise approach is that so few of the studies have been longitudinal, and cross-sectional designs are particularly problematic in this case. Furthermore, while some forms of adjustment (i.e. to the language or the food) may be U-shaped, others may not be.

Once again, studies highlighted both intra- and inter-individual factors that related to sojourner adjustment. Alas, no theoretical framework emerged which may explain how, which and when these variables alone or in combination related to sojourner adjustment.

Psychological research into sojourner adjustment is comparatively new. Large-scale, multi-factoral, longitudinal studies which are theory-derived may help considerably to identify the problems of increasing numbers of sojourners the world over.

6 *Psychology of the short-term visit: tourism and job transfer*

This chapter is concerned primarily with people who travel both within their own country and to other, foreign countries for comparatively short periods of time. Furthermore, they usually travel voluntarily and/or for pleasure but there are of course exceptions.

There is a surprising paucity of psychological literature on both tourism and business transfer. That which exists is not notable for either its theoretical sophistication or empirical rigour. However, this literature will be considered because it throws important light on the relationship between geographic movement and psychological adjustment.

Tourism

Increasingly, tourism has become a vast multinational enterprise that is the backbone of many a country's economy. It is therefore not surprising that most analyses of tourism have been economic, geographic or demographic, rather than psychological: 'The feelings, memories, frustrations, aspirations and disappointments of the tourist are therefore lost in this mechanistic analysis of supply and demand' (Pearce, 1982a, p. 8).

In his review of the social psychology of tourist behaviour, Pearce (1982a) described the roles of various types of travellers, including tourists, and their characteristic behaviour. These are depicted in Tables 6.1 and 6.2.

Through multidimensional scaling, Pearce (1982a) reduced these various roles into five types of tourist travellers: exploitative (e.g. businesspersons); pleasure first (holidaymakers); high contact (journalists, students); environmental (explorers, conservationists); spiritual (missionaries, pilgrims). These various types are presumably related to where, how and for how long people travel and the extent to which they may suffer from culture shock.

The motivation for travel is an important determinant of reasons to

Table 6.1 The five major role-related behaviours for fifteen traveller categories

Traveller category	The five clearest role-related behaviours (in order of relative importance)
Tourist	Takes photos, buys souvenirs, goes to famous places, stays briefly in one place, does not understand the local people
Traveller	Stays briefly in one place, experiments with local food, goes to famous places, takes photos, explores places privately
Holidaymaker	Takes photos, goes to famous places, is alienated from the local society, buys souvenirs, contributes to the visited economy
Jet-setter	Lives a life of luxury, concerned with social status, seeks sensual pleasures, prefers interacting with people of his/her own kind, goes to famous places
Businessperson	Concerned with social status, contributes to the economy, does not take photos, prefers interacting with people of his/her own kind, lives a life of luxury
Migrant	Has language problems, prefers interacting with people of his/her own kind, does not understand the local people, does not live a life of luxury, does not exploit the local people
Conservationist	Interested in the environment, does not buy souvenirs, does not exploit the local people, explores places privately, takes photos
Explorer	Explores places privately, interested in the environment, takes physical risks, does not buy souvenirs, keenly observes the visited society
Missionary	Does not buy souvenirs, searches for the meaning of life, does not live in luxury, does not seek sensual pleasures, keenly observes the visited society
Overseas student	Experiments with local food, does not exploit the people, takes photos, keenly observes the visited society, takes physical risks
Anthropologist	Keenly observes the visited society, explores places privately, interested in the environment, does not buy souvenirs, takes photos
Hippie	Does not buy souvenirs, does not live a life of luxury, is not concerned with social status, does not take photos, does not contribute to the economy

International athlete	Is not alienated from own society, does not exploit the local people, does not understand the local people, explores places privately, searches for the meaning of life
Overseas journalist	Takes photos, keenly observes the visited society, goes to famous places, takes physical risks, explores places privately
Religious pilgrim	Searches for the meaning of life, does not live a life of luxury, is not concerned with social status, does not exploit the local people, does not buy souvenirs

Source: P. L. Pearce, *The Social Psychology of Tourist Behaviour*, Oxford, Pergamon, 1982.

visit new environments. As in general studies of motivation, this is a complex area. For instance, it is often difficult to distinguish between long- and short-term motivation; people may not be able to accurately explain their motives; and there are also problems with how these motives are measured. There are numerous marketing studies on people's choice of destination. Consider the list provided by over 5000 Canadians, presented in Table 6.3.

Both the aims and the methodology of these 'marketing' surveys make them less interesting, indeed even misleading, from a psychological perspective (Crompton, 1979). There is no simple reason or set of reasons why people travel. However, the complexity of the task should not deter investigators from determining how motivation relates to experience.

The tourist literature is perhaps richest when considering the nature and type of contact between tourists and hosts, which has been described by Machlis and Burch (1983) as relations between strangers. There are numerous examples of misunderstandings and of tourist and other authorities attempting to help travellers by spelling out some major differences in social behaviour between societies.

Each of these misunderstandings can cause bewilderment, rage, disappointment, disgust and stress (Bochner, 1982; Pearce, 1982a). These encounters tend to shape the tourists' perceptions of the natives and also serve to change their perceptions of themselves. For instance, Pearce (1982b) showed that contact with Greeks and Moroccans in their native lands led British travellers to change some of their previously recorded beliefs about them. At the same time, their travel experiences also had the effect of changing some of their attitudes to themselves. The proposition that travel results in greater insight into one's own culture has been explored by others (Steinkalk and Taft, 1979) and may begin to explain why some travellers from some countries experience shock. The idea is that travel acts as a looking-glass providing travellers with new

Table 6.2 The five most-applicable traveller categories for all twenty role-related behaviours

Role-related behaviour	Traveller categories (in order of importance)
Takes photos	Tourist, overseas journalist, holidaymaker, explorer, anthropologist
Exploits the local people	Conservationist (−), religious pilgrim (−), explorer (−), overseas student (−), businessperson
Goes to famous places	Tourist, jet-setter, overseas journalist, holidaymaker, hippie (−)
Understands the local people	Tourist (−), migrant (−), jet-setter (−), anthropologist, international athlete (−)
Lives a life of luxury	Jet-setter, hippie (−), missionary (−), religious pilgrim (−), businessperson
Keenly observes the visited society	Anthropologist, overseas journalist, explorer, missionary, conservationist
Interested in the environment	Conservationist, explorer, anthropologist, jet-setter (−), businessperson (−)
Contributes to the economy	Businessperson, hippie (−), tourist, religious pilgrim (−), holidaymaker
Never really belongs	Tourist, traveller, jet-setter, holidaymaker, overseas journalist
Takes physical risks	Explorer, businessperson (−), jet-setter (−), overseas journalist, tourist (−)
Is alienated from own society	Hippie, migrant, missionary, religious pilgrim, explorer
Stays briefly in one place	Tourist, jet-setter, traveller, international athlete, explorer
Has language problem	Migrant, tourist, overseas student, international athlete, traveller
Experiments with local food	Overseas student, tourist, traveller, jet-setter, overseas journalist
Explores places privately	Explorer, anthropologist, conservationist, overseas journalist, traveller
Concerned with social status	Jet-setter, businessperson, hippie (−), missionary (−), religious pilgrim (−)
Searches for the meaning of life	Missionary, religious pilgrim, hippie, anthropologist, conservationist
Seeks sensual pleasures	Jet-setter, missionary (−), hippie, religious pilgrim (−), businessperson

| Prefers interacting with people of his/her own kind | Jet-setter, migrant, businessperson, hippie, international athlete |
| Buys souvenirs | Tourist, missionary (−), hippie (−), conservationist (−), explorer (−) |

Source: P. L. Pearce, *The Social Psychology of Tourist Behaviour*, Oxford, Pergamon, 1982.
Note: A negative sign (−) after the traveller category implies that this traveller role is very low on the particular role-related behaviour.

insights into their own culture, and the new appraisal may not be welcomed. For instance, the sudden realization of the relative economic or cultural poverty of one's country, or of sexual, religious or political discrimination, may lead to feelings of distress. Machlis and Burch (1983) have noted:

> Of course, travelling is bound up with greed, curiosity, adventure and status. That is, the same motives that drive our daily life are part of travelling. The difference is that as tourists we alter the routines for fulfilling our daily life. Consequently, events we normally take for granted – eating, sleeping, bathing, talking, observing, thinking, sex, and so forth – take on larger than life significance. (p. 669)

Nearly all tourism is thought to be enjoyable. Although the motives and roles of individual tourists may be quite different, tourism is valued highly and looked upon as a pleasurable, desirable experience. It often represents a major reason for saving money (Furnham, 1985). Despite tourism – particularly the annual holiday – being so positively rated and being portrayed as interesting and relaxing, not all tourists enjoy their trip. Bewilderment, rage, disgust, boredom and illness may be as much a part of the tourist's experience as delight and recreation (Furnham, 1984b). For instance, many tour operators have complaints departments; radio and television programmes dedicated to holidays devote much of their time to the stories of disgruntled tourists; and drunkenness, brawls and other forms of socially unacceptable behaviour occur more often on holidays. Furthermore, it is not only the tourists who suffer negative effects of tourism, but also the toured.

There are only a few studies that have attempted to understand the negative psychological reactions of tourists – that is negative reactions which are not simply due to unfulfilled promises (hotel bookings, costs), transportation difficulties, theft of money or being cheated, but rather consequences of 'culture shock'.

Prokop (1970) found a high incidence of alcoholism, depression and minor psychiatric illnesses among a group of German tourists visiting Innsbruck. Increased, even excessive, alcohol consumption is frequently associated with holidays abroad. Although this may partly be a function

Table 6.3 Reasons for travel destinations of 5000 Canadians

Reasons for destination choice	*Respondents giving each reason (%)*
To visit friends or relatives	50
Relaxing atmosphere	33
Scenery	41
For oceans and beaches	19
Sports facilities	10
Good camp-sites	11
Good weather	24
Not too many tourists	10
To get better buys	4
Low cost of vacations	11
Warm, friendly people	22
Good roads	13
Outstanding food	7
Attractive customs, life	7
Foreignness	7
Night-life	6
Easier to have fun there	13
Cultural activities	5
Attractive advertising	5
Don't know much about own province's attractions	2
Don't make fun of English	3
Kicks of getting something back through customs	1
None of above	9

Source: P. L. Pearce, *The Social Psychology of Tourist Behaviour*, Oxford, Pergamon, 1982.

of the comparative price of alcohol in the place visited, it may also be due to boredom or anxiety.

In a study of American tourists in Africa, Cort and King (1979) examined three 'behavioural manifestations of culture shock': withdrawal; expression of hostility towards the host culture; and reidentification with the home culture. They hypothesized that tourists with more prior touring experience, and those with higher internal locus of control and more tolerance for ambiguity, would experience less shock, as operationally defined above, than those with little previous experience, external locus of control and tolerance of ambiguity. Prior travel experience – which was confounded by age, did not correlate with the three measures of culture shock, but age did in that older tourists experienced more shock. Locus of control did not correlate significantly with any of the dependent variables, but intolerance for ambiguity did. Because travel in other cultures is often difficult and bewildering, producing numerous incongruous and ambiguous situations to the foreigner, those with high intolerance of ambiguity experience more stress. Multiple regression failed to support the hypothesis that culture shock was a function of several variables working in combination.

In a more recent and more careful research project, Pearce (1981) used diaries to measure the day-to-day moods (both positive and negative) of groups of Australian tourists on two islands off the east coast of Australia. They were also asked to rate nineteen minor health symptoms (such as migraine, nausea and skin rash) prior to and during the holiday. Groups from both islands reported more health problems on the first three days of their visit than either prior to touring or subsequently, suggesting some incidence of environment shock. Furthermore, tourists experienced more negative moods at the beginning of their holiday than later on. This could have been due to health problems, but perhaps also to a dislike of being encouraged to take part in structured, other-initiated activities.

Pearce's study is interesting for three reasons. First, it demonstrates that people report more minor health problems while on holiday than before it, suggesting that the environmental change ('shock') may indeed have negative consequences. Second, it shows some variations in moods but some fairly rapid adaptation to a new holiday resort, once the initial shock is over. Third, organized tourist-role, 'fun' activities were associated with negative rather than positive moods, and the reverse for self-initiated activities. The way in which tourists and their organizers perceived the tourist role appears to have been a critical factor in determining the nature and quality of the tourist experience.

While there is a limited literature on the culture shock of tourists, there is an even more limited, but equally relevant, literature on the shock of being visited. This anthropological and psychological research concerns tourism's impact upon local populations. Anyone who lives in a popular tourist city or town soon becomes aware that it is not only the tourists who are 'culture shocked' by the behaviour and beliefs of the natives, but also the natives, who experience culture shock due to the unusual habits of tourists. The amount and type of shock that tourists can impart to local people depends on a number of things, such as the relative proportion of tourists to natives, the duration of their stay, the comparative wealth and the development of the two groups, and the racial and ethnic prejudices of both groups.

Pearce (1982a) has reviewed the few available studies concerned with host perception of tourists. Studies done in Britain and America, in both large and small towns, suggest that apart from minor complaints like litter, traffic congestion, inflation and noise, most residents are positive about tourists. Other studies in Israel, Turkey and small Mediterranean islands have found similar reactions, particularly when tourism gives marginal or deprived sub-groups an opportunity to broaden their world-view.

However, this can definitely not be said about the majority of the evidence; many studies of poor, small, simple communities have shown the complete reverse to be true. In rural parts of Europe, northern Spain, Iceland and Bali, tourists tend to be disliked. Indeed, in some cultures they are cheated, victimized and verbally and physically abused. Pearce (1982a) has summarized some of the conditions that will lead to tourist–host friction. This friction and its attendant stress might not necessarily lead to simple hostility and anger but could also lead to guilt, and depression.

> In summary, tourists appear to have maximum social and psychological impact on their hosts where the host communities are small, unsophisticated and isolated. This impact may be a powerful one, either in direct interpersonal encounters or in subtle indirect influences on the visited community. When the receiving society is technologically more advanced and the affluence gap between tourists and hosts narrower, the contact experience has less impact. In this instance tourists may develop friendships with the hosts and the visitors can sustain local social institutions as well as prompting pride in the visited community. The negative effects are not restricted to interpersonal friction, but also include indirect stress to the hosts through noise, pollution and environmental degradation. (Pearce, 1982b, p. 208)

The literature on 'sojourner adjustment' has almost totally ignored the shock of being visited, though there are attempts at some institutions to prepare host nationals for foreigners. For instance, some English-language schools give landladies pamphlets telling them what to expect from foreign students staying in their homes.

There is a dearth of literature on the reaction of host nationals to tourists and sojourners. People living in large cities (e.g. Paris, London) become fairly aggressive and even xenophobic during the height of the tourist season. Tee-shirts and badges are for sale, proclaiming the fact that the wearer is not a tourist but a local: typical reactions are aggression, unhelpfulness and discourtesy.

Occasionally tourists form a majority and cause hosts to be a minority. Furthermore, there are cases where the natives find their culture changing around them, that is the tourists (or sojourners, guest workers, etc.) actually give the hosts culture shock by changing their society around them. This is particularly true of the oil-producing countries of the Middle East (El Sendiony et al., 1977).

Finally, although, as we have seen, tourists become victims of culture shock, relative to other sojourners they are much less susceptible. There are several reasons why this is so:

1. *Time.* Almost by definition tourists are on holiday for a comparatively short period of time. Nearly all the empirical culture-shock literature states that initially the experience of the new culture is intriguing and exciting. Hence tourists are usually not long enough in a new culture to fully experience the negative effects of culture shock.

2. *Arrangements.* More and more tourists are going on package holidays, which are pre-planned and booked so that all their accommodation, sight-seeing tours and arrangements are taken care of. Insurance often covers medical emergencies, and there are therefore few reasons for the tourists to come into contact with the natives except when purchasing goods, in which case the shrewder natives will have learnt the tourist's language, monetary system and habits.

3. *Tour leader/guide/host.* Many tourists on package holidays have guides or leaders who are cultural mediators, speaking both languages and familiar with the traditions and requirements of both groups. Those not on package holidays often also visit friends and relations, who act as hosts and allow the visitors very little opportunity to experience the culture alone.

4. *Peers and social support.* Because of the popularity of various holiday destinations, it is unlikely that tourists will not find people of their own culture there. These people act as a social support group, often chauvinistically flaunting their culture.

5. *Tourists tend to be observers* rather than participants in the new culture. The empirical literature on culture shock suggests that visitors' troubles commence when they begin to get involved in their new society; that is, when they start looking for jobs, accommodation, sexual partners, social-support networks, and so forth (Bochner, 1982; Bochner and Wicks, 1972). Tourists almost by definition stay at the periphery of the society they are visiting, and hence escape the satisfactions as well as the frustrations of participation.

Business movement

It is becoming more and more frequent, particularly for people in developed countries, to move from job to job, and/or to be geographically transferred in the course of their working lives. Indeed, some businesses, for a variety of reasons, have an active (and expensive) policy of regular job transferral, while for some occupations (e.g. travelling salesman, diplomat) the job almost by definition involves travel. It is not until comparatively recently that social scientists have begun to consider some of the psychological consequences of business transfer.

There are a number of dimensions or factors that may be used to distinguish one type of transfer from another. These include:

1. *Distance*: how far a person is transferred.
2. *Country*: whether the move involves leaving one's own country or not.
3. *Job*: whether the person is expected to do much the same or a different type of job, at the same or different level in the organization.
4. *Social support*: whether the person moves alone, with others from the work place, with or without family.
5. *Time*: how long are the persons likely to spend in this other place and when can they expect to return.
6. *Returns*: benefits and costs of the move including the possibility of being dismissed or demoted if not agreeing to the transfer.
7. *Volunteering*: to what extent the individuals believe that they had a choice in the move.

These factors are important for the adjustment of the businessperson. For instance, a six-month sideways transfer, alone to an unknown and distant country, is likely to have quite different consequences than a two-year sojourn in another part of the same country, accompanied by one's spouse or family and provided with generous financial and social support. A major theoretical and research problem in this area is to distinguish which of a number of concurrent changes account for the variety of psychological consequences observed. For instance, job transfer within or between different countries nearly always entails some differences in the work itself (e.g. change of status, income, skill utilization), different living arrangements (family, physical environment) and different organizational variables (size, structure), all or none of which may account for change or no change in a person's adjustment, health or performance.

This section is primarily concerned with *geographic* mobility, as it relates to the movement of business people from place to place. However, because geographic mobility is often accompanied by *occupational/social* mobility (in the form of promotion, increment in income), it is difficult to separate the two. More studies have been done on the latter than the former. Indeed, since Durkheim (1897), social analysts have positively related excessive social mobility (change in social class, culture and life-style) with a decrease in mental health. Eaton and Lasry (1978) have reviewed eighteen studies concerned with social–class mobility and mental health. Despite numerous differences in both the dependent variable (instruments used in the diagnosis of mental health) and the independent variable (inter- versus intra-generational mobility) and the occasional absence of a control group, some attempt at drawing a conclusion was made. Much depended on the severity of diagnosis (i.e.

psychoses versus neuroses) but seven out of eleven studies showed mental disorder to be connected with downward mobility, which is in accord with the 'drift' or 'selection' hypothesis, which states that pre-existing psychological disorder leads to low social status. Although the results for less-severe mental diagnoses (depression, neurosis, personality disorders) were more ambiguous, they tended to indicate that upward mobility is also associated with mild psychiatric symptoms. Because these investigations could not specify the direction of causality (does a propensity for neurosis precede mobility or do stresses associated with upward mobility cause an increase in symptoms?), Eaton and Lasry (1978) conducted a study of 2000 North African Jewish immigrants to Montreal. They were careful to partial out various confounding factors such as present and previous job, education, and so on, and found the presence of mild psychiatric symptoms (measured by the Langer 22 index) and job dissatisfaction, to be related to upward mobility. Partial correlation showed a fairly close relationship between comparatively recent mobility and symptomatology, so indicating that upward mobility is causally related to psychiatric symptomatology.

Although this study confounded geographic and social mobility, nevertheless the results and the review seem to support the general conclusion that *severe mental disorders tend to be followed by downward mobility* while *mild mental disorders tend to be preceded by upward mobility*.

Most of the studies in this area have been epidemiological rather than psychological in nature. Few have considered individual differences in response to mobility or the possibility that increased social status itself may compensate for the problems associated with the stress of change, nor have they attempted to explain why these changes lead to illness.

The *occupational/social* mobility literature has been useful in providing a model for those who have studied the geographic mobility of business people. A great number of studies have attempted to test the thesis that *geographic mobility* is associated with stress and reduced mental health.

The problems of the business sojourn, transfer or short-term posting have been known about for some time. After the Second World War, multinational industrial and manufacturing companies found their overseas operations hampered and rendered inefficient by staff not being able to adjust and work efficiently in their new surroundings (Fayerweather, 1959). Even military personnel have showed fairly considerable evidence of problems in foreign countries (Boxer, 1969). Skinner (1968) published an overview of studies and commentaries concerned with identifying the personal factors that predict effective overseas performance. Despite the compilation of a long list, he noted how often the opinions differed, and commented on the poor quality of the research. Studies were difficult to compare because of different dependent variable measures of performance, widely different groups of people going to very different countries, and poor statistical analyses which failed to look at random, confounding and bi-directional effects.

In one of the better-planned and executed studies, Stoner et al. (1972) set out to assess the determinants of effective work performance among young Americans in Africa. Various individual, organizational, and environmental factors were considered. Age, travel experience, and qualifications were not related to performance but perceived ability and marital status were. Early success in the job, similarity between own and organizational expectations and specific task-needs were all correlated with good performance. Furthermore, the closer the country was to independence, the better the Americans performed in it.

Despite the paucity of psychological research on the consequences of job transfer, popularists have been quick to point to the negative consequences of transfer: heart attacks in men, depression in women, maladjustment in children (Packard, 1972). More recently Brett (1982) tested some specific hypotheses about the effects of job transfer, in five different areas of life:

1. *Work*. Mobile employees should be more satisfied (with pay, security, fringe benefits, promotion) than less-mobile employees, whereas working wives of mobile employees are likely to be less satisfied than less-mobile working women.
2. *Self*. Mobile employees should have better, and their wives worse, self-concepts and mental health than their less-mobile counterparts. Further, mobile parents are likely to perceive their children as less mature but more adaptable to new environments.
3. *Marriage/family life*. Because of the conflict of interests in transfer, it is expected that marital instability would be higher in mobile than non-mobile families.
4. *Friendships*. Mobile employees, their wives and children should all have less stable friendship patterns than less mobile families.
5. *Standard of living*. Mobiles should have a higher standard of living than less mobile families.

Despite the apparent reasonableness of the above hypotheses, many of which had been entertained by other writers, Brett (1982) was able to confirm only the hypothesis relating to social relationships – that is mobile families are less satisfied with their friendship networks than immobile families. She comments on her findings thus:

> The challenge of moving may make life interesting. The experience of re-establishing a household after a move may contribute to feelings of competency. Dissatisfaction with social relationships may be due as much or more to the trauma of relinquishing old friends as to the difficulty of making new ones. This interpretation is particularly supported in the children's data. Further, the fact that the family members go through the disruption of the move together and must provide social support for each other until new friendships can be

made explains the mobile adults' relative satisfaction with family life and marriage.

Few families in the transfer sample believed moving is easy. However, the data from this study show that despite their mobility, these families were as satisfied with all aspects of their lives, except social relationships, as were stable families. (p. 462)

Not all researchers have, however, come to this conclusion. Stokols and Shumaker (1982) developed a new theoretical framework for the study of residential mobility and mental health. They state that previous research on the topic has assumed that geographic movement is inherently stressful. Yet findings suggest that most people change residence voluntarily and regularly without any obviously detrimental consequences for mental or physical health. Prior theoretical analyses were simplistic and misleading because they provided an inadequate conceptualization of mobility, failed to delineate the psychological context of relocation, and oversimplified health outcomes. Only when there is prolonged exposure to undesirable places or separation from familiar ones, are psychological and health problems likely to occur. The antecedents of place dependence include the quality of the current residential situation and the relative quality of alternative (past/future) residential situations. Hence moves to lower levels promote stress and illness, while moves to higher levels do not. Stokols and Shumaker also note that current residential satisfaction depends on numerous factors both within and outside the residence.

In a series of studies utilizing this framework (Shumaker and Stokols, 1982; Stokols, Shumaker and Martinez, 1983), a group of over 200 people were tested at two different periods in time. Many of the findings support the model. For instance, those individuals whose mobility is blocked or restricted, thus remaining in low-quality residential situations for lack of better alternatives, have increases in illness. The data suggest that positive experiences within the residence domain may compensate for negative experiences in the work environment. However, they did find that irrespective of situational or dispositional factors, frequent relocation is associated with increased illness.

In summary, Stokol's model says that staying in a place that does not meet one's needs is associated with negative health outcomes, while staying in a place that does meet one's needs is associated with positive health outcomes. The consequences of moving depend on how well the new location compares with previously experienced environments in meeting important needs. Furthermore, various psychological and material benefits of residential change are able to reduce or ameliorate any negative effects.

This may explain why some people find geographic mobility stressful, while the opposite is true for others. Neither simple upward social or geographic mobility is of itself sufficient to explain an individual's reaction. It is the perception of the changes and how these affect the person's needs and the congruence between these needs and the environment, which ultimately determine the relationship between mobility and adjustment.

So far, most of the studies considered in depth have been concerned primarily with job transfer within countries. Some detailed studies have also been done on business people living abroad.

According to Torbiorn (1982), companies have three basic motives in posting people to foreign countries: the control function – to ensure that operations in other countries are being carried out as planned and to secure staff loyalty; the know-how function – to provide technological and administrative services; and the contact/co-ordination function – to evaluate and transmit salient information between company operations. For Torbiorn, overseas businesspersons have a difficult role in that they are required to act in accordance with the expectations of the parent company *and* also fulfil local expectations, the two often being incompatible. Problems with these professional roles include: unclear, ambiguous or even incompatible expectations on the part of the parent company; communication difficulties; a clash between company and personal interests and values; uncertainty about the future; and problems with the adjustment of the spouse and family.

In a large empirical study Torbiorn (1982) set out to establish the determinants of business expatriate satisfaction. In doing so he questioned over 1000 Swedish businessmen and businesswomen in twenty-six host countries. He looked at their personal circumstances (age, education, status); motives for moving abroad; who initiated the move; previous overseas experience; the nature of the country they came from and the country they moved to; their chosen life-style; and spouse satisfaction. Among his findings were that men more than women, and better educated rather than less well educated people, adapt better; that the motive for moving most strongly associated with adjustment was 'a special interest in the particular host country'; that previous overseas experience had no effect on adjustment; that expatriates who spent most of their free time with host country nationals were happier on average than those who turned to their own countrymen; and that the satisfaction of the spouse was a major factor in determining adjustment.

By and large, whichever variable was plotted against adjustment over time, whether sex, age, previous experience, friends, or attitudes to the host country, the pattern was much the same, showing a steady increase in satisfaction, though there was sometimes the indication of a flat U-curve.

The study also covered variables such as the most popular countries to work in, knowledge and adoption of host-country conditions, the adaptation of children and the experience of work in other countries.

Despite all this information, Torbiorn admits to not being able to explain much of the variance in business expatriates' satisfaction and adjustment, the thirty variables he examined together accounting for between 25 per cent and 50 per cent of the variance. Happiness of spouse was by far the most important factor, followed by various features of the external environment such as food and climate. Women tended to feel more isolated than men, which in turn greatly affected the man's satisfaction. A number of cultural barriers – religion, language and socio-economic development – were good predictors of the business people's happiness, adjustment and life-style and hence showed enormous variation between countries: the more the barriers, the less the satisfaction.

Studies such as Torbiorn's have important implications for the selection, training and management of businessmen and businesswomen and their families as they move from country to country. For instance, the study suggests the desirability of selecting people with interpersonal skills and high scores on assertiveness. Similarly, flexible, multidimensional and fairly extensive training programmes can help to ensure not only adaptation but efficiency in the job.

By and large, studies on business people who have moved from one area or country to another have come up with evidence of unhappiness, distress and poor adjustment. Of course, this is not always the case and, as research has shown, there is a large and complex number of variables determining the actual adjustment of particular individuals. At the same time it is probably safe to say that, overall, business people experience less difficulty than say students or other sojourners moving to new environments. There may be a number of reasons for this:

1. Business people are usually posted elsewhere for a set, specific and relatively short period of time. Hence they may see their move as relatively temporary and not requiring much adaptation and change.
2. Businessmen and businesswomen are posted abroad for a specific purpose, usually to deal with particular technical and managerial problems. This is not to say that the problems are simple – indeed, they are often complex and highly intractable – but rather that their problems are confined to work. They do not, as a rule, have to worry about transportation, accommodation and other 'house-keeping' problems. Students and migrants, on the other hand, often have a great many personal and logistical problems in addition to any difficulties they might face at work.
3. Business people have strong sponsorship. Many are given financial incentives for working abroad and often their life-style overseas is an improvement on what they have left behind. Furthermore, the sponsorship is not only financial but may include social and political benefits that increase rather than decrease a person's social standing,

political power and influence in the new society.

4. A tour abroad often increases opportunities for advancement on return. Whereas this may be true of students, it is less certain for them. Indeed, many business people travel specifically to enhance their chances for promotion. Hence any hardships on the trip may be seen as a small price to pay for the rewards to be gained later.

5. In contrast to students (and some migrants), business people tend to be older and are usually more mature. Although the literature is equivocal on this point, it is generally the case that older, more experienced people cope with the problems of geographic movement better.

6. Businesses often provide accommodation enclaves, 'old-hand' guides and a social-support network that insulate the foreigner against the initial difficulties and surprises of movement. The long-term benefits associated with these 'ghettos' are, however, debatable.

7. Because businesses are primarily interested in the work their employees do, the employees' time is carefully structured and scheduled. This, as unemployment researchers have shown, is directly related to a reduction in mental illness.

8. The social relationships both inside and outside the work place are probably more likely to be on an equal footing for businesspeople than for students. Such equal-status peer-group interaction probably goes some way in accounting for the relatively better adjustment of business people compared to students, whose social relationships are more often asymmetrical with respect to status. There are, therefore, practical reasons why business travel is not as stressful as student sojourning or migration.

The literature on the movement of working people is, like all research concerned with the psychological consequences of geographic movement, complex and equivocal. Commonsense ideas have not proved particularly reliable in predicting adjustment or performance. There also remain some fairly puzzling results. Overall it seems that the relative quality of life (social, occupational, familial) between the point of departure and the point of arrival best predicts the adjustment of businesspeople, though there may be initial distress or strain. This is hardly a startling finding. Nevertheless, it does have practical implications. In particular, companies must ensure that their overseas employees are no worse off than they would have been had they stayed at home. However, as we have seen, this is not simply a matter of pecuniary reward but involves a variety of social, psychological and familial considerations that together influence the well-being of the sojourner.

Chapter summary

This chapter dealt with the psychology of two groups of culture travellers: tourists and international businesspersons. In both cases the analysis revealed some hidden aspects and contradictions. Although tourism is universally regarded as enjoyable and relaxing, and indeed is sold to the public on that basis, the evidence indicates that tourists, like most other people venturing into unfamiliar cultural territory, experience some degree of stress. However, tourists tend to be cushioned against the extremes of 'culture shock' by virtue of a number of conditions pertaining to their special circumstances. These include the briefness of their sojourn and the growth in the package-tour industry. Conducted tours tend to sanitize the tourist experience, in providing the travellers with minders in the form of tour guides; in making arrangements that segregate the tourists from host situations and individuals that might create stress; in steering the tourists towards places and people which are culturally palatable; and in providing the tourists with social support in the form of contact with fellow nationals in the group. It is not surprising, therefore, to find that the tourist experience has only a relatively minor effect on the attitudes and perceptions of the travellers. Even so, some studies have shown that occasionally tourists may return home with a better insight into their own culture and a greater degree of world-mindedness.

The effect of tourism on the visited societies tends to be a function of the relative wealth of the tourists and their hosts. The impact is negative when a small, remote and technologically unsophisticated community is visited by wealthy tourists from the developed world. Where the affluence gap is narrower or non-existent, some studies have shown that the host society tends to welcome tourists, and its members express positive attitudes towards their visitors. However, by and large, no one, whether an Oxford don or a Tibetan peasant, relishes being a tourist attraction, an intractable problem which underlies the friction which most studies of tourist–host interactions have noted. Consequently, the idea, sometimes floated by vested interests, that tourism may lead to improved intercultural relations and greater mutual understanding, does not have a sound theoretical base, nor is there much empirical support for it.

Businesspersons on overseas assignment are also not immune from the stresses that result from having to cope with and master an unfamiliar cultural environment. A consistent finding is that the breadwinner's adjustment and satisfaction tend to be higher than those of the person's spouse and children, which in turn has indirect effects on the employee's state of mind. Another variable is the psychological distance between the culture of origin and the visited society, the greater the distance the more problems being encountered. However, in the context of intercultural contact in general, business travellers, like tourists, experience relatively minor stress, in comparison say to overseas students or migrants. This is because their sojourn is relatively brief, they are posted abroad for a set, finite period and they are given a specific task to do. Furthermore, as was the case with tourists, many business travellers tend to be sheltered from the mundane 'housekeeping' problems that tend to loom so large in the lives of students and migrants, such as finding accommodation, transportation, food and social support. Also, many corporate travellers have local counterparts who function as minders, mediating persons and culture friends. Finally, the overseas posting is usually financially rewarding and may provide opportunities for further advancement and career development, considerations which may be regarded as compensation for the cultural inconveniences of the sojourn, and hence make it more acceptable.

Because foreign business people often interact with their local colleagues on an equal footing, the possibility exists that such contacts could lead to improved mutual understanding and better intercultural relations. Working against this hypothesis is the possibility that the context for many of these contacts will be one of commercial competition rather than co-operation, resulting in some degree of hostility and intercultural friction. Research on this specific issue is virtually non-existent, despite its obvious interest and utility.

It should be pointed out, however, that many of the 'traditional' explanations for culture shock (see Ch. 7) as well as the more 'modern' explanations (see Chs. 8 and 9) are more relevant to migration and sojourning than to tourism. That is, the explanations for tourists' reactions may be both quantitatively and qualitatively different from those used to explain the mental health of migrants or the adjustment of sojourners.

Part III
Coping with unfamiliar environments: explaining the relationship

7 *Traditional descriptions of culture shock: grief, fatalism and selective migration*

Introduction

Various attempts have been made to explain the relationship between geographic movement and psychological adjustment. In this chapter we shall consider several rather different approaches. Each of these explanations is far more pertinent to an understanding of the phenomena described in Chapter 4 (mental health and migration) and Chapter 5 (sojourner adjustment) than to the material covered in Chapter 6 (the psychology and sociology of tourism).

First, it is clear that there is a connection between geographic movement and a change in psychological 'well-being'. Most, but by no means all, of the literature has shown a small but positive relationship between long-term migration and psychological disturbance, however measured. Second, it is unlikely that this relationship is simply a consequence of methodological artifact, sampling policies or unreliable and invalid instruments, as it has been found with various groups on various measures and in various countries. Third, it is most probable that only certain features of migration (such as the disparity between the two countries) contribute to the severity and type (e.g. depression, neurosis) of psychological disturbance. Fourth, there are clearly a large number of intervening and confounding variables which are related both to the decision to move (tour, sojourn, migrate) and to subsequent changes in psychological well-being.

A good deal of the research in this field has been epidemiological, the purpose being to establish the facts rather than test theories. There are nevertheless various theories – nearly all borrowed from other areas of research – which attempt to explain, or at least describe, this relationship.

It should be pointed out that these theories are by no means *mutually exclusive*. Many draw heavily on similar ideas, though they differ in their emphases and in which factors they believe to be important. Further, they often lead to similar predictions and recommendations for management.

It is also worthy of note that although each explanation is *necessary*, none is *sufficient*. It is precisely because the different explanations overlap and do not fundamentally contradict one another that each may be necessary for a full explanation. Indeed, what is perhaps most surprising in this area is the extent to which competing explanations overlap and do not contradict or oppose each other.

How then may one evaluate competing explanations for the relationship between geographic movement and psychological well-being? Obviously, the criteria that one uses to judge all theories must apply, such as internal consistency, clarity, predictability, parsimoniousness, and so forth. However, perhaps the most important criterion is: *Do predictions based on the theories fit empirical observations?* That is, do the theories fit the available data? Can, for instance, a theory or explanation for the relationship account for:

1. The difference between various migrant groups' psychological, socio-political and economic responses to the same country.
2. The difference between the same migrant groups' responses to different countries.
3. The change, over time, in the response of migrant groups to the host culture.

Furthermore, what is particularly interesting about the different explanations is what *implication* each theory has for migrant selection or management. Because the explanations emphasize different aspects of the migration experience, they carry differential implications for the way migrants would be selected, given preference or denied access, and how they would be helped after they had arrived at their destination. The value or validity of a theory cannot and should not be judged by its implications for treatment. Nevertheless, the differences between theories can sometimes be most clearly understood when their strategies for intervention are examined.

This chapter will describe four very different approaches to the relationship between geographic movement and mental health. The first draws heavily on the psychological literature on *loss* and regards the migration experience to be akin to grief. The second focuses on attitudes to *fatalism*, assuming that cultural and individual differences in locus of control beliefs predict adaptation to new environments. The third is perhaps the simplest of all and accounts for different adaptation and adjustment patterns on the basis of *selection differences* – the idea that various selective processes, such as the number of criteria that have to be fulfilled before migration is permitted, account for the differences in migration experiences. Finally, a number of researchers have pointed to the importance of migrant *expectations* in their adjustment. The more realistic these expectations are, the better a migrant adjusts and *vice versa*.

These explanations are traditional in two senses. First, they have been around for some time and can be found in scientific and popular writing dating back twenty years or more. Second, they are the ideas often held by lay people and migrants themselves. However, as shall be argued in the next chapter, although each 'explanation' may have some truth in it, they are far from sufficient in explaining the range and complexity of the migration and sojourn experience.

Grief and bereavement: movement as loss

There is a long literature on the psychology of loss (Bowlby, 1969), seen by some as a central theme in psychotherapy. The concept of loss, and more particularly the work on grief, mourning and bereavement, has been applied to many areas of human experience. Furnham (1985) has pointed out that the loss, or bereavement, literature has been used to describe the experience of such diverse phenomena as divorce and, more recently, unemployment. Grief is a ubiquitous, extremely stressful reaction to the real or imagined loss of a significant object or role, which may be resolved when a new object or personal relationship is established.

It has been suggested that concepts from this research area may also be used to shed light on the reactions of migrants. Migration (but to some extent all forms of geographic movement) involves being deprived of specific relationships or significant objects. These include family, friends and occupational status as well as a host of important physical variables ranging from food to weather patterns. The loss may be followed by grief (a stereotyped set of psychological and physiological reactions, biological in origin) and mourning (conventional bereavement behaviour determined by the mores and customs of society). Indeed, it is the similarity between various documented symptoms of grief, and the *stages* or *phases* of grief which have most interested researchers on migration and mental health. And because bereavement behaviour is to some extent culturally determined, this may account for various differences in the reaction pattern of migrants and sojourners from different cultures:

> For example, mourning rites may begin before the expected death of a significant individual, immediately upon his death, or be delayed for various periods of time; they may last for days, weeks or years; they may require abstentions from communication concerning the deceased or they may enjoin public proclamation. The emotions of the bereaved may be publicly displayed in weeping and wailing, suppressed with stoic resolve, or camouflaged behind the mask of some other affect, for example, with smiling and laughter. (Averill, 1968, p. 722)

Studies on grief and bereavement have emphasized not only cultural determinants but also biological ones. For instance, it has been argued that the biological or adaptive significance of grief is that it helps to cement group cohesiveness in all species where the maintenance of social bonds is necessary for survival. What is perplexing is the paradoxical nature of grief. Typical grief reactions – intense mental anguish, reduced resistence to stress, apathy and withdrawal, unreasonable demands – tend to reduce the possibility of establishing or maintaining interpersonal relationships. Yet it has been argued that this paradox is explained when it is recognized that the well-being of the individual is less important than the well-being of the species. The fact that certain physical changes consistent with both anxiety and depression occur after grief, lends some support to the migration-as-loss thesis because similar 'symptoms' often attend migration.

However, it is the psychological perspective on grief that seems most useful in accounting for migrants' reactions to movement. Within psychology, the psychoanalysts have probably paid most attention to grief. They see grief as the breaking of emotional ties (decathecting libidinal energy) to significant people. Since Freud (1957), many psychoanalysts have written about grief, of whom perhaps the most important has been Bowlby (1961). Bowlby placed great emphasis on weeping and anger as a way of recovering the lost object. Bowlby (1960, 1961) asserts that mourning is a biological and instinctual process and that separation anxiety, grief and mourning are all phases of a single process. He takes as his starting point the mother–child relationship which 'is mediated by a number of instinctual response systems which are part of the inherited repertoire of man' (Bowlby, 1961, p. 333). The anxiety and loneliness experienced by the child at its first loss (i.e. when the relationship is first broken) evokes an ancient instinctive response in the child. Bowlby identifies several phases through which the bereavement will pass, although they are all considered as a part of a single process. In the first phase, anger, weeping and ingratitude are seen as expressions of the urge to recover the lost object. The child expresses hostility against others indiscriminately, while also making various appeals for help. Despair, withdrawal, depression and disorganization in the second phase are the result of the failure to recover the lost object. In the third phase there occurs the development of a new structure through which the individuals can relate to their environment. These phases are a useful way of categorizing the data which have repeatedly been found in different studies:

> The internal conflict of grief becomes more manageable, when it is projected, as a social drama to which people can relate their behaviour . . . When loss cannot be articulated, its suppressed tensions in the end prove more profoundly disruptive than the social conflicts which relieve them. Above all, if we deny grief, we deny the importance of the meaning each of us has struggled to make of life. Loss is painful because we are committed to the significance of our personal experience. (Bowlby, 1960, p. 103)

The psychoanalytical formulation of grief is limited in several ways.

Apart from the usual criticisms, the psychoanalyst's 'consideration of social relationships has been included only with a primary conception of the individual as a bundle of instinctual and biological energy and has therefore been given minimal attention' (Smith, 1975, p. 76). Further, the actual objective situation in which the grieving behaviour occurs is ignored, for it is presumed that the 'process' is the same across all people, in all cultures, independently of their social or economic standing. Antecedent, intrapersonal factors are given more prominence than any concurrent variables in the grieving situation. Finally, there are various differences in emphasis in the different psychoanalytic approaches, some theorists stressing learnt behaviour patterns (Freud, Klein) in grief, others favouring a more biological or instinctual conceptualization (Bowlby).

Psychological studies of grief have attempted to describe and categorize different patterns of grief, as well as set out the course or phase of the 'typical grief reaction' to loss (Averill, 1968; Parkes, 1965; Lindemann, 1944). These include:

1. *'Normal'* grief, which is usually characterized by shock, despair, depression and recovery, persists for a period of between three and twenty-four months after the loss.
2. *Exaggerated* grief, where all the symptoms are intensified and prolonged. The behaviour, which may involve deep depression and apathy, undue guilt, or strange identification with the lost person, may have both neurotic and psychotic features.
3. *Abbreviated* grief is described as genuine but very short-lived, either as a consequence of having the lost object or person 'replaced' or being insufficiently deeply attached to the lost object in the first place.
4. *Inhibited* grief occurs when the symptoms or manifestations of the normal grieving patterns are masked or inhibited, only to reveal themselves later in psycho-somatic complaints.
5. *Anticipatory* grief is an abbreviated grief pattern with most of the grieving occurring before the loss takes place.
6. *Delayed* grief is the postponement of the normal grief pattern to long after the loss has occurred.

It is not always clear what determines the various patterns of grief, which differ primarily according to two dimensions: *intensity* and *duration*. Clearly degree of attachment to the lost object is one factor, and the age of the grieving person is also important. Although studies have looked at the effect of age, sex, class and education, no clear conclusions emerge (Kübler-Ross, 1975; Parkes, 1975). However, what is important to bear in mind is that this literature is very conscious of the widely varying individual differences in the reaction to loss. Most studies on grief have noted the complex number of emotions associated with loss –

anger, anxiety, depression, guilt, fear. Some of these emotions are more expected and explicable than others. For instance, grief and anxiety appear overlapping conceptually, but anger seems less expected. Anger may be the result of frustration because behavioural patterns are disrupted, desires ungratified and expectations unfulfilled; or as a defence against sadness. Some emotions – fear, rage, sexual arousal – seem to have strong biological determinants, and are thus culturally invariant, while other emotions like envy, guilt, shame appear to be determined primarily by psychological and cultural factors. Hence it is not surprising that although there is some similarity in the grief reaction and mourning rituals of various cultural groups, there are also some striking differences. This depends partly on religious belief and partly on custom. Jews, for instance, have various rites such as *kriyah*, the tearing of clothes, which is meant to be a visible and dramatic symbol of the internal tearing asunder that the mourners feel in their relationship with the deceased. Further, Jews oppose the repression of emotions, encouraging an open outpouring of grief. Some Africans have two funerals – one 'wet', the other 'dry' – much as some Christians have a memorial service some time after the deceased has actually died and the numbness and shock subsided. It is these differences which may help to account for the different reactions to migration of specific national groups.

The idea of exile or migration as bereavement or grief has been pursued by Munoz (1980), who examined the socio-psychological reactions of Chilean exiles in Britain. Through a number of case studies she spelt out her thesis:

> bereavement experienced by exiles may be interpreted as a result of loss of roots, the geography, the emotional support, the cognitive world and the status which they enjoyed prior to exile. The social isolation resulting from the loss of friends and relatives is felt as particularly punitive. (p. 231)

However, there are a number of problems with the analogy between grief and migration. First, it is presumed that all migrants, sojourners and travellers experience negative, grief-like reactions, which is clearly not the case. For some people migration is a blessed escape. Second, although the grief literature does take into account individual and cultural differences, it makes no specific predictions as to what type of people suffer more or less grief, over what period or what form the grief will take. Third, counselling for the grieving would seem highly inappropriate for migrants, who need information and support as much as therapy.

Fatalism (locus of control)

There is a considerable literature in personality and social psychology, which attempts to link fatalism with distress and depression. Perhaps the most commonly examined concept in the area is that of locus of control. This has been defined by Rotter (1966) thus:

> When a reinforcement is perceived by the subject as . . . not being entirely contingent upon his action, then, in our culture, it is typically perceived as the result of luck, chance, fate, as under the control of powerful others, or as unpredictable because of the great complexity of the forces surrounding him. When the event is interpreted in this way by an individual, we have labelled this a belief in *external control*. If the person perceives that the event is contingent upon his own behaviour or his own relatively permanent characteristics, we have termed this a belief in *internal control*. (p. 1)

Fatalism is therefore the generalized expectation that outcomes are determined by forces such as powerful others, luck or fate and is the opposite of *instrumentalism*, which is the generalized expectation that outcomes are contingent on one's own behaviour. This dimension has also been described as a perception of *general self-efficacy and control* over events in one's own life. Others have referred to it as 'environmental mastery', a sense of coherence or control. Weiner (1980) has noted the similarity between a number or related concepts, and these are depicted in Table 7.1.

For over twenty years researchers have looked at the causes and consequences of fatalistic versus instrumental belief systems. The fatalistic concept has been used to examine the relationship between belief and behaviour in a wide number of areas including mental and physical health, religion, education, politics and organizations (Furnham, 1985), and differences between various cultural and national groups (Furnham and Henry, 1980) have also been studied.

A general trend in the findings is that fatalistic, external-locus-of-control beliefs are associated with a passive orientation, impaired coping strategies and psychological distress (Dohrenwend and Dohrenwend, 1969; Seligman, 1975). Perceived control is important because it affords the opportunity to manipulate the outcomes of behaviour. To lose control over the events in one's life is also to lose control over the ability to achieve important long- or short-term goals or to avoid punishments. Thus, if people or specific groups are prone to fatalistic beliefs – and it has been argued that certain cultural traditions, such as that of Mexico (Ross et al., 1983), are particularly associated with these beliefs – it might be expected that they would cope particularly badly with geographic movement. For instance, in general, women, working-class and old people have more external locus of control than men, middle-class and youngish or middle-aged people and adjust to migration less well, providing some empirical support for the connection between the two

Table 7.1 Approaches to the study of personal responsibility

Concept	Theorist	Antecedents		Consequences	
		Internal	External	Internal	External
Locus of control (Internal-External)	Rotter (1966)	Skill task	Chance task	Information seeking; typical shift in expectancy	Information avoidance: atypical shift
Personal causation (Origin-Pawn)	de Charms (1968)	'Correctly' structured setting	Overly structured setting	Origin feeling: realistic	Pawn feeling: unrealistic
Intrinsic-extrinsic Motivation	Deci (1975)	Low external reward: intrinsic motivation	High external reward	Continued motivation	Lack of continued motivation
Perceived freedom	Steiner (1970)	Equivalent alternatives	Unequivalent alternatives	Perceived choice freedom	Little perceived choice freedom
Reactance	Brehm (1966)	No barriers	Barriers	State of equilibrium	Attitude shift: motivated to restore equilibrium
Learned helplessness	Seligman (1975)	Response-outcome	Response-outcome	Normal functioning	Learning motivation

Source: B. Weiner, Human Motivation, New York, Holt, Rinehart & Winston, 1980. Copyright © 1980 by Holt, Rinehart & Winston. Reprinted by permission of CBS College Publishing.

variables. However, it should be pointed out that various other hypotheses could also explain the association.

Studies have attempted to investigate the relationship between locus-of-control belief and migrant adjustment. Kuo et al. (1976) found a relationship between locus of control, assimilation and the symptoms of psychiatric distress in Chinese immigrants to the United States. In a study of 170 immigrants the authors concluded that locus of control explained more of the variance in accounting for mental illness than did any of the other variables examined, which included sex, socio-economic status, marital status, kinship and friendship ties, an assimilation indicator and the amount of life-change. The results showed that Chinese-Americans who believe that the rewards of life are contingent upon some sort of social force beyond personal control tend to have more psychological distress than do Chinese-Americans who believe that they themselves control their lives.

In a similar study, Krause and Stryker (1984) examined the mediating or buffering effects of locus-of-control beliefs in the relationship between stressful events and psycho-physiological well-being. The results indicated that those men with moderately internal locus-of-control orientation cope more effectively with stress than those whose locus-of-control beliefs may be classified as extremely internal, extremely external or moderately external:

> The underlying factor which separates moderate internals from the remaining locus-of-control types may be the ability to initiate actions that are intended to counteract the effects of stressful occurrences. Moderate externals and extreme externals, on the other hand, may be less likely to initiate constructive efforts to deal with stressful events because they believe that self-initiated actions cannot exert a causal influence on the flow of life events. As a result, the stressful event will continue to be a persistent source of strain for persons in both categories of external beliefs. In the case of extreme internals, effective coping actions may not be undertaken because of paralyzing guilt feelings that are produced by the belief that one's actions are responsible for the occurrence of the initial event (p. 787)

Others have also examined locus-of-control beliefs as mediators between life-stress and psychological disorder (Nelson and Cohen, 1983; Sandler and Lakey, 1982). By and large, where the results are significant, which is not always the case, they tend to suggest that external locus-of-control or fatalism beliefs are related to poor mental health and lack of adaptation.

But some have argued that in specific instances the complete reverse is true, that is that fatalism is adaptive. Ananth (1978) noted that although many Indian women occupy social, political and economic roles that are stressful, they exhibit less psychopathology than one might expect to find in western women under similar circumstances. This is particularly true of the probably more oppressed rural women who exhibit a low incidence of depression. The author argues that this is because the women accept the situation as unalterable and do not aspire to change unfortunate circumstances: 'Thus it seems likely that a total acceptance of one's situation as an existential and unalterable reality may be a cultural protection against depression in Indian society, but one which is now changing at least in urban areas' (p. 178). Of course, to suggest that fatalism is adaptive for a minority group in a Third World country is not necessarily the same as suggesting that it is adaptive for all people. Certainly nearly all the literature in the west would suggest the opposite, namely that the perception of personal responsibility and control enhances coping, adaptation and mental health.

Part of the attraction of this hypothesis should be that it allows one to make predictions on the basis of cross-cultural studies. That is, if one cultural group or sub-group is known to have widely held fatalistic beliefs, it may be predicted that they would adapt badly when migrating. There have been a number of critical reviews in this field (Furnham and Henry, 1980; Hui, 1982; Hui and Triandis, 1983; Krause and Hoelter, 1983), yet all reveal how difficult it is to make generalizations about fatalistic beliefs in a subculture. Hui (1982) has noted: 'Findings of cross-cultural and cross-ethnic similarities and differences are generally inconsistent and inconclusive. Neither do studies of antecedents, correlates and consequences of the construct enhance our faith in its universal generality' (p. 301). Others have come to the same conclusion while also pointing out that the concept is multidimensional and that whereas groups may differ on one factor they do not differ on another. The literature is therefore not particularly helpful for making predictions about immigrant adjustment, as it does not reveal any consistent or coherent patterns of fatalistic beliefs about groups or sub-groups.

The fatalism or locus-of-control explanation for the relationship between migration and mental health is potentially interesting but does have problems. The explanation should be able to account for the different distress rates of different immigrant groups. For instance, immigrants from a country whose religion is fatalistic should have more difficulty in adjusting than migrants from a country where personal responsibility is valued. However, there is ample evidence to suggest that this is not the case. For instance, Cochrane (1983) has shown that Indians adjust particularly well when immigrating to Britain (see Ch. 4) yet supposedly come from a fatalistic culture. Thus the data do not support the hypothesis in this case.

Another problem lies in self-selection. In order to voluntarily migrate (as opposed to being a refugee) one has to assume considerable personal responsibility and control over one's own affairs – financial, social and familial. It may be argued therefore that most people who migrate have, by definition, an internal locus of control and are therefore relatively homogeneous irrespective of their culture or origin. There must therefore be other factors which account for the relationship between geographic movement and psychological well-being.

Selective migration

One of the oldest and most popular explanations for the different patterns of reaction to new environments by migrants is the neo-Darwinian idea of selective migration. It is an extension of the principle of natural selection, which states that all living organisms that cope best with the exigencies of the environment become the prevailing type. When people are selected for a new environment to which they are particularly suited, they will cope better than others who are not so matched.

There are a number of appealing features to this approach. First, it describes why different migrant groups to the same country at the same time may adapt differently because of different selective processes. Second, it tends to highlight which combination of general coping strategies are most appropriate to the particular requirements of a certain country. Hence it can explain why people who were 'selected' by similar processes from the same country may adjust well in a particular 'new' country but not in others. The explanation therefore pays special attention to the types of selection processes and the coping strategies of various groups. One should, however, be aware of the fact that, being nearly always retrospective, the selective migration thesis is tautological rather than explanatory.

The idea of selection is, however, not very clear, and it does not necessarily imply free choice on the part of the prospective migrants or the immigration authorities in the country to which they plan to go. For instance, it could be argued that the descendants of slaves should be weaker than their ancestors who remained in their home country because they were captured. On the other hand, only the very fittest survived the appalling conditions of transportation or slave labour and thus their descendants may be seen as particularly strong and adaptable. Similarly, not all refugees can be seen to be those wise enough to move away from impending disaster. The selective process is twofold: certain people select to migrate in spite of various difficulties, while all countries select prospective migrants in terms of a number of criteria such as age, sex, health, skills and nationality. These latter selective criteria may or may not be based on studies looking at the actual predictors of migrant adaptation.

However, before proceeding further with the problems associated with the application of the selective migration, some relevant literature should be considered. As we noted in Chapter 4, various researchers, particularly those interested in psychiatric epidemiology, have proposed the selective migration explanation for observed differences in adaptation and coping. For instance, in Britain Cochrane (1983), attempting to explain the excellent adaptation of Indians on all levels, noted:

> there has undoubtedly been a very highly selected migration from India to Britain. Not all those who wish to migrate have been able to do so and to overcome the very strong formal and informal barriers to achieving migration the potential immigrant has to display considerable powers of ambition, ability and psychological stability. To contemplate migration in the first place, involving as it does a complete cultural transition as well as unknown hardships and dangers, implies a high degree of ambition and adventurousness. To implement the migration once it is decided upon, even obtaining sufficient finance, is also a great achievement for someone from the rural areas of India. The same characteristics which made migration possible in the first place also produce the upwardly mobile, ambitious, psychologically stable person who appears to be typical of Indian immigrants in Britain. (p. 100)

Similarly, it may be inferred that the poor adaptation of the Irish is due to the ease of immigration in terms of distance, language and finance.

The theme of selective immigration can also be found in the work of Krupinski et al. (1973) concerning migrants to Australia. In a study of eastern European refugees in Australia, Krupinski et al. (1973) examined the effect of severity of war experiences, paying particular attention to Jewish, Polish and Russian, and other eastern European groups. Despite the severity of their wartime persecution, the Jewish immigrants appeared to have *lower* rates of psychotic illnesses, but were higher in neurotic symptoms. He argues:

> One has to remember that the survival rate of Jewish inmates of concentration camps was much lower than that of other nationalities. Those who showed psychotic traits would be the first to be selected for the gas chamber. On the other hand, those Jews who managed to survive must have had considerable ego strength to cope with the daily assault on their ego and superego. Still, the massive psychic trauma, to which they were exposed, could not but have resulted in a neurotic reaction in the vast majority of victims. The survival rates of persecuted Poles, Russians and Ukrainians was eighty to ninety times greater and this can account for a genocidal selection of Jewish refugees. (pp. 45–6)

There are many other references in the literature on mental health and migration which explicitly or implicitly refer to a selective-migration hypothesis. However, this hypothesis has a number of limitations. First, considering the selective processes of the migrants themselves, it is not clear which barrier or obstacles select for adaptation and which do not. The sheer number of obstacles alone may predict a certain type of fitness or motivation but does not imply that those people necessarily adapt well. For instance, education, physical fitness, language ability and financial security may be important positive factors with regard to selection, while others such as religion may not. Rarely, if ever, do the optimally adaptive selectors exist in isolation from those factors that do not discriminate. Furthermore, the positive selector obstacles may differ from country to country.

Second, as well as personal obstacles in the way of the prospective migrant and those obstacles imposed by their country of origin, nearly all receiving nations have specific criteria for the admission of prospective migrants. There are social, political and economic reasons for these criteria, which change over time. Nations also differ in the criteria used, which are nearly always based on the perceived economic needs of the country rather than on the needs of the migrants.

Hence, though there may be some truth in the selective-migration hypothesis, it is extremely difficult to test unless the precise nature of the adaptive selectors in both countries of departure and arrival are specified and examined. Otherwise a range of moderator variables could explain the adaptation rate of different groups of migrants. Finally, the adaptive argument is highly unappealing for some because it smacks of racism, suggesting that it is some genetic or biologically predetermined trait on the part of one race or another that makes them particularly prone to healthy or unhealthy adjustment.

Expectations

As Feather (1982) has pointed out, expectancy-value models have long existed in various areas of psychology. Though there are numerous differences between the models proposed by different writers such as Lewin, Tolman or Atkinson, the basic idea is that a person's behaviour is directly related to the expectations that they hold *and* the subjective value of the consequences that might occur following the action. Feather (1982), overviewing the current research in this area, concludes:

> The theoretical analysis does not involve a static set of variables but explicitly allows for changes in expectation and valences and, therefore, for changes in positive and negative tendencies. It also acknowledges that persisting, unsatisfied sources of motivation may carry over from the past. The approach is not situation bound but acknowledges the importance of including both person and situation variables in the analysis. It recognizes that behaviour is always ongoing and involves an active organism making its own distinctive contribution as it

interacts with the environment and processes information from it. The expectations and valences involved in the analysis apply to segments or frames from the continuing stream of a person's behaviour and they relate to that person's own structuring of reality. These variables together capture the cognition and purpose that most of behaviour displays and, in their combination, provide a powerful lever for the understanding of human action. (p. 90)

Although this overlaps with the section on values (see Ch. 8), the stress in this explanation is on expectations of conditions in the new country. Applying the model to migration, the relationship between a migrant's expectations of the chosen country and the fulfilment of those expectations is a crucial factor in determining adjustment.

Most of the research has suggested that high expectations that cannot or do not get fulfilled are related to poor adjustment and increased mental illness. Although he does not refer directly to the expectancy-value hypothesis, Cochrane (1983) clearly believes that positive expectations are inversely related to adjustment. As regards British immigrants he notes:

> West Indians typically come to this country with high expectations of achievement in terms of material well-being and also probably in terms of achieving integration within the wider community. Alienation results from a failure both to meet these expectations and to reach the assimilation goals that the immigrant has set for him or herself (p. 97)

In attempting to explain Pakistani mental disorder in Britain, Cochrane (1983) noted that 'It appears that those who migrated for positively material reasons (for better jobs and better living conditions) also experience more psychological difficulties' (p. 102).

There are numerous other examples, both of internal migration within a country and external migration to other countries, where there is *post hoc*, impressionistic evidence that certain groups have not adjusted well as a function of either unrealistic or unfulfillable expectations. For instance, Littlewood and Lipsedge (1982) have written:

> Even isolated individuals can function adequately if their expectations are met and they enjoy a certain degree of economic and psychological security. European missionaries in China were more likely to break down than those in Africa. In China they met a powerful urban culture which was able to challenge their beliefs and teaching. In Africa, as part of a dominant political structure themselves, there was less reason for them to doubt their own values. (p. 102)

People who migrate for financial reasons usually have high expectations. European migrants to Australia, whose professional qualifications were not recognized, had a comparatively high rate of mental illness. While

Asian immigrants to Britain usually experience a rise in socio-economic status relative to their original position, West Indians may actually experience a fall. Job difficulties are particularly great for those West Indians with the highest educational qualifications. In Jamaica educational advantages are much more significant than skin colour in obtaining a job: not so in Britain. There is also some evidence that low expectations lead to better adjustment. Krupinski (1985: personal communication) has noted that many Vietnamese refugees expected a poorer standard of living and more discrimination than they actually encountered, which may account for their relatively successful adaptation. Clearly one implication of these findings is the need to educate prospective migrants to set realistic and realizable goals in various spheres.

Expectancy-value theories have proved useful in predicting people's reactions to unemployment. Yet this theoretical approach is not without its problems. First, it should be pointed out that the migrants have a wealth of expectations, some relating to social, economic, geographic and political aspects of life in their new country. They are bound to be wrong about some, expecting too much or too little. What is unclear is which expectations about what aspect of life in the new country are more important to adjustment than others. Second, the way in which unfulfilled expectations lead to poor adjustment is far from clear. For instance, do disappointed or unfulfilled expectations lead to anxiety, depression or anger? Third, from the above literature it would seem that having low expectations may be better for adjustment but worse for overall social mobility. Further, apart from refugees, few people would voluntarily migrate if their expectations were too low.

However, research on applying expectancy-value theory to the area of migration and mental health is comparatively new, and many of the above problems have simply not been addressed.

Chapter summary

This chapter reviewed four theories which have been applied to explaining the relationship between migration and mental health. The first was the psychology of *grief and bereavement*, which sees migration as the experience of loss; though the theory allows wide variations in the intensity duration and stages of grief it seems unable to account for individuals who experience no negative consequences of grief. The second theory concerned beliefs about *personal control* over the environment, which implies that as opposed to people with fatalistic beliefs, those with instrumental beliefs adapt better when migrating. Evidence for this theory is highly equivocal, as other cross-cultural studies have shown. The idea of *selective migration* was the third theory reviewed. It suggests that the more rigorous and salient the selection procedure for migrants, the better they will be at adapting to the new environment. The theory tends to be non-specific, tautological and very difficult to test. Finally, *expectancy-value* theory has been applied to this area. This suggests that accuracy of a migrant's expectations of life in the new country are directly related to his/her adjustment. However, the theory does not specify which or whether expectations about particular features are more or less important than others. Nor does it explain how unfulfilled expectations lead to poor adjustment.

Despite the limitations of, and problems associated with, each of these explanations for culture shock, each highlights some important factors associated with mental health and migration. They are, in turn, the experience of loss, control beliefs, individual fitness and expectancy values. The four explanations come from three rather different academic traditions. The grief and bereavement literature as applied to culture shock is firmly rooted in the psychoanalytic tradition. Both the locus-of-control and expectancy-value theories are firmly based in applied social psychology. Finally, selective migration theories are closely linked to socio-biological forms of explanation. The importance of the epistemological origins of these explanations should not be overlooked as they give insight into what constitutes both suitable evidence and an acceptable explanation. Therefore the same researchers who favour an 'experience of loss' explanation will be happy to validate their theories by in-depth interviews with a few (unhappy but probably eloquent) migrants, while those favouring a selective migration thesis would probably be content with archival and historical material relating how the circumstances under which migrants were permitted to migrate and/or were selected are directly related to mental health or any other appropriate statistics. On the other hand, other applied social psychologists may test locus-of-control or expectancy-value theories by experimental or survey methods.

8 Recent explanations for culture shock: negative life-events, social-support networks, value differences

In the previous chapter four rather different explanations for culture shock were considered. None of these 'theories' or 'explanations' were developed in the context of, or specifically for, the culture-shock experience. Nevertheless, they have all been more or less successfully applied to literature on mental health and migration, and sojourn experiences.

More recently, work in other fields has led to the application of other rather different ideas to the notion of culture shock. What they have in common is that they are concerned with how various social variables contribute to psychopathology. At first glance there is only a tenuous link between them and the topic of the book – culture shock – but it is hoped that this chapter will spell out this link and show that each of these three areas of research provides a rich source of theory and data with which to understand culture shock. None of the theories would claim to account for all or even most of the variance, but rather each emphasizes a factor which is clearly important in explaining the relationship between geographic movement and culture shock. It would however be unfair to argue that this literature is particularly useful in understanding the reactions of particularly short-term visitors like tourists, though it may shed some light upon it.

It should be noted that these three approaches are not competing but complementary. The first two areas – *negative life-events and illness* and *social-support networks* – are closely related and often examined together. Early findings from the negative life-events literature suggest that the experience of major changes in one's life often leads to mental and physical illness. The social-support hypothesis is not so much concerned with origins of stress as with its alleviation and predicts a close positive relationship between the *quality* and *quantity* of support from others and the ability to cope with stress (such as culture shock). The third research area has less of a clinical flavour than the above two and is concerned with what occurs when people holding different values live together. This literature is more concerned with describing the major dimensions of *value differences* between various groups than in explaining how or why value differences lead to stress, anxiety or lack of well-being.

Nevertheless, this increasingly sophisticated research area provides very interesting insights into the causes of culture shock.

It is encouraging to note that many recent studies and theories have been looking at the combined effects of numerous variables. Although early research in each area was primarily concerned with the effect of a single factor (e.g. negative life-events) as an independent variable on some specific (often single) dependent variable, current research employs multiple independent and dependent variables and examines which independent variables predict or explain which dependent variables. All three explanations in this chapter appear able to cope with multiple variables of both kinds.

Negative life-events

For nearly twenty years psychologists, psychiatrists and sociologists have been collecting evidence on the relationship between recent stressful life-events and psychological and physical illness (Rahe et al., 1964). The basic idea is that negative life-events, such as the death of a spouse, divorce or losing one's job, make people ill; the more negative in terms of intensity the duration and consequences of the event, the more severe is the illness. Some research has also shown that *any change* in one's daily routine, not necessarily a negative one, has similar deleterious effects, although these findings have been questioned (see later in this chapter). Negative life-events have been associated with responses as varied as depression, neurosis, tuberculosis, coronary heart disease, skin diseases, hernias and cancer. Although the mechanism by which negative life-events influence health and illness is by no means clear, most studies have demonstrated a significant relationship between the two (Dohrenwend and Dohrenwend, 1974). Monroe (1982) has listed three reasons for the growth in this research area: first, it allows one to examine the attractive but elusive link between psycho-social processes and physical/psychological functioning: second, its conceptual basis is congruent with other areas of research; and third, the clinical implications seem clear and straightforward.

The applicability of the life-events literature to migration and geographic movement should be apparent (Guthrie, 1981). The act of migration (indeed, even tourism) often involves a number of important life-events – changes in routine patterns of behaviour. For some forms of migration are asterisked. These are numerous, and if the total score is life-events are measured. Table 8.1 shows the social readjustment rating scale often used in determining the magnitude of recent life-events (even though the psychometric properties of this scale have not been properly established). Those events which might reasonably be associated with migration are underlined. These are numerous, and if the total score is calculated, it exceeds 300. By any standard this is a large score and might

Table 8.1 Social readjustment rating scale

Rank	Life event	Mean value
1	Death of spouse	100
2	Divorce	73
3	Marital separation	65★
4	Jail term	63
5	Death of close family member	63
6	Personal injury or illness	53
7	Marriage	50
8	Fired at work	47
9	Marital reconciliation	45
10	Retirement	45
11	Change in health of family member	44
12	Pregnancy	40
13	Sex difficulties	39
14	Gain of new family member	39
15	Business readjustment	39★
16	Change in financial state	38★
17	Death of close friend	37
18	Change to different line of work	36★
19	Change in number of arguments with spouse	35
20	Mortgage over $10,000	31
21	Foreclosure of mortgage or loan	30★
22	Change in responsibilities at work	29★
23	Son or daughter leaving home	29
24	Trouble with in-laws	29
25	Outstanding personal achievement	28
26	Wife begins or stops work	26★
27	Begin or end school	26
28	Change in living conditions	25★
29	Revision of personal habits	24
30	Trouble with boss	23
31	Change in work hours or conditions	20★
32	Change in residence	20★
33	Change in schools	20★
34	Change in recreation	19★
35	Change in church activities	19★
36	Change in social activities	18★
37	Mortgage or loan than $10,000	17
38	Change in sleeping habits	16
39	Change in number of family get-togethers	15★
40	Change in eating habits	15★
41	Vacation	13
42	Christmas	12
43	Minor violations of the law	11
		339★

★ indicates those events or changes that frequently occur with migration.
Source: T. H. Holmes and R. H. Rahe, 'The social readjustment rating scale', *Journal of Psychosomatic Research*, 11 (1967), 216.

be associated with serious psychological and physical breakdown. For instance, a score of 164 was considered very high by Rahe et al. (1967). Therefore, because migration involves a great number of potentially stressful changes, the development of psychological or physical illnesses may be attributable directly to them. In short, the life-events index may be a simple but complexly derived score that predicts culture shock – the greater the score, the greater the shock. However, there are many problems with this simple formulation, including the objectivity of the score, the causal links between life-changes and any illnesses and individual differences.

However, it has also been demonstrated that when stressful experiences are *shared* by a group or a community, beneficial effects for mental health may often result (hence the link between this and the social-support hypothesis):

> The feeling of confronting a common threat might lead to increased group cohesiveness, increased social interaction, provide a distraction from strictly personal worries, offer new roles and perhaps status to people who previously were isolated, and finally offer to the person experiencing some degree of personal distress an external reason for their state of mind, which means they do not have to resort to an explanation based on personal inadequacy or illness. (Cochrane and Sobel, 1980, p. 155)

Thus, for some the experience of geographic movement and its consequent life-changes may be positively beneficial. The question remains of for whom this is true. But what does emerge from this literature of importance is that both positive *and* negative changes can have both positive and negative consequences. It is by no means the case that all positive changes (i.e. increase in living standard, better education and health facilities) lead to positive results (increased mental and physical health) or that negative changes (difficulty in acquiring a new language, lack of close friends or family) necessarily lead to negative results (depression, neurosis, etc.). Rather, the results suggest that the absolute amount of positive or negative change can have serious negative health and other effects if various social conditions are not so arranged as to prevent it. Therefore it is not surprising that there are highly equivocal findings on the benefits of positive life-events (Cohen and Hoberman, 1983; Lewinsohn et al., 1980; Zantra and Reich, 1980; Reich and Zantra, 1981).

Some (but surprisingly little) of the research in the negative life-events literature has made specific reference to migration. An article by Guthrie (1981) has the title 'What you need is continuity' and the theme is that going to live in an alien culture almost always involves changes of sufficient magnitude to produce psychological and physical stress in the sojourner. Hinkle (1974) studied migrant groups in America (especially the Chinese and Hungarians) who had experienced major socio-cultural changes as a consequence of migration. Hinkle and his colleagues looked at the relationship between the range and type of major life event changes and any resultant physical and mental illness. They were surprised by the large number of Chinese who, though they had experienced major 'life changes', seemed little affected by them. Overall the Hungarians appeared to experience more physical and psychological illness. Case studies:

> suggested that when these people had had difficulty in making a satisfactory adaptation to their social environment in the past, and most notably during the periods when they felt insecure, frustrated, or threatened, they had had an increase number of episodes of many varieties of illness. This again has been especially true of those who had been frequently ill. (Hinkle, 1974, p. 28).

Numerous individual differences were noted, as was the importance of the perceived nature of the threat. The more that people perceived life-events and life-changes as threatening, challenging, demanding and frustrating, the more they were likely to succumb to illness. This led to three conclusions:

1. Exposure to culture change, social change and change in inter-personal relations may lead to a significant change in health if (a) a person has pre-existing illness or susceptibility to illness, and he perceives the change as important to him, or (b) there is a significant change in his activities, habits, ingestants, exposure to disease-causing agents, or in the physical characteristics of his environment.
2. Exposure to culture change, social change and change in interpersonal relations may lead to no significant change in health if (a) a person has no significant pre-existing illness or susceptibility to illness, or if he does not perceive the change as important to him, and (b) there is no significant change in his activities, habits, ingestants, exposure to disease-causing agents or in the physical characteristics of his environment.
3. If a culture change, social change or change in interpersonal relations is not associated with a significant change in the activities, habits, ingestants, exposure to disease-causing agents, or in the physical characteristics of the environment of a person, then its effect upon his health cannot be defined solely by its nature, its magnitude, its acuteness or chronicity or its apparent importance in the eyes of others. (p. 42)

Research in this area has developed in a number of different directions. One promising avenue has attempted to clarify which aspects of life-events are associated with symptomatology. Various dimensions of the events have been proposed, including the amount of *change*; their subjective *desirability* or undesirability; perceptions of *control* over the events; and the long-term *threat* of the events. While some researchers have argued that it is essential to distinguish between these various life-events, others have argued that a simple count of life events is an adequate, robust and parsimonious measure. Second, researchers have worked on developing normative scores, or weights, for each life-event, though there are clearly problems with using an objective 'group mean', as individuals differ in the extent to which life-events cause them stress. Third, researchers have set out to specify those moderator or intervening variables which mediate between life-events and illness. Yet surprisingly perhaps, very little of this research has been or appears to be being done on migrants, sojourners or tourists, who appear – in terms of the magnitude of the changes they experience – to be an ideal group. It should be noted, however, that the *culture-distance hypothesis* mentioned in Chapter 5 is very similar to the *life-event hypothesis*. Both suggest that the absolute amount of difference between country of origin and country of destination leads to *changes* in life-style which can lead to various illnesses. Thoits (1982) has suggested that the psychological vulnerability of certain groups, such as older adults, women, unmarried persons and those with less education, income and prestige, is because they are exposed to the occurrence of many stressful events and have fewer psychological resources (i.e. social support) to cope with such events. Although she found strong support for the vulnerability hypothesis – relatively disadvantaged lower socio-demographic groups suffer more from the effects of life-events – social support failed to buffer stress to any degree in most of the groups. Interestingly, it is precisely the vulnerable groups listed above who appear to cope poorly with geographic movement.

Many studies have begun to concentrate on the relationship between change (life-events) and help (social support), suggesting that the latter buffers or protects against the former (Brown and Harris, 1978; Smith et al., 1978; Williams et al., 1981; Monroe, 1983). Thus Monroe et al. (1983) found some connection between life-events, social support and symptom specificity. Certain dimensions of stress (control) and particular aspects of social support (living at home) were directly related to certain symptoms; perceived dimensions of events *and* social support interactively predict symptoms: 'Thus it appears that those individuals who either experience or perceive events to be mostly undesirable (and without desirable qualities) and who have fewer close friends are especially likely to exhibit diverse types of symptoms during final-examination stress' (p. 347). Similarly Lin and Ensel (1984) found that vulnerability to depression of various groups in the population is affected by three factors: previous states of depression, an *increase* in undesirable life-events and a *decrease* in social support. Thus social support did show a mediating or buffering effect between life-events and depression.

Certainly both 'common sense' and a recognition of the complexity of the relationship between life-events and illness suggest that moderating or buffering variables such as social support should play a part. However, as the research appears to suggest, a number of other interactive variables render the simple buffering hypothesis inadequate as it stands.

There are, as may be expected, various measurement and methodological problems in this area. The various scales in use, e.g. Schedule of Recent Experiences, Social Readjustment Rating Schedule, Life-Events Inventory (Cochrane and Robertson, 1973; Holmes and Masuda, 1974) have been criticized on a number of grounds. All the questionnaires require subjects to indicate if they have experienced each of the stipulated events over a specific retrospective period, these events having previously been assigned numerical weights based upon their estimated magnitude. The greater the change or social adjustment required, the higher the score. In turn, the magnitude of this score is used to predict the amount of stress and ill health in the subjects. There are numerous criticisms of this method, which include the possibility that subjects may not accurately recall what happened to them; the quality versus the quantity of the events; and perceptions of their stressfulness (Hurst, 1979; Mechanic, 1974; Thoits, 1981). Monroe (1982) has pointed out that perhaps the major criticisms concern scale content and scoring procedures. Because the actual content of the event scales must relate to a particular research question and population, Monroe has advocated that 'the most prudent strategy for present research is to examine various sub-groups of events separately in relation to the different stages of the disorder's clinical course (e.g. onset, maintenance, remission)' (p. 439). Similarly, there are serious problems in comparing the results of studies because of differences in scoring methods, including which events are thought most important, the *dimensions* of proposed importance and the resultant weighting procedures, and the time period over which the incident is assessed. As a result, Monroe (1982) considers a number of alternative approaches, including looking at overlapping or synonymous items, the causal sequence of events and the common underlying causes of events. All of these points are of course pertinent to the interviewing of migrants and sojourners in general, who often retrospectively interpret their experiences for the benefit of investigators.

As with the social-support hypothesis (see p. 184) the importance of life-events (absolute change from country of origin to country of destination) in illness (physical or psychological) has probably been overemphasized. Correlational studies have found the relationship between measures of life events and illness to range from 0.2 to 0.4, so accounting for between 4 per cent and 16 per cent of the variance. For instance, in a review of nearly twenty studies Cochrane and Sobel (1980) found an average correlation of 0.35, while Sarason et al. (1975) described the correlation as 'on the border between tiny and small' (p. 338). Hence the aetiological impact of life-changes as a function of migration in mental (and physical) illness may be grossly exaggerated. Yet it should be pointed out that this literature has not been undertaken within the context of geographic movement (migration, sojourning), nor has the adaptation variable very often been mental health. It may well be, therefore, that within this specific area, life-style changes as a function of geographic movement do account for much more of the variance. As Rahe et al. (1964) pointed out more than twenty years ago, life-events may be a *necessary*, but by no means *sufficient*, precipitator of major health changes. Furthermore, the relationship may be moderated or confounded by other individual differences (neuroticism, sensation-seeking) or belief (locus of control) variables. For instance, it has been suggested that social class is a powerful and important intervening variable. Others have argued that social class is a composite summary factor and that lack of intimate relationships, number of children and lack of a job are the important factors. Brown et al. (1975) have suggested that the aforementioned factors lower self-esteem, which in turn lowers stress resistance and hence makes the person more vulnerable to illnesses. However, attempts to specify intervening personality variables have not met with much success (Hendrie et al., 1975; Robertson and Cochrane, 1976). Finally there is, once again, the sticky problem of cause and correlation. Do psychologically distressed people cause the occurrence of many negative events, or do randomly occurring life-events lead to depression? As always the relationship is likely to be bi-directional, though it is probable that the major causal direction is from events to illness rather than the other way around.

What is perhaps most surprising is how little the life-event literature appears to have filtered into the migration and mental-health literature. Although the importance of previous experiences has been noted by some researchers (Krupinski et al., 1973), they have concentrated only on refugees and on extreme examples, such as the effect of the holocaust. Though it may not serve to account for a great deal of variance, the range, intensity and perceived threat of a migrant's life-changes may go some way towards explaining the nature of the link between mental health and migration.

Social support networks: reduction in social support

There is a rapidly growing, already considerable body of literature in clinical, community, medical and applied psychology regarding the supportive functions of interpersonal relationships. In the main these findings suggest that social support is directly related to increased psychological well-being and to a lower probability of physical and mental illness. Thus the various types of support provided by interpersonal relationships play a crucial role in determining a person's general adaptive functioning and sense of well-being. This literature draws on various traditions, including attachment theory, social-network theory and various ideas in psychotherapy. Of relevance in the present context are the findings that the social networks of neurotics differ significantly from those of normal people and that persons with a well-developed primary group are substantially protected against neurotic symptoms (Brown et al., 1975; Henderson et al., 1978). Because migration often involves the leaving behind of family, friends and acquaintances, such as work colleagues and neighbours, sources of social support are reduced and there is, according to the theory, a consequent increase in physical and mental illness. Supportive relationships with family and friends are no longer available to the same extent to sustain migrants and sojourners. Henderson and Byrne (1977) have noted that for some migrants, deficiencies in social support are related to the emergence of psychiatric symptoms, rather than to a personality attribute which antedated the migration itself. They point out that where migrant groups have developed dense and liberally available support networks, the distress and breakdown of these groups is lessened. In a relevant study Holahan et al. (1983) looked at social integration and mental health in a biracial community. They found that those American blacks who had low levels of social integration showed more psychiatric symptoms than either white respondents or blacks with a high level of integration. They argue that black communities are usually characterized by particularly well-developed, culturally responsive, informal networks which make them highly sensitive to the absence of social support.

If the social-support hypothesis is true, then what is clearly important for migrants and sojourners is that they have access to a supportive (possibly co-national) group. This may explain the preference for living in immigrant ghettos. Yet many agencies have attempted to prevent migrants living in homogenous geographic groups because they believed that it prevents adaptation and assimilation and can even cause or encourage prejudice. Of course, living in a co-national group does not ensure support, but as we noted in Chapters 4 and 5, friendship networks and indeed the absolute number of co-national migrants in a community is a good indication of adaptation.

As is probably true with all areas of research, the social-support literature is somewhat equivocal, and fundamental structures and processes have yet to be fully described. Differences in populations, measures, as well as social-support definitions and stressors may account for the contradictory findings in this area. Nevertheless, there is enough consistent literature to indicate that a relationship does exist between social support and psychological disorder. What is perhaps most lacking is a clear, interactive, feedback model, rather than a simple undirectional causal model, that can explain the nature and sequence of the interaction between stress, support and coping over time and across settings. Three possibilities exist: that social support may have direct, protective, or compensatory effects on mental health. The question, therefore, is whether social support is an important aetiological variable on mental health in its own right (direct); whether it affects mental health outcomes under certain circumstances only (protective); or whether it may compensate for or be compensated by other forms of help and support (compensatory). Probably, as Syrotuik and D'Arcy (1984) suggest, social support has an effect in all of these circumstances.

The first problem one confronts in this literature is the definition of, or agreement on the dimensions of, social support. Some definitions are tautological (Lin et al., 1979), others extremely vague (Beels, 1981). Most researchers have relied on Cobb's (1976) definition, which sees social support as information telling the person that they are cared for, held in high esteem and a member of a communication network with mutual obligations. Some have emphasized the cognitive aspects of support (Caplan, 1974) while others have stressed emotional or instrumental factors. Most researchers have attempted to spell out the various dimensions of support theoretically (Kahn and Antonucci, 1980; House, 1981; Wills, 1984; Barrera and Aislay, 1983). Essentially, the sort of dimensions that occur are *affective* (emotional, self-esteem), *instrumental* (behavioural assistance) and *informational* (feedback), though these have sometimes been divided further.

There are other taxonomies, most of which overlap with the above. All authors see the dimensions as oblique rather than as orthogonal, that is as interdependent rather than as independent, leading to a complex concept of social support. This is clearly very important as the type of support people receive affects their psychological adaptation. For instance, Cohen and Hoberman (1983) found that self-esteem and appraisal were more effective as buffers to various stresses than tangible or belonging support. Further, a particular type of support may meet one need and alleviate one source of stress but not another (Cauce et al., 1982). Equally, if support is sought but not met, additional stress may arise leading to depression (Fiore et al., 1983).

A problem with the above definitions is that they confound qualitative and quantitative aspects: social support must therefore be seen as the availability of helping relationships and the quality of those relationships – *both* the structure and the content of the phenomenon. Social support has a *structure* (size, setting, reciprocity, accessibility and make-up of interpersonal relationships), *a content* (what form the help takes such as emotional, financial) and *a process* (the way in which an individual develops, nurtures and uses supportive networks). Recent studies have concluded that different modes of support and different measures of adjustment should not be treated as if they are equivalent or interchange-able (Fondacaro and Heller, 1983; Hammer, 1981; Porritt, 1979; Hirsch, 1979; Holahan and Moos, 1983; Willis, 1984; Henderson, 1984).

The ways in which researchers have gone about demonstrating the relationship between social support and psychological disorder have been as follows (Leavy, 1983): to compare the social-support structures of 'normal' with 'clinical' populations; to compare the social support structures of groups with different degrees of a specific type of disorder (e.g. depression); general population epidemiological studies that have attempted to look at the separate or interactive effects of social support and life-stress on mild forms of psychological difficulty and psychiatric morbidity; to compare the coping response of groups of individuals with different social-support networks to the same stressful life-event; and studies aimed at specifying personal or demographic characteristics which differentiate the supported from the non-supported. Furthermore, social support has been related to a large number of medical behaviours ranging from patient compliance (Leavy, 1983) to cancer (Reverson et al., 1983).

Clinical studies have yielded various results which may be considered salient for migrants. First, more disturbed clinical populations tend to rely on non-family members, while less-severe cases have more family members as sources of social support. Although the results are not completely consistent, they do tend to point to the importance of close family members. Many migrants have to leave their families behind in the process of migration and hence may become bereft of their primary support network precisely when they are needed most. Second, whereas almost by definition social support is a *mutual, interactive* process with obligations of reciprocity, many of the severely disfunctioning persons tend to be only recipients rather than providers of support. Being able to provide support of any kind involves having psychological or material assets that the immigrant may not have access to. That is, there appears to be an element of normative reciprocity in support in that if it is not offered, it is not received. Often migrants are not in the position to offer support (except perhaps to fellow migrants) and hence get offered very little, which in turn may render them particularly vulnerable to mental breakdown.

Studies done within a culture-shock context have lent support to the thesis. Two studies of immigrant Americans – Chinese (Lin et al., 1979) and eastern European (Biegel et al., 1980) – showed that social support was negatively correlated with psychiatric symptomatology. Unlike the control groups of young, non-ethnic, upper socio-economic status Americans, for whom neighbourhood attachments had only a buffering effect on their symptoms, a lack of neighbourhood attachments had a powerful effect on the symptomatology of the migrants. One advantage of the social-support hypothesis is that it can allow for cultural and national differences in adapting to a new culture. These differences would depend on the quantity and quality of support previously experienced, expected and needed, and the difference in support network in the country of migration. The size, structure and cohesiveness of co-national migrants would also be an important factor in predicting migrant adjustment, as was shown in Chapter 4.

There has been some work done on individual differences in social support (Leavy, 1983). Consistent sex differences have been found: women of all ages tend to have more supportive relationships than men, especially those of an intimate and confiding nature. Women who work, and hence have available larger and more varied social-support networks, have lower psychiatric morbidity (Roberts et al., 1982). Studies have also shown that the sexes seem to differ on the components of support which are associated with emotional well-being (Phillips, 1981) as well as the consequences of support (Holahan and Moos, 1981).

Social support is often best provided at work, and this may explain some of the more intriguing culture-shock findings (Nathanson, 1980). Many studies have shown that in migrant families it is the non-working mothers who adjust least well, partly because they are not able to learn the appropriate skills of the culture but also because they do not have the opportunity to develop a rich, work-related social-support network. Yet Holahan and Moos (1982) found that qualitative measures of support in family and work environment predict various symptoms of depression and psycho-somatic illnesses. More importantly, they found the work environment to be a more important source of support for men than women, and the family environment to provide an especially powerful source of unemployed women.

Although the social-support hypothesis is intuitively appealing, a host of studies using dependent measures as varied as weight loss (Brownell et al., 1978) and compliance with medical instructions (Baranowski et al., 1982) have found only weak support. This may be either because the measures of social support are too insensitive or psychometrically unsound, or because social support may not be as important as previously thought. Indeed, both might be true, and research in this area must continue to determine which aspects of support lead to which psychological processes.

As has been pointed out there are a host of findings in Chapters 4 and 5 which can be interpreted within the social-support conceptual framework. These include the finding that there is a significant inverse relationship between the density of an ethnic migrant group and the rate of mental illness in that group (Muhlin, 1979). Also it was pointed out in Chapter 5 that students' friendship networks were a good indicator of their health and adjustment. There are many other examples.

Clearly there is much that is unknown about how social support prevents psychological problems. Many of these issues were raised but it remains the case that the overwhelming bulk of the literature suggests a modest but important relationship.

Value differences

The differences in values that exist between many cultures have also been used to try to account for the misunderstandings, distress and difficulties experienced by cross–cultural travellers. Qualitative and quantitative differences in values between the person's country of departure and country of arrival were assumed to be directly proportional to the amount of difficulty experienced by that person. Ever since the work of Merton (1938) on the relationship between social structure and anomie, sociologists and psychologists have seen a link between deviance, delinquency and mental disorder, and a conflict in cultural values. There is a rich, interdisciplinary literature on the definition and consequence of values. Several distinctions have been made, including terminal versus instrumental (Rokeach, 1973) and intensity and direction (Hofstede, 1984). However the theoretical/philosophical literature far outweighs the empirical (and particularly psychological) literature on the topic.

Furthermore, because the study of values is concerned with the effect of society and culture on the individual, it has attracted a good deal of cross–cultural research (Zavalloni, 1980). Some of this research has been concerned with the establishment of valid and reliable measures of values (Allport et al., 1960; Kikuchi and Gordon, 1966; Rokeach, 1973; Triandis et al., 1972), while other studies have been concerned with differences between cultures, groups and individuals. A few studies have directly addressed the relationship between value differences and psychological distress. The literature on cultural differences and similarities in values will be first briefly reviewed, followed by a look at how value differences lead to misunderstandings and difficulties.

Despite the fairly extensive and very interesting research on cultural differences in values, the literature is difficult to review for two reasons. First, different researchers have chosen different instruments (with surprisingly little in common) and used them on quite different populations. Hence the results are hard to compare; there is a mass of interesting findings from a variety of studies that do not fall into any pattern. Second, and perhaps most importantly, few of these studies are theoretically, as opposed to empirically, driven. Most of them are descriptive rather than aiming to test a particular theory or model, though there are certain notable exceptions.

Some of the cross–cultural value studies have been quite extensive in that they have compared equivalent samples from many countries. Ng et al. (1982) studied the values of students in nine South-East Asian and Pacific countries (e.g. Bangladesh, Tasmania, India, Japan) using the Rokeach scale. Multivariate analysis revealed numerous and large differences between the groups from each nation. Two factors, derived from discriminant analysis, seemed to differentiate the groups most strongly. One factor differentiated cultures with societal-orientated values characteristic of underdeveloped countries (Papua New Guinea, Malaysia, India) from those with self-orientated, Dionysian, values characteristic of developed societies (New Zealand, Japan).

More ambitious projects using long, specially developed, standardized interviews of a random general population sample have been conducted. The European Value Systems study group (1982) interviewed approximately 1200 people in each of ten European countries. The hypotheses of this enormous study were:

1. (a) There is no single European values system. Rather, at any one point in time there co-exists a number of alternative interacting systems which can be defined and analysed. (b) These alternative systems have distinct appeal to different groups within the population.

2. (a) During the twentieth century the relative emphasis placed on the component values and beliefs which make up the various systems has changed. (b) Furthermore, the relative importance within a given society (in terms of the number of adherents) of the alternative systems has also changed.

3. Changes in values systems can be systematically linked to major social and political events and processes which have occurred at different times and to varying degrees in different parts of Europe. These have resulted in important national variations in values systems.

4. Variables previously thought to provide causal explanations of values such as social class, income and education are less important as predictors of moral values than the age, spiritual and political disposition of the respondent and his or her stage in the life cycle. Indeed, social-psychological indicators may ultimately prove to be the best predictors.

5. The underlying profile of values and beliefs which a respondent exhibits, conditions his or her perception of reality and provides the basis for the code of conduct and behaviour adopted. Consequently, there is a reciprocal relationship between values and behaviour.

6. (a) A majority of Europeans continue to express a range of important spiritual needs despite the loss of attachment to religious institutions. (b) The decline in religious affiliation has been reinforced by the failure of institutions adequately to respond to changes in the European values systems.

7. The apparent change in social morality is correlated in particular with the changing relative emphasis of religion and political values.

8. Commitment to the institution of the family remains high but differential changes in expectations regarding the family have occurred in response both to changes in values and to political and social developments. (b) The increasing incidence of marital breakdown is indicative of both the changing expectations regarding the family and the increasing emphasis on individual freedom.
9. Political minorities in Europe exhibit distinctive and predictable values profiles.
10. Attitudes towards the morality of work, respect for authority and the organisation of corporate enterprise show fundamental differences according to the structure of values and belief systems.
   (European Value Systems Study Group document, 1982, p. 3)

Although the results of this study covered a great deal of ground – including attitudes to the police, church, legal and educational system, government, industry, and most of the hypotheses were confirmed, the study was more descriptive than analytic. Indeed, it explicitly aimed to be descriptive rather than explanatory, and tested few direct hypotheses concerning different values between different countries.

One of the most extensive and ambitious cross-cultural projects is Hoftstede's (1984) study of international differences in work–related values. The study was based on data from hundreds of individuals from forty countries, at two points in time. From a literature survey, theoretical reasoning *and* a statistical analysis of all his data, Hofstede concluded that cultures differ along four orthogonal dimensions that show significant correlations with demographic, economic, geographic, historical and political indicators. The first dimension is *power distance* and refers to the extent to which various societies put different weights on inequalities in such areas as prestige, wealth and power. The second dimension is labelled *uncertainty avoidance* and refers to the extent that cultures cope with uncertainty through technology, law and religion. The third dimension is labelled *individualism* and refers to the way in which people live together and the relationship that exists between the individual and the collectivity in any one society. The fourth and final dimension is labelled *masculinity* and refers to the sex roles socialized in families, schools, in peer groups and through the media. The author then proceeded to integrate the four dimensions via a number of analyses enabling countries to be plotted in space and absolute distances, one from another. Because the study was primarily concerned with work–related values, much of the policy and implications section of the book takes the form of advice on how to improve organizational effectiveness. For instance, a motivational 'map of the world' suggests four quadrants:

1. (USA, great Britain, and their former dominions and colonies): motivation by personal, individual success, in the form of wealth,

recognition and 'self-actualization'. This is the classic McClelland–Maslow–Herzberg pattern.

2. (Japan, German-speaking countries, some Latin countries and Greece): motivation by personal, individual security. This can be found in wealth and especially in hard work. Second-quadrant countries have grown fastest economically in the 1960–1970 period (contrary to McClelland's theory).

3. (France, Spain, Portugal, Yugoslavia, Chile and other Latin and Asian countries): motivation by security and belonging. Individual wealth is less important than group solidarity. It is no accident that Yugoslavia, with its worker self-management system, is in this quadrant.

4. (North European countries plus the Netherlands): Motivation by success and belonging. In this quadrant, success will be measured partly as collective success and in the quality of human relationships in the living environment.

(Hofstede, 1984, p. 256)

There are many advantages to creating a robust and sensitive taxonomy. First, it provides a 'map' on which countries may be compared. The map was derived both theoretically and empirically, and though it reveals some interesting geographic, historical and political anomalies, it does not contradict other studies or 'commonsense' classifications. This map allows one to achieve some understanding of the amount of difference between value systems on the four specified dimensions held by people in those cultures, which in turn presumably has implications for difficulties experienced by people moving from one country to another. For instance, one might expect extreme differences between people going from Colombia to Finland, moderate differences between Belgium and Greece, fairly close similarities between Yugoslavia and Portugal, and very close similarities between Belgium and France, Brazil and Turkey, Taiwan and Pakistan, or Norway and the Netherlands.

Hence the map provides one with a set of readily testable hypotheses regarding the relationship between overall as well as major value-dimension difference and adjustment.

Second, the study suggests not only the quantity of difference but also the quality of difference on each of the four dimensions. Thus value differences in the society at large, in religious and political life and in organizations are spelt out. This is an important point as a person may be in an organization or a community which for one reason or another does not share the values of the dominant culture.

Hofstede's work is an extraordinary achievement but not without certain problems. Comparatively few African and eastern European countries were tested – where many migrants come from. It is not certain to what extent there is homogeneity within a country on the four values.

The mechanism whereby these values change is not made explicit. Perhaps most importantly for the value-difference hypothesis, the actual psychological consequences of a cultural clash are never spelt out; what occurs to individuals who hold one value system when confronted by another is not made clear.

Many studies have used the Rokeach value survey, which measures both terminal values (end-states of existence) such as freedom, equality, wisdom; and instrumental values (modes of conduct) such as courageous, independent and logical. Rokeach and Parker (1970) found seven significant differences in the rank ordering of terminal values, and six in the rank ordering of instrumental values when comparing black and white Americans. However, once the socio-economic differences were controlled, the number of significant differences dropped dramatically, which has important implications for cross-cultural research, notably in the careful matching of subjects. The only major difference between black and white Americans appears to be their ranking of equality, which is high for blacks and comparatively low for whites.

The Rokeach value survey has also been administered to students from various cultures: America (Rokeach, 1973), Australia (Feather, 1970), Canada (Rokeach, 1973) and Israel (Rim, 1970). Rokeach (1973) has made some comparisons between these groups, using the method of inspecting the data. The largest terminal value differences among the four groups were found for a world at peace and national security, both of which Israelis valued very highly, but upon which Americans, Canadians and Australians placed comparatively little value. The Americans tended to care more for a comfortable life, social recognition and being ambitious and less about being helpful than the other three groups, while the Israelis valued capable, intellectual, logical, helpful, clean, obedient and self-controlled more than the other groups. Australians, on the other hand, tend to rate true friendship, equality, wisdom and a sense of accomplishment higher than the other groups, while the Canadians appeared least achievement-orientated, placing less value on a sense of accomplishment, wisdom, ambitions and being capable. Rokeach (1973) noted that these findings are only tentative given the problems of sample equivalence. However, it should be pointed out that many of these results are consistent with the prediction of Lipset (1963), who in a theoretical paper conducted a comparative analysis of the links between national institutions and central value systems in Australia, Canada, Britain and the United States.

In two studies (Feather, 1980; Feather and Hutton, 1973) Feather compared the value systems of students in Papua New Guinea and Australia. The predictions were based on general considerations about the effect of affluence and education on the two societies and about specific factors relating to the history and traditional culture of Papua New Guinea. The Papua New Guineans gave much higher priority to equality, national security and salvation and less to happiness, inner harmony and self-respect than the Australians. Feather (1980) tested the hypothesis that the extent of social interaction will be positively related to the degree to which individuals of one group perceive that members of the other group share value systems similar to their own and see that they have something in common. This hypothesis was found true for the Australian group only with respect to instrumental values, but was not true for the Papua New Guinea group.

Feather (Feather, 1980; Feather, 1981; Feather and Hutton, 1973) traced these results to characteristic differences between the cultures in their socio-economic status, cultural-religious patterns and needs. Furnham (1984) found the same explanations accounted for the differences in the terminal and instrumental values in white (European), brown (Indian) and black (African) South Africans. For instance, Africans assigned higher priority to a world at peace, equality, salvation, national security and social recognition, than the other groups, while the Europeans assigned higher priority to true friendship, family security, mature love, a world of beauty and an exciting life. Overall the individualistic-privatistic outlook of the whites contrasted starkly with the collective/socially-orientated outlook of the Africans. Other studies have looked at differences in values between the Pueblo Indians and Anglo values (Trimble, 1976) and the values of foreign students (Furnham and Alibhai, 1985b).

However interesting and useful these descriptive studies may be, they do not explain how, why or when value differences between people lead to misunderstandings when they come into contact via tourism, a sojourn or migration. To overcome this limitation, Feather and colleagues (Feather and Wasejluk, 1973; Feather and Rudzitis, 1974) have studied migrant subjective assimilation as a function of value difference. In these studies it was argued that adult migrants have an already established, fairly inflexible set of values and attendant behavioural repertoires. Their children, however, because they come into closer and more regular contact with the host culture *and* because their value systems are not fully developed, are more likely to change towards those of the dominant host culture. This hypothesis was confirmed with Ukrainian migrants (Feather and Wasejluk, 1973) and Latvian migrants (Feather and Rudzitis, 1974).

Feather's studies have not demonstrated how value differences lead to difficulty or, indeed, how they change, but rather how second-generation migrants adopt the dominant cultural values. However, he has speculated on the nature of the difficulty:

> When they leave their own country to settle in a new culture, they will be subject to a wide range of experiences that are discrepant from what they have been used to previously. The physical environment itself

(e.g. its light, colour, vegetation, landscape, climate, and so on) may be strange and unfamiliar. They may find that the new society involves a different language, different economic opportunities, different social and political institutions, different forms of social stratification, different norms and values – indeed, a host of differences, some obvious, some subtle. They have to learn to adapt to these discrepancies, and in the course of doing so may have to modify existing responses or develop completely new ones. . .

The degree to which they feel comfortable in the new environment will relate to the nature and extent of the discrepancies that they encounter. When the environment satisfies their basic needs and abilities and is congruent with their already developed systems of beliefs, attitudes and values they should feel more satisfied and adjusted than when the person–environment fit is imperfect, involving serious discrepancies that demand resolution. As they learn more and more about the new environment, some discrepancies (e.g. those involving beliefs, attitudes and values) may be found to be based upon false perceptions of reality, and these discrepancies may then be modified in the light of more accurate information. In this way, the migrants may build up a veridical perception of the new environment. If this is to happen, obviously a considerable amount of interaction with both the physical and social aspects of the new environment will be necessary. In the case of values, for example, the adult migrants might start with rather vague and undifferentiated perceptions of the dominant values of the host society. These perceptions may become more refined and more accurate as they expand their network of social interaction within the host community. The initial pattern of value discrepancies may be modified in the light of this experience, giving rise to new satisfactions, or perhaps to new dissatisfactions, with the environment.

Some person–environment discrepancies that develop as the migrant interacts with the new culture are more important than others. For example, if persons cannot satisfy their basic needs because they cannot find outlets for their skills and abilities in a work situation, they are obviously confronted with a dramatic discrepancy that demands quick resolution – in the short term, by obtaining forms of social support and temporary relief where they are available, and in the long term, by learning new skills that enable them to cope. At the level of higher-order concepts such as values, some discrepancies that occur between migrants' value systems and those that they attribute to particular social environments are more important than others, involving more pressure for resolution. (Feather, 1979, p. 125–6)

Feather has recognized that there are individual and group differences in the ability to tolerate discrepancies in values. More importantly perhaps, he has pointed out that value changes are not just one-way, so that migrants may influence the host nationals with whom they interact. Finally, societies differ in the extent to which they tolerate people holding divergent values, some societies being much more tolerant than others. To understand the consequences of value differences for migrants it is important to take three variables into consideration: the quality and quantity of difference in salient values between the hosts' and migrants' societies; the tolerance for varying cultural value systems within the same society; and the individuals' cognitive complexity, ability and motivation to change their cultural value system.

Thus it may be predicted that migrants who have strongly internalized the moral values of their original culture are likely to feel more strain if these values are seriously questioned. For instance, self-confident, morally righteous Christian missionaries at the turn of the century suffered fairly high rates of mental illness when faced with a different culture and value system to the one they had left, while they appeared to cope moderately well in countries where, for a variety of reasons, their values were not challenged (Price, 1913). Therefore the strength, sophistication and complexity of a value system may also be an important determinant of adaptation.

Finally, it should be pointed out that value systems are dynamic and ever-changing due to social, political and economic influences. Hence it is likely that in some cultures there is as much within-cultural as between-cultural value variance. This is particularly the case where societies are undergoing radical or swift change. The idea, therefore, of adapting to the values of a particular culture or country may be meaningless if there is no one generally accepted or coherent system. Under these circumstances it may be necessary to specify the subcultures which will be salient for the sojourner.

There have been only a few attempts to explain precisely why value differences lead to difficulty. Robertson and Cochrane (1976) have proposed a value-change model to explain the relationship between life-stresses and psychological consequences. They noted the large increase in deviant behaviour and psychological disturbance over the past twenty years, particularly among the young (and more particularly young, working-class British males). They argued that these have occurred because two fundamental values have changed – at least for the young. The first is the belief that all individuals have intrinsic and *equal value*, and the potential for self-actualization, irrespective of their station in life. The second is that the fulfilment or frustration of these potentials depends on the social and physical *environment* of the person. Older values stress self-reliance, personal achievement and accomplishment as a function of personal responsibility, whereas recent values stress self-development as a function of environmental, social, political and economic justice. Thus for the young failure, illness, unemployment and even lack of personal worth are a function, not of personal misfortune, lack of effort or ability, but public injustice:

> There is no room in the new value system for the equivalent of stoicism or fulfilment through suffering which may moderate the responses to stress of those guided by the precepts of self-help, individual initiative and self-denial which are fostered by the old value system. The prediction is that those imbued with the new world-view will have a diminished threshold of tolerance for stress. They will feel that they should not be called upon to undergo frustrations to any degree because these constitute an affront to expectations about freedom to develop and a betrayal by the society seen as responsible for guaranteeing these freedoms. Upon encountering life-stresses, such an individual is more likely to resort to one or more forms of deviance and to experience more psychological problems. It is suggested that possessors of the new value system will tend to interpret relatively minor feelings of tension, anxiety, or depression, brought about by life-stresses, as evidence of mental disturbance, whereas individuals whose perceptions are governed by the old value system will define these same feelings as a morbid preoccupation or as indicating that they need to 'get a grip' on themselves. Individuals in the former group are therefore predicted to report more symptoms and to be more likely to seek professional help when stressed than are the possessors of the old ethos. (Cochrane, 1980, p. 167)

This work suggests that certain values – like stoicism and self-help – are perhaps more adaptive than others. It may, however, be that the values relate more to the reporting or not reporting of illness and unhappiness than to how people cope with stress, yet this is unlikely. Value systems, then, may be useful predictors of both how much strain travellers feel and how they cope with that strain. Again, it is not being argued that values are the only important variable in determining culture shock but rather that they account for a significant proportion of the variance.

Chapter summary

This chapter reviewed three areas of research which may be usefully applied to the culture-shock literature. *The life events and illness* explanation suggests that it is the experience of *change* and adaptation to new conditions that is stressful and a possible cause of ill health – the greater the change, the more likely or vulnerable is the person to illness. The theme of difference, distance or change arose consistently in Chapters 4 and 5, as did the idea that the amount of adaptation necessary is directly related to stress and illness. A number of concepts in this literature are important for the theme of culture shock. First, both positive and negative events can cause stress: it is the adjustment to these events that is important. Second, there may be various dimensions of change such as control, desirability and threat which need to be distinguished and which may lead to quite different consequences. Third, the consequences of stress are quite different for different people and it is virtually impossible to predict which person will suffer from precisely which mental or physical illness. Fourth, the effects of change and life-events may be modified, ameliorated or reduced by other factors. There are a number of difficulties in this research literature, not least of which is the modest relationship between life-events and illness. Nevertheless, it provides a useful theoretical framework with which to conceptualize the causes and consequences of culture shock.

The second area of research reviewed in this chapter was concerned with the reduced *social support* as a function of fragmented social networks. The focus of this area is not so much on threatening life-events but on the provision of various forms of support from established social networks. The idea is simply that support from other people has direct, protective or compensatory effects on mental health and well-being. Quite naturally this support usually comes from family and friends, and geographic movement nearly always involves a physical separation and considerably reduced opportunities for support. Although there is no agreed-upon taxonomy of support features, it is agreed that support is multidimensional, having such dimensions as emotional, instrumental and informational components. It may well be that different dimensions of social support are important for different people at different times. Hence foreign migrants might first require informational, followed by instrumental and then followed by emotional support. Not only is social support multi-dimensional it is also qualitative as well as quantitative, which of course presents a problem for measurement.

Studies done on migrants tend to confirm clinical findings, namely that social support is negatively correlated with psychiatric symptomatology. Similarly, findings on those people particularly vulnerable to mental illness as a consequence of reduced or inadequate social support seem to mirror the culture-shock literature which shows that women, adolescents, the poorly educated, and so on, are all more vulnerable to illness as a function of poor support networks. Once again, it is not being claimed that social support is the only or even the major factor in explaining the association between mental health and migration. Rather it is being suggested that it provides a conceptual framework within which to interpret many of the findings from the extant culture-shock literature.

The final area of research focuses on one aspect of difference between travellers and their hosts: the difference in fundamental human values. It has often been suggested that a clash of values causes stress which in turn leads to mental illness. However, because of the subtlety and complexity of values, much more work has gone into the description and taxonomizing of these values than in explaining the mechanism whereby clash leads to illness. The descriptive studies are, however, very useful as they provide a 'map' of the major differences, which allows one to get some idea of the amount or degree of difference in values in different migrant or sojourning groups.

However, some researchers have attempted to explain how value differences lead to strain and poor adaptation. It has been suggested that a person's beliefs, attitudes and values should be considered as a total *system* that is concerned with such issues as competence and morality and that is derived in large part from societal demands. These systems are organized summaries of experience that capture the focal, abstracted qualities of past encounters, have a normative or 'oughtness' quality about them and which function as criteria or frameworks against which present experience can be tested. Furthermore, they function as general motives. When people move to other cultures, value differences between them mean that previously established expectations and predictions are invalid. This poor fit between person and the environment may lead to distress and anxiety until the values of the new society are understood and internalized.

Of course, values change over time, and they are by no means unanimously endorsed by all members of a group; some values may be more adaptive and flexible than others – all of which indicates it is by no means simple to predict who will experience what sort of distress as a consequence of value difference. Nevertheless, this literature has been particularly useful from a descriptive and toxonomic viewpoint in that it has attempted to delineate the major dimensions by which cultures and countries differ one from another.

This chapter has applied the rapidly developing literature in three areas of social and clinical psychology to the problem of culture shock. Though there remain various problems with each of these areas of research, each offers new insights and also a conceptual framework for interpreting many of the findings reported in Chapters 4, 5 and 6.

9 *Beyond culture shock: social skills and culture-learning*

In Chapter 7 we reviewed some of the more traditional explanations that have been offered to account for the psychological reactions of individuals to novel environments, such as the notion of grieving for lost familiar surroundings. In Chapter 8 we described some more recent formulations, in which culture stress is regarded as resulting from a lack of social support in the new setting, and the changes in values and life-style that a move from one culture to another usually entails. In this chapter we shall present a model of culture stress that is based on a social-learning/social-skills approach. After describing the theory and some of its empirical support, we shall, as in previous chapters, draw out the implications of this approach for intervention and remedial action. A more detailed description of culture training programmes based on social-skills training (SST) will be found in Chapter 11.

Argyle and Kendon (1967) were among the first to suggest that the social behaviour of persons interacting with each other can be construed as a mutually organized, skilled performance similar to other motor skills. Difficulties arise when this performance breaks down or cannot be initiated in the first place. There is now an extensive empirical literature on the causes and correlates of social-skills deficiencies (Ellis and Whittington, 1981, 1983) as well as manuals on the methods and effectiveness of social-skills training (Spence, 1980; Trower, Bryant and Argyle, 1978). Empirical research has identified some of the interpersonal skills that socially incompetent persons lack or perform unsatisfactorily, although it should be noted that there is no general agreement on what these are, that is different workers emphasize different skills and come up with different lists (Furnham, 1983). The Oxford tradition has always given prominence to the interactive elements that regulate social encounters, in particular the non-verbal aspects of social interaction. Consequently, their list (which this chapter also favours) includes elements such as expressing attitudes, feelings and emotions; adopting the appropriate proxemic posture; understanding the gaze patterns of the people with whom they are interacting; carrying out ritualized routines such as greetings, leave-taking, self-disclosure, making or refusing requests; and asserting themselves (Trower, Bryant and Argyle, 1978).

A distinction is also sometimes made between knowing what to do, and converting that knowledge into action, which in the interpersonal sphere translates into perceptual sensitivity, on the one hand, and behavioural flexibility, on the other. Not only must individuals be sensitive to how others respond to them, to what is going on around them psychologically, but they must also acquire a flexible behavioural repertoire which can respond appropriately to various social milieux. Furthermore, not only will there be variations between different situations, but each episode will have its own dynamic ebb and flow which a participant must take into account.

Thus it can be said that socially inadequate individuals have not mastered the social conventions of their society, either because they are unaware of the rules of social behaviour that regulate interpersonal conduct in their culture or, if aware of the rules, are unable or unwilling to abide by them. From this perspective it may be argued that socially unskilled persons are often like strangers in their own land, suggesting that people newly arrived in an alien culture or subculture will be in a similar position to indigenous socially inadequate individuals. There is empirical evidence to indicate that the elements of social interaction listed earlier vary between cultures (Argyle, 1982; Furnham, 1979, 1983; Hall, 1959, 1966; Hall and Beil-Warner, 1978; Leff, 1977) and that many travellers do not easily learn the conventions of another culture. It is ironic to note that individuals in this predicament, such as foreign students, business people, diplomats and missionaries, often tend to be highly skilled in the customs of their own society and find their sudden inadequacy in the new culture to be quite frustrating, not having had many similar experiences of failure previously.

The culture-learning/social-skills model has clear implications for the comprehension and management of cross-cultural difficulties. Cross-cultural problems arise because sojourners have trouble negotiating certain everyday social encounters. Indeed, this was the very point made by all the early writers on culture shock (Oberg, 1960). Therefore it seems necessary to identify the specific social situations which bother a particular sojourner, and then train the person in the skills that are appropriate for effective interaction in those situations.

As we will discuss in more detail later, the actual list of skills will depend on the demographic characteristics of the clients (their age, sex, social class, culture of origin, and so forth); the new culture whose skills they will be learning; and on the purpose of their sojourn. As numerous intracultural studies have shown that subjects who are incompetent in their culture of origin will benefit from remedial social skills training (Argyle, 1979), it may be presumed that intercultural training would have similar beneficial effects.

Although there are substantial differences between social-skills trainers in their aims and methods, such as the length of training, the specific behaviours being trained, the relative reliance on modelling, feedback, homework exercises, and so forth, they nearly all follow a similar sequence in their training. The first stage is a diagnosis or description of the verbal and non-verbal behaviours that are lacking in the clients, followed by exposure to models, role-playing with feedback, and often in-site training. The precise skills being trained depend on the needs of the client and may be easily and usefully applied to the problems of 'foreigners'.

The social psychology of the cross-cultural encounter

A meeting between two culturally disparate persons is in principle no different from any other social encounter.

There are various ways of conceptualizing troublesome social encounters. One approach (e.g. Argyle, 1982; Bochner, 1982) is to regard unsuccessful social episodes, particularly cross-cultural ones, as instances of failed verbal and non-verbal communication. An analysis of such encounters usually reveals that implicitly or explicitly the exchange of information and/or affect has not been successful. Thus, from the point of view of the sender, the intended messages may not have reached the receiver, or if they did, they were incomplete, garbled or distorted. From the point of view of the receiver, the messages may have been difficult to interpret, were ambiguous and, in more extreme cases, offensive. And since receivers are also senders, once the spiral of miscommunications has commenced, it can accelerate very quickly into a vicious circle of misunderstanding, the final result often being the breaking-off of the contact. At the institutional level, the same process usually leads to the establishment of two hostile camps ritually 'communicating' with each other through mutual complaints and accusations, which often have a mirror-image quality about them (Bronfenbrenner, 1961).

The miscommunication model of cross-cultural disharmony has fairly specific implications for remedial action. First, it is necessary to halt the vicious circle of misunderstanding. However, by itself that will not solve the problem, since the participants may still not know how to go about establishing a mutually positive relationship. These skills will have to be acquired by the persons involved, either gradually by trial and error or through a systematic learning approach such as in SST.

An analogy can be made with the process of learning a new game. There are two possibilities: where the game is known to one party and not the other, and where neither party knows the game. Cross-cultural learning usually but not necessarily follows the first-mentioned pattern, in which the sojourner has to learn the rules of the game and then learn the game itself. From the game perspective this places the sojourner at a disadvantage since the people with whom the game is being played already know both the rules and the moves and, what is more, expect everyone else to have that knowledge and those skills. The positive effect of this imbalance is to create an incentive for the sojourner to learn the game as rapidly as possible. On the negative side, experiences of failure may discourage sojourners and ultimately induce them to withdraw from the game, that is from the culture they set out to acquire. In the case of an intercultural SST those managing the experience will have to be alert to such a possibility.

One further general assumption needs to be made, namely that the encounter is taking place between reasonable people (or groups) of good will, whose hostility for each other is due to mutual misunderstandings, and not because one or both of the parties are maniacs, sadists or wicked, evil and malevolent persons. If such an assumption cannot be sustained or, as is more likely, the participants are unwilling to entertain the idea, then SST interventions are unlikely to be effective. All that SST can do is to teach the participants the social skills they lack; it is not a technique for the moral re-education of real or perceived scoundrels. In other words, some minimum degree of mutual good-will, or at least a recognized desire to improve relations, is a prerequisite for interventions aimed at reducing the incidence of cross-cultural miscommunications. Hence some trainers have suggested that no programme should begin without the establishment of a 'learning contract' which sets out the mutual responsibilities of both the trainers and the trainees (Furnham et al., 1980).

In his analysis of cross-cultural friction, Triandis (1975) distinguishes between external (to the persons) and internal determinants of conflict. For instance, external factors may include major differences in the distribution of resources, leading to the exploitation of one group by the other – what LeVine and Campbell (1972) called 'realistic conflict'. Reducing externally produced conflict is predominantly a task for economists and legislators and can be most effectively addressed through political rather than psychological processes. In contrast, internal sources of conflict, according to Triandis, stem from different perceptions of the environment, or the subjective culture of the participants, leading to misunderstandings, disconfirmed expectations and role conflicts. This is the province of the applied social psychologist, and the social-skills trainer.

Another category needs to be added to Triandis's distinction between internal and external sources of conflict, namely the values held by the various parties in contact and the extent to which their moral stance may differ (see Ch. 8). Although values are internal in Triandis's sense, they function like external factors in that they are highly resistant to change. Thus no amount of SST is going to train devout Catholic parents to accept sexual 'promiscuity' in their teenage children, nor are these young people going to be easily persuaded from their view that their parents are repressive and authoritarian. Or to use a cross-cultural rather than a subcultural example, Filipino school children give and receive a great deal of assistance from each other in the classroom (Guthrie, 1975); what they call co-operative behaviour, other cultures may regard as cheating, and an English or American teacher working in the Philippines could disapprove of what is deemed locally to be acceptable and even desirable behaviour.

• The conclusion to be drawn is that SST is most appropriate in dealing with what Triandis called 'internally based conflicts', which we have identified as communication problems. SST is unlikely to be very effective in reducing 'real' conflict, nor is it going to make much of an impact on people locked into morally or politically divergent positions. The difficulty is that many real-life conflicts are a complex mixture of all three types. For instance, when white police arrest an unemployed non-white suspect, the accused may quite justifiably complain about their relative powerlessness to answer the charge; at the same time, the police may dislike the accused because the suspect is on the dole, which is contrary to their belief in the work ethic; and both parties may send out verbal and non-verbal messages that are misunderstood by all concerned. Only the latter component of the conflict is amenable to SST intervention, and it would be a disservice to SST to claim otherwise. What is also apparent from this analysis is that effective intercultural orientation programmes must deal with the three components of conflict in an integrated way, taking political, economic, 'moral' (i.e. value judgement) and psychological factors into account as part of an overall approach to the problem.

It should not, however, be thought that SST is without its critics. A period of enthusiastic expansion and optimism was followed by more sceptical assessment and evaluation. Criticisms of SST fall into three main areas: criticisms of the theory, methodological criticisms of research and therapeutic criticisms (Furnham, 1983a,b). It has been suggested that Argyle's (1979) model, though it is heuristically useful, is deficient in a number of respects; for instance, its neglect of cognition and affect, and the fact that it is not interactive. Methodologically, research has been hampered by a paucity of valid and reliable assessment techniques, sampling and analysis problems and a neglect of follow-up studies. Also, studies on its therapeutic effectiveness have been flawed by confounding treatment and therapist effects as well as problems in the measurement of change. Despite these criticisms, Furnham (1983a,b) and other reviewers have argued for the positive effects of SST, pointing out that nearly all studies on various groups (prisoners, alcoholics, school-children and disabled people) have shown positive effects after a comparatively short time.

Cross-cultural differences in how people communicate

A prerequisite of cross-cultural SST is an understanding of the characteristic differences in communication patterns. Research has shown that there are consistent and systematic cultural differences in the way in which people send and receive information, prescriptions (commands and wishes) and affect (e.g. Argyle, 1982). When persons from two different cultures meet, they will have difficulty in communicating with one another to the extent that their respective 'codes' differ, and to the extent to which they are unaware that these differences exist. The latter is a particular problem in encounters between two groups that may share the same linguistic forms (or at least speak mutually intelligible dialects), because the similarities in language may obscure any differences that might exist in their subjective cultures. Consequently, the participants may not realize that they are sending unintended messages and distorting incoming information. For instance, when an American says 'Would you like to . . .?' (e.g. as in 'write a report on the sales prospect of a particular product'), this is not a question but a polite order; if an Australian subordinate were to answer 'No', the American might be offended and the Australian out of a job. In general, however, the evidence indicates that as differences (including differences in language) between the cultures of the participants increase, so do the difficulties in communication, due mainly to differences in the elements that enter into and regulate interpersonal behaviour. The psychological literature describing these processes is voluminous, and a comprehensive review is beyond the scope of this chapter. What follows is a brief list of those aspects of interpersonal communication that are known to differ cross-culturally and which contribute significantly to the effectiveness of information exchange. Both emitted and received/perceived behaviours can and often do occur within a complex socio-cultural context, each with its particular rules and conventions. The main aim of an SST programme would be to train people to emit the behaviours that are appropriate to a particular setting, interpret the feedback they are getting (e.g. what a sender means with a V-sign), and also be aware of the rules that apply to those particular sorts of interactions.

Polite usage: etiquette

Cultures differ in the extent to which people are direct or indirect, how requests are made, and more importantly, how requests are denied or refused. For instance, Philippine social interaction is based on what Peace Corps Volunteers came to call 'SIR', or 'smooth interpersonal relationships'. Yet Americans assigned to the Philippines were initially told to be perfectly frank in their dealings with the locals, which turned out to be a devastating piece of advice; the directness of the Americans was regarded as tactless and brutal, and totally contrary to the principles of SIR as practised in the Philippines (Guthrie, 1966).

In many Asian countries the word 'no' is seldom used, so that 'yes' can mean 'no' or 'maybe'. There are many stories of westerners extending an invitation to an Asian acquaintance, receive what they consider to be an affirmative reply, and then become angry when the visitor does not show up (Brein and David, 1971). Furthermore, rules surrounding invitations, and how these are to be extended and accepted, are highly culture-bound. Triandis (1975) relates how an American visitor asked his Greek acquaintance what time they should come to his house for dinner. The Greek villager replied 'any time'. Now in American usage the expression 'any time' is a non-invitation that people give to appear polite but which they hope will not lead to anything. The Greek, however, actually meant that the Americans would be welcome any time, because in his culture putting limits on when a guest can come is deemed insulting. Triandis does not reveal how the incident ended, but it is quite likely that the Americans would have taken what they thought was a hint and withdrawn from the engagement, thereby seriously offending their Greek host.

Some cultures use linguistic forms like 'thank you' to show their appreciation, whereas in other cultures 'thank you' is signalled non-verbally. A visitor from a 'linguistic' culture unaware of this custom may come to regard the hosts as rude and uncouth, who in turn will wait in vain for the visitor to exhibit the appropriate gesture of appreciation. The intensity with which speech is uttered is also a variable. For instance, Arabs speak loudly, which Europeans interpret as shouting. Americans speak louder than English persons, to whom they sound as brash and assertive. The list of examples is endless, and some guide-books try to provide tips on how to behave in foreign countries. Yet few attempts have been made to document and explain the origins of responses to the infringement of cross-cultural etiquette.

Non-verbal communication

Non-verbal signals play an important role in communicating attitudes and affect, in expressing emotions, in supporting speech by elaborating on what is said, by providing feedback from listener to sender and by synchronizing verbal interactions so that the participants know when it is their turn to speak and when it is their turn to listen, when it is appropriate to interrupt, and so on (Argyle, 1975, 1980). Cross-culturally there are both similarities and differences in how non-verbal signals are used depending on the particular culture and behaviour concerned, and a comprehensive treatment is outside the scope of this section. Communication elements that have been studied include the face, eyes, spatial behaviour, bodily contact and gestures (Duncan, 1969; Ekman and Friesen, 1972, 1974; Mehrabian, 1972; Sommer, 1969). For instance, Japanese display rules forbid use of negative facial expressions (Shimoda, Argyle and Ricci Bitti, 1978), making them indeed relatively 'inscrutable'. Filipinos may smile and laugh when they are very angry (Guthrie, 1975), so that outsiders could get a completely false impression of the impact they were making. Levels of mutual gaze vary across cultures, Arabs and Latin Americans having high while Europeans have relatively low levels (Watson, 1970). When persons from high- and low-gaze cultures meet, the behaviour of the low-gaze participant is interpreted as impolite, not paying attention and dishonest; while the high-gaze person is seen as disrespectful, threatening or insulting. Spatial behaviour varies between cultures, some groups standing much closer to each other than others (Aiello and Jones, 1971; Baxter, 1970; Brein and David, 1971; Hall, 1959, 1966; Jones, 1971; Scherer, 1974; Watson and Graves, 1966).

Cultures also vary in the extent to which they allow bodily contact (Argyle, 1982). Contact cultures include Arab, Latin American and southern European groups. In non-contact cultures, touching is only allowed under very restricted conditions, such as within the family, in brief handshakes with strangers or in specialized role relationships (e.g. doctors, dentists, tailors). Contact outside these approved settings can be a source of considerable anxiety. When a high-touch culture meets a low-touch one, the low-contact person is seen as aloof, cold and unfriendly, whereas the high-contact person may be seen as a perverted creep.

In one of the few controlled experiments conducted in the area of non-verbal cross-cultural communication, Collett (1971) trained English subjects in Arab social skills (e.g. more mutual looking, position themselves closer, touch each other slightly during interaction, more smiling and handshaking). A control group were merely given general information about the Arab world. Arab participants then interacted with one English experimental and one English control subject, respectively. The Arabs were later asked to make a sociometric choice between the two Englishmen they had met. The results showed that the Arabs chose the trained (i.e. experimental) subjects significantly more often than they did the untrained or control subjects. Thus, consistent with theoretical expectations, the Arabs preferred Englishmen who employed Arab-like non-verbal behaviour over those who behaved in a more characteristically English fashion.

Gestures and their meaning vary widely between cultures (Collett, 1982; Morris, Collett, Marsh and O'Shaughnessy, 1979). Some gestures are used in one culture and not in others, and the same gesture can have quite different, indeed opposite meanings in various cultures. For instance, in the United States a raised thumb is used as a signal of approval or approbation, the 'thumbs up' signal, but in Greece it is employed as an insult, often being associated with the expression 'katsa pano' or 'sit on this'. Another example is the ring sign, performed by bringing the tips of the thumb and finger together so that they form a circle. For most English-speaking people it means O.K. and is in fact known as the 'O.K. gesture'. But in some sections of France the ring means zero or worthless. In English-speaking countries disagreement is signalled by shaking the head, but in Greece and southern Italy the head-toss is employed to signify 'no'.

In a recent study, Pearce and Caltabiano (1982) administered eleven typically Italian and eleven typically Australian gestures to either Italo-Australian or Anglo-Australian children, who had to decode and encode them. In the decoding task the children were shown photographed gestures and asked to describe what the signs meant; in the encoding task the children were instructed to use their hands to convey various messages. The results indicated that Italo-Australian children were better acquainted with the Italian gestures than the Anglo-Australian children. However, there was no significant difference between the two groups of children in their recognition of the Anglo-Australian gestures. In other words, the Italo-Australians tended to be bicultural in their knowledge of gestures, whereas the Anglo-Australians were monocultural, being familiar only with their own gestural code. This highlights both the problems that minority groups face, the opportunities they have to develop a wider, more varied and enriched perspective on life by virtue of their position in society. Italo-Australian children are exposed to both cultures and hence tend to learn the respective communication codes of the two groups. On the other hand, Anglo-Australians are primarily exposed to the dominant culture, and unless their social circle extends beyond that group (e.g. Crowley, 1978), will tend to acquire only the mainstream code. One implication of studies such as these is that communication difficulties between mainstream and minority members may be asymmetrical, in the sense that minority persons can probably decode the messages they receive from dominant members more easily than the signals that dominant persons receive from the minority groups in their midst.

Social-skills training has always placed a great deal of emphasis on the measurement and training of non-verbal behaviours. Their complexity and variety across cultures attests to their importance in effective cross-cultural interaction. However, it should be noted that some aspects of non-verbal behaviour are more important than others. For instance, facial expressions and gaze play a greater role than spatial behaviour. Nevertheless, in specific instances even the smallest variation in non-verbal behaviour could lead to a major failure in communication.

Rules and conventions

Finally, cross-cultural differences in the rules that govern interpersonal behaviour are a major source of difficulty in intercultural communication. For instance, rules about punctuality vary from culture to culture (Argyle, 1982; Brein and David, 1971). Thus Levine, West and Reis (1980) found that Americans regard someone who is never late for an appointment as more successful than someone who is occasionally late, who in turn is perceived as more successful than a person who is always late. Exactly the opposite is the case in Brazil, where arriving late for an appointment is indicative of success. These differences suggest a poor prognosis for meetings between American and Brazilian businesspersons who are unaware of the rules governing punctuality in each other's cultures.

In an unobtrusive study of attitudes to punctuality, Levine and Bartlett (1984) checked the accuracy of clocks in cities in Japan, Taiwan, Indonesia, Italy, England and the United States They found clocks to be most accurate in Japan and least accurate in Indonesia. In another aspect of the same study, the walking speed of pedestrians was measured in the same cities. Again, the Japanese were the fastest and Indonesians the slowest strollers. Data such as these can be interpreted to reflect cultural differences in attitudes to pace of life.

According to Telberg (cited in Krech, Crutchfield and Ballachey, 1962), cultural differences in time perspective create difficulties in international organizations such as the United Nations. Telberg provides the following illustration:

> *'Gentlemen, it is time for lunch, we must adjourn,'* announces the Anglo-Saxon chairman, in the unabashed belief that having three meals a day at regular hours is the proper way for mankind to exist.
> *'But why? We haven't finished what we were doing,'* replies – in a puzzled manner that grows rapidly more impatient – an Eastern European delegate, in whose country people eat when the inclination moves them and every family follows its own individual timetable.
> *'Why, indeed?'* placidly inquires the Far Eastern representative, hailing from a country where life and time are conceived as a continuous stream, with no man being indispensable, with no life-process needing to be interrupted for any human being, where meetings, theatre performances, and other arranged affairs last without interruption for hours on end, while individuals come and go, are replaced by others, meditate or participate as the occasion requires, without undue strain, stress, or nervous tension. As one or the other group persists in its own conception of the time perspective, mutual friction grows, murmurs of 'unreasonableness' are heard around the room; and, when the issue under discussion is an important one, overt accusations are hurled across the room of 'insincerity,' 'lack of a serious approach to the problem,' and even 'sabotage.' (p. 346)

Conventions about punctuality are only one instance of the many social rules that cross-cultural travellers must take into account. Furnham and Bochner (1982) identified forty routine social situations which sojourners have difficulty in negotiating to varying degrees, partly because the rules according to which these encounters are played vary from culture to culture and may not be obvious to an outsider. Different subcultures within a particular society also vary in the extent to which they have social difficulties.

According to Welford (1981), friction between members of different social classes can be attributed in part to differences in their respective life-styles, interests and concerns, all of which become salient when these diverse strategies of living come into contact with each other. Welford's solution is not to do away with class differences but to teach each group to interact more skilfully with other non-similar groups, in other words to train people for bicultural competence, a point we shall return to later in this chapter. Welford does not quote any evidence in support of his analysis of between-class conflict, but there are data to indicate that social-class differences do lead to interpersonal problems. In a survey of students at Oxford, Trower, Bryant and Argyle (1978) found that those from working-class backgrounds reported significantly more difficulty in social situations than middle-class students. Furnham (1983c) administered the social situations questionnaire to African, Indian and European nurses in Natal, South Africa. He found a significant difference in reported difficulty between the three groups, with the Europeans expressing least and the Africans expressing most problems. In this case, although all the subjects were in a sense insiders, black Africans are kept separate from the dominant sectors of their society, and hence have fewer opportunities to acquire and rehearse mainstream socially skilled acts and their respective ground rules.

In a more direct demonstration of the existence and effect of cultural differences in social rules, Noesjirwan (1978) contrasted Indonesia and Australia on three general cultural themes: first, that Indonesians valued maintaining friendly social relationships with everyone, in contrast to the Australian preference for a few exclusive relationships and personal privacy; second, that Indonesians valued conformity to the group and the community in contrast to the Australian emphasis on individuality; and third, that Indonesia's interpersonal life-style is smooth, graceful and restrained in contrast to the Australian preference for an open, direct social manner. On the basis of these themes, Noesjirwan then generated a number of common social situations and predicted that Indonesians will consistently select one course of action while Australians will consistently select a different one; and that the same actions will be regarded positively by one culture but negatively by the other, depending on how congruent they were with each culture's rule structure.

For instance, a preference item read:

Mr A is in a waiting-room waiting for an appointment. There are several other persons also waiting. One is the same age and sex as Mr A. Would Mr A: (a) do nothing, just read a book; (b) try to talk to the other person, to get to know him?

Affective reactions were measured with items such as:

> You are in a waiting-room waiting for an appointment. There are several other persons also waiting. One is your age and sex. He pays no attention to you, just reads a book. How do you feel about that (on a five-point scale from negative to positive)?

Noesjirwan also included items representing the three general value themes, for example (a) it is more important to have a few really close intimate friends than many casual friends; (b) it is more important to have good relationships with everyone than a few close friends.

The three questionnaires were translated into Bahasa Indonesia using a back-translation technique (Brislin, 1980) and administered to 125 Indonesians and 129 Australian subjects matched on various dimensions. The results of all three questionnaires significantly discriminated between the two groups in the predicted direction. Thus the study provides direct confirmation that common, everyday social episodes are governed by different rules in the two cultures, and that when the rules are contravened their transgression arouses disapproval. The results also show that a few general principles or cultural themes can account for the operation of particular rules in specific interpersonal encounters, and predict the reaction of the participants when the rules are broken.

The study carries several implications for setting up intercultural SST programmes. It is not unreasonable to make the generalization that any given culture can be analysed for its rule and value structure, and contrasted with any other given culture. From such a comparative analysis it then becomes feasible to isolate the likely sources of misunderstanding and conflict between the respective cultures, which in turn will suggest particular action sequences for inclusion in the SST. The study also provides further support for a recurring theme in this chapter, namely that effective intercultural SST programmes must be tailor-made for the population, task and milieu. It does not make sense to look for some universal rule that might apply to intercultural communication in general, because even if such a principle existed, it would be too abstract to be of any use in a particular, concrete situation. If two cultures are to be bridged, their specific social skills, interpersonal rules and underlying values must form part of the curriculum, information that can only be derived from ethnographic research and a sound knowledge of both cultures and not from some general principle of behaviour. Although most cross-cultural SST programmes are likely to concentrate primarily on teaching their clients the actual behaviour patterns which they lack, it would be desirable for the curriculum to include a cognitive or information-giving strand that places the behaviours in their wider social context (Furnham, 1983a). An efficient way of doing this would be to describe the general rule or principle that gives meaning to the actions. Indeed, it has been suggested that SST in general has neglected social cognition, in the sense of failing to impart an understanding of the range and meanings of social rules in different cultures and subcultures. Cross-cultural SST would certainly need to take this aspect very much into account.

In the last section of this chapter we will briefly describe some specific problems that either have been or lend themselves to intercultural SST. In keeping with the distinction made earlier (Ch. 2), the material has been organized according to whether the contact is between culturally diverse members of a pluralistic society or whether the contact occurs between members of different societies, which in practice means between sojourners and hosts.

Social relations in multi-cultural societies

Earlier in this book we distinguished culture-contact occurring within multi-ethnic societies from contact taking place between members of different societies. We then went on to illustrate inter-society contacts by referring to various kinds of sojourners, such as overseas students, businesspersons and Peace Corps Volunteers. In this section we would like briefly to deal with the issues, problems and training concerns that arise in connection with intra-societal contact between culturally diverse groups.

There are very few culturally homogeneous societies in the world today. Most countries have or are becoming culturally pluralistic, either through a deliberate policy of immigration or inadvertently due to circumstances not entirely to their liking or choosing. The fact remains that many nations contain within their borders sizable groups of people who consider themselves and are seen by others to possess distinct ethnic identities, and whose practices, customs, linguistic forms and often appearance clearly distinguish them from other groups. Although there is a great variety of such groups, most of them fall into one of the following categories: descendants of the dispossessed aboriginal in-habitants of a land overrun by a technologically superior invader, subsequent waves of immigrants, guest workers, refugees and, as time progresses and nature takes its course, their spouses and children, the latter being labelled as second-generation immigrants.

Elsewhere in this chapter we distinguished between real (external) and psychological (internal) sources of conflict. This distinction is particularly relevant in an analysis of intra-society contact, since both sets of determinants play a major part. With the exception of the dispossessed aboriginal population, the groups concerned are usually newcomers, or seen as such even if this is not strictly true. Their status is low, they have little political clout and they are usually relatively poor. Even so, the established inhabitants tend to be threatened by such groups, psycho-logically in the sense that the newcomers are intruding on what they regard as their territory (Bochner, 1982), and to some extent realistically, because immigrants put pressure on the welfare system, the schools, health services and other societal institutions. It is also widely believed that immigrants take jobs away from the locals. The arguments advanced by economists that newcomers create more jobs than they fill does not seem to convince the person in the street. The justification offered for the favoured treatment that some nations are now providing for their aboriginal populations as a form of reparation for past deeds and neglect, is also not meeting with universal approval, again on the grounds of economic equity. On top of all that, these people look, dress and speak differently, and engage in all sorts of strange and unfamiliar customs and practices.

Although there is undoubtedly a great deal of friction, on a one-to-one interpersonal basis, between the mainstream inhabitants of a multicultural society, and those newcomers and aboriginal groups that also live there, the evidence for this conclusion can only be regarded as circumstantial. Certainly there have been many studies of cross-racial helping (Bochner, 1980), prejudice towards and the stereotyping of outgroups (Katz, 1976) and other similar investigations, but the incidence of these processes and the extent to which they characterize a particular society can only be estimated.

There are better opportunities for assessing, quantifying and dealing with the problem when the contact occurs at the institutional rather than the individual level. The main institutions that become involved on a day-to-day basis with ethnically diverse groups are the welfare services, the police and the schools. A good deal has been written about each of these categories of contact, but relatively little has been done about training the personnel involved to become better cross-cultural communicators, and there is even less in the literature written specifically from the point of view of SST.

In the welfare area the main effort is taking place in the United States, particularly in the field of counselling (Higginbotham, 1979; Pedersen, Lonner, and Draguns, 1976). Therapists and counsellors tend to belong to the dominant middle-class culture, whereas their clients are often members of minorities. The major concern is to make counselling and psychotherapy culturally more relevant and sensitive, which in practice means training the counsellors to take the cultural identities of their clients into account, both with respect to the goals being set, as well as the techniques used to achieve these aims. SST is particularly appropriate in this context and a study employing this approach will be described in Chapter 11.

Turning now to the school system, problems arise when the pupils come from a variety of cultural backgrounds, such as in educational institutions servicing areas that contain large concentrations of second-generation immigrants. The problem is exacerbated when the teachers and administrators come predominantly from the mainstream of society while the children are members of a minority. Again, the most systematic, or at least the most visible, treatment of this problem seems to be occurring in the United States. An outstanding example is the intervention which took place over several years in a school in Hawaii where the pupils were the descendants of the original Hawaiian population (now in the minority) and the school was run according to mainstream American practices (Gallimore, Boggs and Jordan, 1974; Jordan and Tharp, 1979). Before the intervention, the school had an appalling record, which included abysmally low academic achievement, violence and poor staff morale. Gallimore and his team of psychologists gradually persuaded the administrators and teachers to adopt techniques and practices that were more appropriate to the particular culture of their student population, and the school now performs above the national norm. As a group, Hawaiian children are vigorous, mutually helpful, affectionate, talkative and aggressive. In the school as in their homes, they continue to be peer and sibling orientated, and as in their houses they typically avoid adults. These traits and values can produce chaos in an ordinary classroom, and it is therefore not surprising that traditional teachers described them as rowdy, restless, inattentive, lazy, cheating, uninvolved and provocative. The intervention consisted of making the two cultures fit together better, in some cases changing the behaviour and attitudes of the teachers, in other cases producing changes in the children. Thus teachers were encouraged to use more praise, introduce group incentives and rewards, and organize the class into small continuing groups that provide their members with mutual support. Teachers were also shown how to use a 'storytelling' technique of exposition, which is more in keeping with traditional Hawaiian methods of education, representing a group of children under a tree with a friendly adult all enthusiastically creating or recalling a story together. These interventions were formulated after three years of ethnographic research into Hawaiian culture in general and after systematic observation of the particular school and its community. Although SST as such was not employed in this project, the general approach serves as an excellent model for interventions in multicultural schools.

The third area where institutions and ethnically diverse groups intersect is in the field of law enforcement. Again, not much work appears to have been done in this area. In Britain, according to Taylor (1983) recent developments in police education have either ignored or distorted the contribution psychology might make. Furthermore, psychology was seen to be of little use by British police, unlike in the United States, where psychology is regarded as having a role to play in police work. Taylor argues that police should be given systematic training, both with respect to general theoretical and conceptual topics such as a contextual analysis of the society into which they fit their activities, as well as practical skills. In particular, Taylor sees the need to teach police interpersonal communication skills. However, in an otherwise comprehensive discussion there is no mention made of intercultural skills, an omission that is remarkable considering that the article purports to set out how psychology can contribute to police education in Britain in the 1980s. In a more recent paper, McKenzie (1984) suggests that Taylor has understated the psychology content of British police training curricula, and defends his assertion by describing the sorts of skills being taught to recent recruits. Included are a number of periods in language laboratories, the aim of which is:

> to develop an understanding of the potential difficulties of communication which may exist with some groups in society, not simply those from minority ethnic backgrounds or those who may have English-language problems but also those who are disadvantaged in some way such as the mentally ill, the physically disabled, the deaf. (p. 146)

Superintendent McKenzie may not realize it, but he has strayed on to the losing side of a fifteen-year-old debate between those who account for minority underachievement and problems in terms of a deficiency model (e.g. Jensen, 1969) based on the hypothesis that certain ethnic groups are genetically inferior and/or culturally deprived from realizing their true potential; the cultural-difference model, on the other hand, states that minority underachievement is due to a lack of congruence between the assumptions, norms, values and behaviours of the dominant society and its institutions, and the respective minority groups (e.g. Cole, 1975; Cole, Gay, Glick and Sharpe, 1971). By implying that minority groups are disadvantaged, and linking them with the mentally and physically handicapped, McKenzie could not be more explicit as to where he stands on this issue. It would appear that although deficiency models are not much in favour in the social sciences today, they are clearly alive and well in the world of affairs.

Host–sojourner relations

In this section we will briefly describe one area where SST has a high degree of application: the field of international educational exchange.

Some work has been done on diagnosing cultural social-skills deficit among overseas students. Thus Furnham and Bochner (1982) asked 150 foreign students in Britain how much difficulty they experienced in each of forty different social situations. A control group of British students were also given the questionnaire. The foreign students were classified into three regional groupings, according to their cultural distance from British society (near, intermediate or far). The results clearly showed that culture-distance and social difficulty in the host culture are strongly related: the greater the distance the more difficulty these sojourners experienced. Two other findings are of direct interest in the present context. A factor analysis of the forty situations revealed six factors: (1) formal relations/focus of attention; (2) managing intimate relations; (3) public rituals; (4) initiating contact/introductions; (5) public decision-making; and (6) assertiveness. Similar factors have been found in previous (non-crosscultural) studies of social-skills deficit (e.g. Trower, Bryant and Argyle, 1978), providing empirical justification for regarding second-culture learning as a social-skills problem. The other finding related to those situations that were particularly troublesome for the students. The ten most difficult social situations, in descending order of difficulty, were as follows: (1) making British friends of your own age; (2) dealing with somebody who is cross, aggressive; (3) approaching others/starting up a friendship; (4) appearing in front of an audience (acting, speaking); (5) getting to know people in depth, intimately; (6) understanding jokes, humour, sarcasm; (7) dealing with people staring at you; (8) taking the initiative in keeping the conversation going; (9) being with people that you don't know very well; (10) complaining in public/dealing with unsatisfactory service. All of these situations to some extent involve establishing and maintaining personal relationships with host nationals, thereby providing empirical justification for giving a high priority to teaching interpersonal skills in cross-cultural training curricula.

Studies such as Furnham and Bochner (1982) have clear implications for setting up limited SST programmes for selected target groups. For instance, counsellors wishing to assist overseas students in Britain may, on the basis of that study, wish to develop a training package that teaches the students how to approach strangers and make friends, deal with aggressive locals, make complaints and appear in front of an audience like a tutorial or a class. Alternatively, the counsellor can administer a diagnostic questionnaire, such as the one described, and develop tailor-made exercises for specific clients. If resources permit, they can build an evaluation component into their programme, along the lines suggested earlier.

Chapter summary

The theme of this chapter was that the distress that many culture travellers experience is largely due to their lacking the social skills of the new society. This creates barriers to effective communication between visitors and hosts, and sows the seeds for a vicious circle of misunderstanding, friction and hostility among the participants. Social interaction can be regarded as a mutually organized, skilled performance. The synchronization that is the hallmark of an effective and satisfying encounter, results from the participants having a shared, although often only implicit understanding of the bases on which the interaction is taking place. These include the method of signalling turn-taking, the appropriate manner in which to effect self-disclosure, what different gestures signify, the correct interpersonal distance within which to conduct the encounter, and so forth. However, there is ample evidence that these forms are not universal but that there exist systematic cross-cultural differences in communication patterns, that is in how people send and receive information, express emotion and influence each other, both verbally and non-verbally. The rules and conventions that regulate interpersonal encounters also vary between cultures.

The communication patterns and social conventions of a given society are usually taken for granted by its members. Consequently, people tend not to be explicitly aware of the operation, or even the very existence of these rules, which often only come into prominence after they have been broken, either inadvertently or by someone not familiar with them. What has been called the hidden language of interpersonal interaction is a major source of cross-cultural misunderstanding and friction. In an intercultural encounter, the greater the difference that exists in the respective, culturally determined communication patterns of the participants, the more difficulty they will have in establishing a mutually satisfying relationship. When this idea is applied to the typical sojourner, the visitor can be regarded as lacking in the social skills of the host culture, and this formulation can also explain why so many sojourners have difficulty in negotiating ordinary, routine social encounters with local people. The principle can also be used to account for inter-ethnic friction in multicultural societies. This is particularly evident in institutional settings such as the schools, the provision of health, and law enforcement.

The SST model of cross-cultural interaction has clear implications for setting up culture training and orientation programmes, a topic that will be discussed in greater detail in Chapter 11.

Part IV
Culture learning and management

10 An evaluation of theories for culture shock

The various theories, models and explanations for the relationship between geographic movement and adaptation have their origin in a wide number of social-science disciplines, including psychoanalysis, social psychology, psychiatry, clinical psychology, epidemiology and sociology. As a consequence they both benefit and suffer from the theoretical and methodological strengths and weaknesses of each approach. Thus psychoanalytic theories of grief and loss as applied to culture shock may be accused of being unfalsifiable, while social psychological theories of value differences may be thought of as caught-in-time or culture-specific.

Nearly all of the theories for culture shock have been devised in another setting or for other problems and then applied to culture shock. They are thus theories applied to the culture-shock literature rather than theories arising from it. However, surprisingly little theory-testing research has been done. Cross-cultural research is notoriously difficult but has innumerable benefits. Triandis and Brislin (1984) have spelt out four major benefits of cross-cultural research, all of which are applicable to this area. They include theory expansion, increasing the range of manipulable variables, unconfounding variables that occur together in a culture and the study of the influence of the socio-physical context within which behaviour occurs.

Nearly all research in this area has shown that demographic variables by themselves lead to only modest levels of statistical prediction and explanation and that the addition of psychological variables is necessary to arrive at a satisfactory account of the effects of geographic movements.

In Chapters 7, 8 and 9 we set out some of the major theories that attempt to describe, explain and understand *culture shock* – in particular the relationship between mental health and geographic movement. Some of the key ideas were grief (Arredondo-Dowd, 1981); values (Bhatt and Fairchild, 1984; Sharma, 1984) and interpersonal relations (Scott and Scott, 1982).

One of the weaknesses of the culture-shock literature is that theories are rarely if ever set out in a formal, propositional manner and then subsequently tested. There are some notable exceptions, such as a study by Kim (1977) on communication patterns of foreign immigrants in the process of acculturation. He tested nine propositions that followed logically from the stated communication theory:

1. The more immigrants participate in interpersonal communication with members of the host society, the more complex will be their perception of the host society.
2. The more immigrants use mass media of the host society, the more complex will be their perception of the host society.
3. The more competent immigrants are in the host language, the greater will be their participation in interpersonal communication with members of the host society.
4. The more competent immigrants are in the host language, the greater will be their use of most mass media.
5. The greater the immigrants' acculturation motivation, the greater will be their participation in interpersonal communication with members of the host society.
6. The greater the immigrants' acculturation motivation, the greater will be their use of host mass media.
7. The greater the immigrants' interpersonal interaction potential, the greater will be their participation in interpersonal communication with members of the host society.
8. The more access immigrants have to host mass media, the greater will be their exposure to host mass media.
9. The complexity with which immigrants perceive the host society will be influenced by language competence, acculturation motivation and channel accessibility, mediated by interpersonal and mass-communication experience.

Results showed that effects of all three causal factors (language competence – propositions 1 and 2; acculturation motivation – propositions 3 and 4; channel accessibility – propositions 5 and 6) were all significantly related to intercultural communication. The study also showed that sex, age at time of migration, time spent in the host society, and education are the most important factors in predicting the immigrant's language competence, acculturation motivation and accessibility to host communication channels. It would seem that the influence of interpersonal communication is stronger than that of the mass media in developing a subtle, complex and refined system for perceiving the host society. What was most interesting about Kim's (1977) work was that the study was analytic and of the hypothesis–testing rather than inductive type. The lack of studies comparing and contrasting different theoretical perspectives in this area is one of its major weaknesses.

In Chapter 7 we set out four 'explanations' for culture shock: *grief and bereavement*; *external locus of control*; *selective migration*; and *migrant expectations*. In Chapter 8 three further 'explanations' were described: *life-*

events and illness; *social support*; and *value differences*. Chapter 9 contained a fairly lengthy description of the *social skills* hypothesis. As has been noted at the beginning of Chapter 7, these explanations are not mutually exclusive, although they differ in their theoretical origin and in their implications for intervention. Various criticisms of each approach have been noted in the text of Part III and they will not be repeated here. However, some attempt will be made to compare and contrast these theories, and this is set out in Table 10.1

Rather than presenting the evidence for and against each approach (as this has already been done in Chapters 7, 8 and 9), Table 10.1 compares the theories in terms of whether they can account for or predict the numerous subtle and complicated differences between migrant groups, host societies and their responses to one another over time. A consistent theme of reviewers and researchers in this field is that there are a large number of variables relating to culture shock and a great variety of outcomes. One criterion of a good theory is therefore the extent to which it can and does predict and account for these various reactions.

Table 10.1 shows the extent to which each 'theory' as such accounts for differences in motives and expectations, responses, temporal factors, host cultural variables, generational differences and consequent therapy and training. In one sense the *grief and bereavement* hypothesis – as it has been applied to migration and mental health – is least specific, in that it predicts universal negative experiences of loss irrespective of motivation, expectation and the reactions of the host culture. However, in another sense it is highly specific because it considers individual-difference factors as they relate to adaptation. The *locus of control* thesis appears to be able to account for many different response factors and emphasizes the role of expectations and motivations. However no temporal, generational or therapeutic aspects are considered.

One of the simplest, least-psychological theories – namely *selective migration* – appears to account for a number of the differences. However, as Table 10.1 indicates, because there is no carefully stated formal theory of the relationship between selective migration and adaptation, these predictions can only be inferred. Certainly there appears to be some mileage in this neo-Darwinian approach, but its obvious appeal may conceal numerous methodological and theoretical difficulties. Similarly, the *expectation* (or expectancy-value) approach appears to be sensitive enough to cope with numerous subtle differences in the reactions of different groups. However, this relatively sophisticated theoretical framework (Feather, 1982) has not as yet been sufficiently adapted to explain or test the relationship between migration and mental health.

The *negative life-event* and *social support* hypotheses have many features in common. They appear to be able to account for a number of the observed individual and group differences in the literature, while also having some implications for therapy. The *value difference* hypothesis,

Table 10.1 An attempt to compare the eight 'theories' on various specific criteria

CRITERIA	THEORIES							
	Grief and bereave-ment	Locus of control	Selective migration	Expect-ations	Negative life-events	Social support	Value differences	Social skills
Motives and expectations								
1. Does the theory presume that different motives of different groups lead to different reactions?		x	o	x	o	o	o	o
2. Does the theory presume that different expectations of different groups lead to different reactions?		x	o	x	?	o	o	o
Responses								
3. Can the theory account for different migrant groups' responses to the same country?		x	x	x	o	x	x	x
4. Can the theory account for the same migrant groups' responses to the different countries?		x	x	x	o	x	x	x
5. Can the theory account for different response patterns in the same migrant group?			o	x	o	x	x	x
6. Can the theory account for the same response patterns in the different migrant groups?		x	o	x	o	x	x	x
7. Does the theory allow for positive as well as negative responses to migration?	?	x	o	x	o	x	x	x

Time						
8. Does the theory predict any temporal pattern of response?	x	?	o	?	?	x
Host culture						
9. Does the theory suggest host-culture factors that are relevant to adaptation?	x	?	x	o	x	x
Generational differences						
10. Does the theory predict different responses from people from different generations?	?		o	o	o	x
11. Does the theory predict different responses from second- and third-generation immigrants?	?		o	o	o	o
Therapy and training						
12. Does the theory have an explicit therapy/training method?	?	?			?	x
13. Has the therapy/training method proved effective?	?				?	x

x Theories definitely do this   o Theories appear to consider this factor relevant   ? Possibly being rather specific, cannot predict the precise nature of responses once value differences occur, nor does it have any recommendations regarding therapy. Work in this area remains fairly minimal and further developments may prove more promising.

The theory – examined in some detail in Chapter 9 – which appears to be most useful is the *social skills* approach. Not only can and does it predict and explain different reactions of different groups, but it appears to have a reliable and adaptable method of training culture travellers which follows on directly from the theory.

Social-skills training has attracted the attention of a great deal of research in recent years, which shows no signs of diminishing (L'Abate and Milan, 1985). As Furnham (1983) has pointed out, critical and comparative studies have produced good evidence for the effectiveness of social-skills training, though there is some doubt about the generalizability of these effects. Surprisingly, perhaps, social-skills training has not as yet been extensively applied to the area of 'culture' shock, although Argyle (1981) has argued for training in what he calls 'intercultural communication'.

Social-skills training is not without its problems, but it certainly seems to be one of the more promising theoretical approaches to asking which, why and when different groups of cultural travellers experience difficulty. More importantly, perhaps, it is the only approach which offers a clear, well-documented and very carefully researched therapeutic and training method.

In looking at the various theories and approaches to culture shock it has become apparent that certain important topics have been neglected, which will now be considered.

Neglected groups

In this book we have dealt mainly with tourists, business personnel, students, guest and volunteer workers, and migrants. There are, however, other categories of travellers who have not been considered, mainly because little has been written about them. However, these neglected categories of migrants may be particularly relevant in evaluating the various theories of culture shock, because of their special and unusual circumstances. Three such groups are children, missionaries and diplomats, about whom psychology has been relatively silent.

Children
At various points in Chapter 4 references were made to studies done on the children of migrants, and there is a growing interest in the adaptation and integration of first- and second-generation migrants. However, by far the most work on migrants has been done on adults. With regards to sojourners, there is almost no material at all on children, despite the fact

that many sojourners (diplomats, business people, even students) travel with their families. A major exception is the work of Torbiörn (1982) who argued:

> In concrete terms children are likely to be more dependent than their parents on purely local conditions, which will affect their chances of making friends and will probably decide which school they attend. In some of their contacts with the local culture they will probably feel under considerable pressure to conform to its attitudes and norms. To a child, the move abroad also often involves more than an overall adjustment to the host-country culture as a whole; it may also mean frequent changes of school, friends, and so on. (p. 138)

However, it may equally be possible that children are more adaptable and flexible than adults. Finally, it should be pointed out that there is practically *no* work on children as tourists.

In view of the comparative paucity of studies in this area it may be worthwhile considering which are some of the most interesting and important questions that need to be addressed. The first, and perhaps most obvious question is the extent to which the experience of, and adaptation to, new cultures (for whatever period of time) is basically similar in adults, adolescents and young children. If not, it behoves researchers to specify in which ways they are different and to explain why different variables are important in the culture-shock experience of adults and children. Second, one would want to know if culture-shock experience is somehow passed on to or felt by first- and even second-generation children of migrants. Some work has been done on first generation children but precious little on second generation. Also one would want to know whether the experience of being the child of a multiple-sojourner or a very frequent tourist had any beneficial or negative consequences. Another question concerns differences in adaptation as a function of the migrant experience itself, that is do voluntary, prepared, well organized migrants adjust more happily or quickly than refugees who may have suffered considerable hardship and difficulty while moving?

More and more work is being done in this area, but as yet comparatively few major findings have emerged.

Missionaries
Psychologists interested in the ministry have noted that it is a fairly stressful profession and no doubt even more so for missionaries working abroad. Collins (1977) identified nine sources of stress in missionaries: loneliness; pressures of adjusting to a foreign culture; constant demands on one's time; lack of adequate medical facilities; overwhelming work-load and difficult working conditions; pressure to be a constant positive 'witness' to the locals; confusion over one's role within the local church;

frequent lack of privacy and inability to get away for recreation and vacation.

In an empirical study of 549 missionaries, Gish (1983) looked at their major sources of stress. These are given in Table 10.2. Clearly the second

Table 10.2 Items identified as sources of stress by 30% or more of respondents (N = 549)

	% rating considerable to great stress	% rating great stress
Confronting others when necessary	54	27
Communicating across language-cultural barriers	53	26
Time and effort maintaining donor relationships	50	22
Amount of work	48	25
Work priorities	47	18
Time for personal study of the word and prayer	37	14
Progress on my work	36	14
Need for pastoral care	35	15
Making decisions affecting others' lives	35	15
Need for confidant	34	19
Self-acceptance, including self-forgiveness	34	14
Conflicts between my values and those of host culture	34	13
Gold-fish bowl existence	33	13
Certainty about my future	33	13
Freedom to take time for myself	32	12
Extended family concerns	31	12
Frequent moving	31	18
Task orientation versus 'servant attitude'	31	11
Recreation and exercise	30	09

Source: D. Gish, 'Sources of missionary stress', *Journal of Psychology and Theology*, 11 (1983), 243–50.

most common source of stress related to culture shock. However, none of the independent variables – sex, age, marital status, nationality, years of service or amount of time on the job – appeared to be significantly related to this variable.

In a more rigorous predictive study with a fairly large N, Britt (1983) asked which of a number of factors – personality, interpersonal-skill attitudes and biographical information – predicted missionary success overseas. He used a multidimensional criterion measure. A stepwise multiple regression analysis was then performed followed by an analysis of variance. Some of the discriminating items came from the 16 PF. Thus better-adjusted missionaries were more controlled, less moody, more astute, while demographic discriminants showed that first-born younger subjects had adapted better. Those who scored high on perseverance and flexibility also tended to adapt better. The author notes:

A very important conclusion of this study is that the history of one's behaviour, past responses and experiences tend to be the best predictor of the future. God's call and motivation are important, but in the ambiguity and stress of another culture, past experience and events tend to shape how an individual will respond . . . The importance of interpersonal relationships and adaptability has been indicated upon examining the group of predictor variables . . . Accommodating, more passive persons who would respond to more authoritarian supervisors tend to be less successful overseas (p. 211)

Certainly missionaries are a group of people on whom useful future work may be done.

Multiple-sojourners

There is a surprising paucity of studies on short- to medium-term multiple-sojourners. In Chapter 6 we considered the business community, many of whom were multiple-sojourners in the sense that they spend fixed contract periods, of anything from six months to five years, at one particular foreign site before moving on to another equally novel unfamiliar setting. Another group who have received very little attention are diplomats.

In a study of diplomats' wives O'Cuneen (1984) interviewed twenty-three women in Zimbabwe who had moved from one country to another over a period of time spending in each an average of three years. Her interview covered issues such as culture shock, integration in local affairs, social support and expectations. She found that diplomatic experience, status, community involvement, control over next post, family life and the quality of local education were positively related to satisfaction. There was little evidence of a U-curve or reverse culture shock. However, many factors did not correlate with satisfaction, including number of previous postings, age, length of sojourn, local activities and marital adjustment. Social support seemed relatively important in predicting satisfaction, as was happiness in the role of diplomatic wife.

Diplomats and their wives/husbands occupy central positions of power and responsibility. It is therefore quite important to pursue studies on the factors that lead to their successful adaptation.

The psychology of host cultures

Surprisingly little research has looked at the effect of culture-contact on the host culture of immigrants, sojourners or tourists. In Chapter 6 we considered the impact of tourism on local people but, other than that, not much work has been done on the psychology of the receiving party. Boekestijn (1984) has noted some important social-psychological characteristics that may be used to describe and compare 'host' societies:

1. *Territoriality*: the extent to which the host culture protects and defends its own territory.
2. *Ethnocentrism*: the extent to which a culture boosts its own identity and looks with contempt on outsiders.
3. *Competitiveness*: the extent to which a culture seeks out or feels competition from other cultures/groups.
4. *Positive identity*: the extent to which a culture assumes a need for a positive identity.
5. *Shunning of dissimilarity*: the extent to which a culture experiences differences from itself in terms of arousal and negative affect.
6. *Search for control:* the extent to which a culture requires people to accept its belief and value systems that function to ensure predictability and control.
7. *Interaction fatigue*: the extent to which members from one culture experience fatigue and hence shun members of other groups.
8. *Cultural heterogeneity and tolerance*: the extent to which a culture through explicit (legal) or implicit means ensures or eschews cultural heterogeneity.

As Boekestijn (1984) has noted, these factors are closely interrelated and are reminiscent of Tajfel's (1981) theory of inter-group behaviour, that the more a society or culture is territorial, ethnocentric, competitive and in search of a positive identity and control, the more intolerant it would be of immigrants.

There has been some empirical work on national difference in ethnic tolerance. For instance, Kalin and Berry (1980) examined the relationship between geographic mobility and ethnic tolerance in a large group (N = 1277) of Canadian adults. The results showed that total geographic mobility is associated with tolerance, and that when the relationship between geographic mobility and socio-economic status is partialled out, tolerance and mobility remain significantly related. Overall the results indicated that geographic mobility was positively associated with general ethnic tolerance independently of the respondent's ethnicity, socio-economic status and type of mobility (intra-nationally or internationally). This suggests that a culture in which people are well travelled is likely to be more tolerant than one in which people have experienced few other cultures.

More recently, Berry and Pleasants (1984) examined ethnic tolerance in plural societies, arguing that confidence in one's own group identity can provide a basis for the respect of other groups and a corresponding willingness to share ideas, attitudes and assumptions. This idea – that positive group identity leads to tolerance, and threats to that identity to intolerance – received empirical support in a Canadian study. Hence they conclude: 'it is no longer a mark of ethnocentrism to be interested in one's own group's survival; indeed, confidence in such survival may be a prerequisite for the tolerance which appears to be antithetical to ethnocentrism' (p. 11). This finding and argument thus contradict the approach of Boekestijn and Tajfel as set out above. However, the contradiction may be resolved: if ethnocentrism and attempts to improve positive identity stem from a poor self-image, these variables are likely to be associated with intolerance, but if they reflect a healthy satisfaction with self-image and identity, they are more likely to be associated with tolerance.

Implications for training/therapy

One way to evaluate a theory is to examine the effectiveness of cross-cultural training techniques and therapies that are derived specifically from them. For instance, Triandis and Brislin (1984) have identified six training methods: information/fact-orientated training; attribution training; cultural awareness; cognitive-behaviour modification; experiential learning; and the interaction approach. If any therapy/training methods can be shown to be more effective than the others, and if that method is theoretically derived from a particular theory, this may suggest the parsimony of that theory over others. However, no such studies exist.

One major problem with this approach is that there is not always a clear relationship between a theory as it applies to culture shock and the therapy supposedly derived from it. Indeed, of the eight theories evaluated earlier, only the social-skills model leads to any sort of explicit therapy or training method.

Summary

Any good theory of culture shock should integrate known empirical findings within a logically consistent and parsimonious framework. Shaw and Costanzo (1970) have suggested that a good theory has a number of components: the propositions of the theory should be logically consistent; the theory should agree with known facts; the theory should be able to be tested in order to determine its usefulness; and the theory should usefully generate further research. Many of the theories of culture shock only approximately fulfil these criteria, and a great deal of further work still needs to be done.

11 Culture-training strategies

This chapter briefly reviews the main strategies and approaches that have been used to prepare people for cross-cultural contacts, and the theoretical considerations on which these techniques are based. The chapter concludes with a further elaboration of the social-skills/culture-learning approach to second-culture orientation, and the principles which inform such training programmes.

Cross-cultural preparation in historical perspective

Within-culture training, that is trying to systematically improve relations between various sub-groups in multicultural societies, seems to have been relatively neglected by social scientists. Most of the psychological literature deals with orientation programmes which are aimed at persons who will or have become sojourners in cultures or subcultures other than their own original one. The reason is that the problems of sojourners are usually highly visible, have distinctive boundaries that enable them (the persons and their problems) to be identified, and often have consequences that are economically, politically or socially expensive. For instance, if a firm has to repatriate executives because their spouses cannot cope with the culture to which they have been posted (Torbiorn, 1982), and this happens often enough, it may become cost-effective to set up company training, counselling and supportive programmes for overseas personnel which may reduce the incidence of premature terminations. If too many foreign students commit suicide, fail their exams or get into trouble with the police, awkward questions get asked in parliament (Zwingmann and Gunn, 1983). As a matter of empirical fact, the categories of sojourners who have received the greatest amount of attention have all shared the following characteristics: they are numerous; their failure would embarrass, or cut into the profits of, or interfere with the projects of influential organizations; and there are funds available to set up research and training programmes for them. Leading the field and setting the pattern was the massive effort surrounding the development of the American Peace Corps, which ultimately involved a large number of social scientists as the programmes grew and their problems became evident

(Guthrie, 1966, 1975; Guthrie and Zektick, 1967; Harris, 1973; Smith, 1966; Textor, 1966). Other target groups attracting the interest of applied cross-cultural psychologists have included overseas students (Bochner and Wicks, 1972; Eide, 1970; Klineberg, 1976, 1981; Klineberg and Hull, 1979; Selltiz, Christ, Havel and Cook, 1963); overseas business people (Fayerweather, 1959; Skinner, 1968; Triandis, 1967; Wilson, 1961); technical-assistance experts (Boxer, 1969; Brislin, 1979; Seidel, 1981); and military personnel (Guthrie, 1966).

In addition to the large sojourn literature, a great deal has also been written about intra-societal multicultural relations, dealing with the problems of groups such as immigrants (Eitinger and Schwarz, 1981; Stoller, 1966; Taft, 1966, 1973; Watson, 1977); guest workers (Boker, 1981); black-white contact in Britain, the United States and South Africa (Banton, 1965, 1967; Bloom, 1971; Katz, 1976, Klineberg, 1971; Pettigrew, 1964, 1969); and the aboriginal inhabitants of countries such as Australia (Kearney and McElwain, 1976; Throssell, 1981; Stevens, 1971, 1972), New Zealand (Ritchie, 1981), the United States (Darnell, 1972; Daws, 1968; Gallimore, Boggs, and Jordan, 1974, Trimble, 1976), and Canada (Berry, 1975). However, until quite recently, culture-training has not been a major concern in this area.

Training models

The type of intervention that will be carried out is dependent on assumptions about what needs to be remedied. Various approaches have been influential in shaping the programmes actually in use. These will now be briefly reviewed.

The pseudo-medical model

The pioneers in the area concentrated on the more noxious aspects of cross-cultural contact, used terms and constructs with a decidedly clinical flavour, and gradually developed a pseudo-medical model of cross-cultural stress that has persisted to this day (e.g. Eitinger and Schwarz, 1981). This model has already received extensive treatment previously in this book. The purpose of briefly recapitulating these ideas here is so that we can then proceed to examine the implications of this approach for the design of culture-training programmes. Three 'clinical' concepts have had wide currency and influence. The first and earliest was embodied in a book called *The Marginal Man* (Stonequist, 1937), itself a development of previous work by Park (1928) dealing with the problems of persons caught between two cultural systems, not belonging to or fully accepted by either group. The construct is not without its critics (e.g. Mann, 1973) but is nevertheless widely used in accounts of the adjustment problems of culture travellers. The second concept is the notion of culture shock, originally attributed to Oberg (1960) and subsequently extended and elaborated by many others (Byrnes, 1966; Guthrie, 1966; Hall, 1959; Smalley, 1963; Taft, 1977). This construct refers to the confusion and disorientation that many sojourners experience when they enter a new culture. At about the same time a third concept was introduced into the literature, again with negative connotations for the psychological welfare of culture travellers. This was the notion of the U–curve of adjustment, which proposed that cross–cultural sojourners progress through three main phases: an initial stage of elation and optimism, replaced by a period of frustration, depression and confusion (presumably the period labelled by Oberg as culture shock), followed by a gradual improvement leading to optimism and satisfaction with the new society (Coelho, 1958; Deutsch and Won, 1963; Du Bois, 1956; Gullahorn and Gullahorn, 1963; Jacobson, 1963; Lysgaard, 1955; Selltiz and Cook, 1962; Sewell, Morris and Davidsen, 1954).

Adopting a clinical approach to culture stress can be criticized on several grounds. The most general point which can be made is that a medical model presupposes that the psychological well–being of individuals is dependent largely on the smooth functioning of their intra–psychic elements, in the same way as a person's physical health is supposed by the model to depend on the satisfactory functioning of the subject's circulatory, glandular, digestive and other physiological systems. Such an approach, whether in the psychological or physical sphere, tends to ignore or de–emphasize the role of the person's socio–cultural milieu in the aetiology, diagnosis and treatment of whatever problems might present themselves. When the model is extended to sojourners in difficulty, the implication is that they have somehow suffered a breakdown in their normal healthy psychological functioning, that they are ill and need treatment or at least counselling. Even if this were true, labelling persons unable to cope with a cross–cultural experience as failures, weaklings and as undergoing a mental breakdown, stigmatizes these individuals and probably just aggravates their problems. In any case, there is very little evidence to suggest that culture stress can be regarded as some form of mental illness, or that counselling or 'therapy' are the most appropriate or effective means of alleviating such stress and promoting 'healthy' personalities and satisfactory social relationships.

There is another problem with the pseudo–medical model, and that is its heavy reliance on the concept of 'adjustment'. Two objections can be raised in relation to the notion of adjustment. The first is its already discussed implication that the failures of the sojourner are symptoms of some underlying pathology requiring treatment. Intervention programmes that take this view seriously will probably concentrate on the internal dynamics of their clients and largely ignore their social psychology. For instance, the goal of therapy may be to reconcile sojourners to their social isolation from the host society rather than to help them to form and extend new social networks. We shall return to this point later in this chapter. Furthermore, it may not be psychologically healthy to adapt or adjust individuals to societies that are themselves 'sick' in some sense. For instance, it is questionable whether the mental health of immigrants to South Africa would be served by adjusting them to that society's view on race relations. The second problem with 'adjusting' a person to a new culture is that it often has overtones of cultural chauvinism, the implication being that all the troubles of the newcomer would be over if they could only be persuaded to embrace the values and customs of the host society and abandon their culture of origin. It should be noted that this is a pseudo-solution to the problem of harmonizing relationships between culturally diverse people, in that it proposes to resolve the difficulty by eliminating the differences between the participants, by 'adjusting' the newcomers to make them indistinguishable from their hosts. The real issue, which is how to improve relations between culturally diverse persons, is not tackled. This latter goal can only be achieved with a theoretical model of cultural accommodation that does not rely on the concept of adjustment as its key idea. The next two models to be presented lead to such an alternative construction of culture stress, propose solutions that preserve the ethnic identities of the participants and do not stigmatize those who have difficulty in accommodating themselves to a new culture. These models liken cross-cultural exposure to a learning experience and, instead of therapy and adjustment, propose programmes of preparation, orientation and the acquisition of culturally appropriate social skills.

Culture-learning

Because of the unsatisfactory nature of earlier approaches, Bochner (1972, 1981, 1982) (see also Ch. 2) developed a culture-learning model of contact. The key idea is that the major task facing a sojourner is not to adjust to the new culture but to learn its salient characteristics. Unlike the notion of adjustment, acquiring a second culture has very few ethnocentric overtones. There are many examples in life when it becomes expedient to learn and practise a custom that one may not necessarily approve of, and indeed abandon the behaviour as soon as cultural circumstances change. A foreigner to Britain may find the English habit of queuing for everything slightly absurd, but will quickly learn the rules and abide by them to avoid being hit over the head with an umbrella wielded by an irate native. Similarly, if English visitors in Japan queued up to board a Tokyo subway car, it is likely that they would remain forever on the platform. In order to be able to use the system, these tourists would need to push and shove like the natives do, irrespective of how distasteful this might seem. Presumably, they would revert to their normal, more restrained behaviour after returning to England. The point is that a particular practice, and the possession of the skill to carry it out, is not intrinsically desirable or undesirable, but must be judged in relation to the cultural circumstances that render the behaviour appropriate or inappropriate. Indeed, the performance attracts notice only when the appropriate skill is lacking or when the act is performed in inappropriate circumstances. We shall return to this point later.

Culture-learning is not something that occurs in isolation from the rest of the sojourner's activities, nor does it necessarily commence at the onset of the sojourn and cease at its termination. Perhaps the best illustration of this is Klineberg's (1981) treatment of the academic sojourn as a life history. Klineberg points out that predeparture experiences, levels of competence and degree of preparation will affect what happens to the person while abroad, which in turn will influence the individual's course after returning home. The various stages in the life history of a sojourn will usually include selection for overseas travel; preparation, including the provision of practical and cultural information about the host society; language-training; professional experiences while abroad, particularly whether these lead to formal success or failure; general adaptation to the new environment, including the making of friends with host members; and finally the return home, including the extent to which the individual is accepted back into the culture of origin and given support in the form of a suitable job, status recognition, and respect (Chu, 1968). This approach conveys the idea that the difficulties that sojourners might experience, including contracting 'culture shock', are not due to purely intra-psychic deficiencies and weaknesses, but the result of a complex set of social-psychological influences played out over a long period. As Klineberg notes, the seeds of many during-sojourn disasters are sown years previously due to poor selection and preparation.

Training techniques

In the final section of this chapter we will provide some guidelines for devising cross-cultural orientation programmes based on the social-skills training (SST) model. First, however, we will briefly describe the other existing techniques, their strengths and weaknesses, and the training models from which they are derived.

Information giving

The most common type of cross-cultural orientation takes the form of providing prospective sojourners with information about their new culture. Travellers are presented with all sorts of facts and figures, either in written form or in lectures or films, about topics such as the climate, food, sexual relations, religious customs, and anything else the trainer may consider important. The advantage is that this kind of information is relatively easy to assemble and deliver. However, the effectiveness of such cognitive programmes is limited, because: (1) the facts are often too general to have any clear, specific application in particular circumstances;

(2) the facts emphasize the exotic, such as what to do in a Buddhist temple, and ignore the mundane but more commonly occurring happenings, such as how to hail a taxi; (3) such programmes give the false impression that a culture can be learned in a few easy lessons, whereas all that they mostly convey is a superficial, incoherent and often misleading picture which glosses over that culture's hidden agenda (Hall, 1966); (4) finally, even if the facts are retained (itself a doubtful proposition) they do not necessarily lead to action, or to the correct action. It would be absurd in the extreme to teach people how to drive a car by only giving them information about how to do it, yet that is exactly the principle on which programmes relying mainly on information-giving are based. If cognitive training is to be of any practical use, it must be combined with some form of experiential learning.

Cultural sensitization

Programmes based on the idea of cultural sensitization set out to provide trainees not just with information about other cultures, but at the same time also to heighten their awareness about the cultural bias of their own behaviour and how the practices of their society differ from those of the host country. The aim is to compare and contrast the two cultures, look at various behaviours from the perspective of each society and thus develop a sensitivity to and awareness of cultural relativity, leading to the view that very few human values, beliefs and behaviours are absolute and universal and that what a particular individual believes to be true and good will depend on the norms prevailing in that person's society, norms that other societies may reject. Such programmes often operate at two levels: (1) they aim to achieve self-awareness about the modal values and attitudes that are typically held by members of one's society; and (2) to gain insight into one's own personal traits, attitudes and prejudices. The latter approach can become heavily 'clinical', with its emphasis on personal growth and development. Culture sensitization and self-awareness programmes, being essentially cognitive techniques, suffer from the same limitations as information giving. For instance, it is all very well for a westerner to accept intellectually that in some cultures ceremonies featuring ritual cannibalism have the same socially cohesive function as say the Trooping the Colour in England, but it is another matter to then willingly observe such occasions and regard them in the same light as the indigenous spectators do.

Isomorphic attributions

According to Triandis (1975) a major obstacle to effective cross-cultural communication is the inability of the participants to understand the causes of each other's behaviour, that is to make correct attributions about the other's actions. Effective intercultural relations require isomorphic attributions, which corresponds to the idea, 'I assign the same cause or reason for their behaviour as they would for themselves'. According to Triandis, the likelihood of making isomorphic attributions decreases as the divergence between the subjective cultures of the participants increases, and explains why intercultural relations are often characterized by mutual hostility, misunderstanding, and poor affect. The solution, according to Triandis and his followers (Fiedler, Mitchell and Triandis, 1971; Foa and Chemers, 1967), is to train the individuals to understand the subjective culture of the other group, which in practice means teaching them how to make 'correct' behavioural attributions. This is done through a device called the culture assimilator, which in effect is a programmed learning manual. The booklet contains descriptions of episodes in which two culturally disparate individuals meet. The interactions are unsuccessful, in that each incident terminates in embarrassment, misunderstanding or interpersonal hostility. The trainee is then presented with four or five alternative explanations of what went wrong, which correspond to different attributions of the observed behaviour. Only one of these attributions is correct from the perspective of the culture being learned. For instance, if the meeting is between an American and an Arab, and the American is the person being trained, then the 'correct' attribution is the one that most Arabs would make. The other three attributions are plausible and usually consistent with the attributions that Americans would make in such a situation, but wrong in the Arab context. The trainees select the answer they regard as correct, and are then instructed to turn to a subsequent page, where they are either praised if they selected the 'right' answer, or told why they were wrong if they selected an 'incorrect' answer.

The technique relies on cognitive learning, and hence suffers from the already-mentioned limitations inherent in such an approach. A great deal also depends on which particular critical incidents are selected to form the basic curriculum. Inevitably, exotic, strange and hence less common events tend to be given greater prominence than the less interesting but more frequently encountered day-to-day problems that make up the bread-and-butter content of intercultural contacts.

Learning by doing

The limitations of information-based orientation programmes led to various attempts to expose trainees to supervised real or simulated second-culture experiences. Perhaps the most elaborate of these schemes was undertaken by the Peace Corps in the 1970s, which built a model South-East Asian village on the Big Island of Hawaii and hired natives of the target countries to inhabit the site. American trainees spent several days or weeks in this village under expert guidance, gaining first-hand experience of what it is like to live in an Asian rural settlement.

Most organizations do not have, or are unwilling to commit such massive resources to experiential culture-training. More typically, behaviourally based culture-training programmes rely on role-playing encounters between trainees and persons pretending to come from some other culture, or if other-culture professional personnel are available, with them. In this respect the techniques are similar to those employed by SST practitioners, but there is a fundamental difference, in that these programmes lack the specific rationale that informs SST. We shall return to this point shortly. Some programmes also contain a behavioural evaluation component, which may take the form of a team of psychologists evaluating and perhaps fine-tuning the performance of the candidates in the field (Textor, 1966).

Finally, to put the entire preceding material into perspective, the vast majority of culture travellers, or those who come into contact with members of other cultures in their own societies, receive no systematic culture-training whatsoever. The little 'training' that does occur is done informally, by 'old hands' who pass on useful information to the 'new chums'. This in itself may not be such a bad thing. One of the requirements of a successful culture-trainer is to be a mediating person (Bochner, 1981), that is a person who is intimately familiar with both cultures and can act as a link between them, representing each to the other. In theory 'old hands' should have that rare capacity, but in practice some may have highly specialized, distorted or even prejudiced views of one or both of their cultures, and perpetuate these distortions in the informal training they impart to highly impressionable newcomers.

SST and culture-training

As has been indicated earlier, most of the culture-training programmes have vague, largely unspecified aims, reflecting their lack of a systematic rationale. The stated goal of most orientation programmes is to make travellers more effective in their jobs and in their interpersonal encounters with their indigenous counterparts, but exactly how this is to be accomplished is usually not made explicit. Consequently, the content of these programmes is a mixture of information, the resolution of critical incidents, and heightened awareness of the cultural bias in construing reality. Such a curriculum in turn reflects the somewhat vague ideas about what determines the difficulties. If pressed, most trainers will say that they are trying to alleviate culture shock (Oberg, 1960), role shock (Byrnes, 1966), culture fatigue (Guthrie, 1966) and other similar conditions. However, these concepts are vague, overinclusive and mostly used to refer to states of mind in the person, when the real locus of the problem resides in the transactions between the individuals and their other-culture counterparts. These limitations led to the development of a training model that is firmly based in theory, takes the social psychology of the cross-cultural encounter seriously, has clear-cut implications for applied intervention, can draw on an already-existing technology for its implementation and avoids some of the ethical, ethnocentric and stigmatic connotations inherent in an approach based on the notion of adjusting the sojourner to some therapist-defined criterion. The model has been extensively described in Chapter 9. We wish to concentrate here in particular on its training implications. This will be done by reviewing a major study which illustrates the assumptions, methods and problems inherent in such an approach. Finally, the chapter ends with a list of the major principles on which SST-based training programmes rest.

A recent study dealing with the mental-health problems of American Indians (LaFromboise and Row, 1983) is based on the premise that traditional psychotherapy is more destructive than helpful to Indian people. Instead, the authors argue that psychotherapeutic intervention should follow what they call a general skills training model. In particular, they suggest that the criteria for determining social competence should be pragmatic, in the sense of relating to the optimal personal development and satisfaction of the individuals concerned, and that these criteria can be looked at from the point of view of both cultures, in this case the Indian and non-Indian worlds, respectively. The primary aim of an intervention should be to increase competence, that is to concentrate on modifying behaviours rather than dealing with abstractions such as personality traits or other inferred states. They point out that skills-training is less culturally biased than other approaches, since it does not adhere to any necessary model of appropriate or correct behaviour, thus allowing programme designers and participants to select target behaviours and outcomes which they, rather than some dominant group, regard as desirable.

The authors state that SST has application to a wide range of problems relevant to Indian people, such as effective assertiveness, handling stress, problem-solving, job-interviewing, parenting, substance abuse, leadership training, handling depression, and marital relations. But in each case special attention must be given to the cultural adaptation of a technology that is largely culture blind. They recognize, however, that no approach can be totally neutral culturally. Thus the skills approach itself, regardless of content, implies an action-orientated problem-solving outlook that is not characteristically Indian. What it does do is to improve the ability of the Indian to cope in a white person's world, with fewer negative consequences than other approaches currently available. Furthermore, the approach makes it possible to teach bicultural competence. Thus assertiveness training may take the form of teaching clients to make their desires or preferences known in both Indian and non-Indian settings. It should be noted in passing that such a dual (or at its most general, multiple) approach is already implied in those unicultural SST models that link the actions being taught with the particular behaviour settings where the encounter is taking place (e.g. Furnham and Bochner, 1982). A bicultural approach simply extends the range of potential situations that can serve as behaviour settings for the target skills being taught.

LaFromboise and Rowe (1983) describe an assertion programme based on these principles. The following target situations were included: challenging employers who stereotype Indians; openly expressing disagreement with Indians and non-Indians; maintaining composure when one is called names like 'Chief', 'Injun', 'Squaw' or 'Brave'; standing up to programme administrators; dealing with interference and unwanted help; refusing unreasonable requests from both Indians and non-Indians; and making complaints. The list was formed after lengthy discussions with mental-health providers, tribal leaders and programme administrators. Video and live-modelling techniques were used and concentrated on such variables as eye contact, timing, loudness of voice, content of message and cultural appropriateness. Both Indian-to-white and Indian-to-Indian feedback was provided, and the effectiveness of the programme for bicultural competence was evaluated by rating videotapes of the participants in pre- and post-training role-plays. The LaFromboise and Rowe (1983) study provides an excellent model for setting up SST projects aimed at improving the social competence of minority persons, both in their dealings with the majority culture and particularly its officialdom, as well as in their contacts with members of their own ethnic group. It also does not ignore the all-important issue of the impact that SST may have on the original culture of the minority members. Indeed, one effect of such a programme model may be to strengthen the culture of origin, or at least ensure its preservation in a modified form (Bochner, 1979).

SST for cross-cultural competence

Although some of the training projects presented in this book may seem rather elaborate, the principles on which they are based can be scaled down to devise programmes for a variety of target groups, from police stationed in multicultural districts, to managers of international houses and hostels. In particular, the advantages of such an approach include the following:

1. The training procedures are based on a specific theory, namely that interpersonal difficulties across cultural boundaries stem from the participants not possessing the requisite social skills. The theory avoids vague statements about 'mutual understanding' and instead emphasizes behavioural-skill deficits.
2. The theory is 'practical' in the sense that it has at its centre everyday, common, even apparently trivial situations which nevertheless cause friction, misunderstanding and interpersonal hostility. The theory avoids vague statements about culture shock. Instead, it attempts to quantify social difficulty on various dimensions and then reduce it.

3. The programme can be tailor-made to the trainee, in that a particular person's social-skills deficiencies are diagnosed and the person is then given culturally appropriate remedial training aimed at removing those specific deficiencies. The training programme avoids general, non-specific lectures and films about superficial and/or exotic aspects of the host culture, preferring to concentrate on those specific features of the culture that the clients find problematic.

4. The training uses well tried, behavioural techniques such as video feedback, role-playing and modelling to realistically simulate real-life situations. In-field training is also employed. The training does not rely exclusively on cognitive or information-giving procedures, partly because these do not generalize readily across to real life situations, and partly because they are readily forgotten.

5. The training focuses on the management of interpersonal encounters. Its emphasis therefore is on the social psychology of the sojourner and avoids vague assumptions about achieving personal growth and insight. The stress is on the acquisition and execution of skills.

6. Evaluation of the theory, training content, training techniques and impact of the programme can be built into a project from the start and not tacked on as an afterthought. At its completion, it is possible to indicate if and exactly how well the various aspects of the project performed in accordance with expectations.

The disadvantages are that because of the systematic nature of such programmes, they are likely to cost more, intrude into and disrupt the activities of the institution whose members are being trained and require an interdisciplinary team of trainers, unless relevant bicultural mediating trainers (Bochner, 1981) are available.

Finally, as our discussion in the areas of host–sojourner relations, immigration, minority welfare, schooling and law enforcement has shown, using SST to improve intercultural communication is not just a matter of developing effective techniques. In addition, those constructing such curricula must be aware of and take into account the model of intercultural relations that is implied in the programme being developed. Is the ultimate aim to assimilate the newcomer, the second-generation migrant or the descendant of the original inhabitants of the land and regard their present un-British, un-Australian or un-American state as a deficiency to be made good, or is the aim to teach the clients those skills which they need in order to perform effectively in their new or the dominant society, without, however, taking away from them their culture of origin, those core characteristics that distinguish them from other human groups? Are we going to pursue the notion of bicultural or multicultural competence, or are we simply going to adjust those that do not conform to a universal standard that is defined by the mainstream of society? Both alternatives can be defended, although this is not the place to debate them. Furthermore, by identifying whether a programme is informed by a unicultural or a bicultural model, the aims are brought out quite explicitly and the SST can then be evaluated not just internally on its own terms, but also regarding its wider impact. For instance, one can think of programmes that are highly successful in achieving their goals but where the goals themselves are regarded as undesirable, or desirable by some groups and undesirable by others. Unless the wider aims and consequences of a programme and its underlying assumptions are clearly articulated, such judgements cannot be made. Nowhere is this more important than in the field of applied intercultural relations.

Chapter summary

Culture-training has application in two broad areas. The first and major effort has been to provide predeparture orientation to individuals about to undertake an extended sojourn abroad. A second, less-developed field has concentrated on teaching members of multicultural societies to become more aware of and sensitive to each other's values and practices.

Several training models exist, each with its own implications for intervention and practice. In the past, the pseudo-medical model has been quite influential, with its clinical approach to culture-training, intrapsychic explanations of culture shock and the aim to adjust sojourners to their new cultures. The model has been criticized on the grounds that it de-emphasizes the social context of the sojourn, stigmatizes those who are having problems with coping, and that the concept of adjustment has ethnocentric overtones.

The culture-learning model regards persons who are exposed to a new society to be engaged in a learning process. Instead of therapy and adjustment, this approach emphasizes the acquisition of culturally appropriate skills. The model also emphasizes the social psychology of the sojourn, in stating that most of the problems that culture-learners face relate to their interpersonal encounters with host members. Consequently, a high priority is to identify those social situations that sojourners find particularly difficult, and then teach them the requisite culturally relevant social skills to enable these situations to be more effectively negotiated. The main advantages of this approach are that culture-learning, unlike the notion of adjustment, has fewer ethnocentric overtones; and programmes can be tailored to suit the needs of particular clients.

The main training techniques include information giving, cultural sensitization, attribution training, learning by doing, and more recently, culture-based social-skills training, or SST. The evidence suggests that although all of the methods have some utility, the more practical and less abstract they are, the more effective they will be. The preferred method would be one that combined a cognitive and informational approach with systematically developed exercises using SST procedures.

SST techniques are particularly suited for the training of minority members in multicultural societies to become competent in both of their cultures, that is to learn and maintain the social skills of their own ethnic group, while also adding to their repertoire the social skills of the dominant culture. SST also has wide application in teaching sojourners to become competent in their new culture, in that the model provides clear guidelines as to what should be included in the curriculum. There also exist well established techniques that can be readily adapted to culture-training. Finally, SST programmes, probably more than any other approach, are capable of being strictly evaluated, so that at their completion it can be stated how well the various aspects of a project performed according to expectations.

12 Conclusion

The aim of this book has been to draw together the scattered literature on the psychological reactions of persons exposed to unfamiliar environments. This review has revealed a number of unresolved issues, problems and controversies, and consequently raised almost as many questions as it answered. However, at the same time the inquiry also produced positive results, both in terms of clarifying some of the conceptual difficulties in the area, as well as establishing a number of empirical generalizations about the determinants of 'culture shock'. In this chapter we will summarize what we regard to be the main issues and findings, and their implications for the other major concern of this book – the containment and management of culture stress.

Descriptions and definitions

Virtually everyone working in this area seems to have agreed that exposure to unfamiliar cultural influences is stressful. We have referred to this phenomenon previously with the catch phrase that 'life was not meant to be easy for culture travellers'. However, this should not be misunderstood to indicate that contact with alien cultures is uniformly noxious. Some aspects of culture travel have effects which can be regarded as positive, such as developing a greater insight into one's own society, a broadening of one's culture-bound perspective and, in some instances, developing a tolerance for other ethnic groups and their 'strange' customs and values. As in most areas of human endeavour, a cost–benefit analysis can be usefully applied to culture travel. However, the consensus seems to be that in general terms the negative psychological consequences of culture travel outweigh the positive ones for most categories of travellers, although there are large and systematic differences in how the ratio applies in specific circumstances. The first half of the book was concerned with identifying those determinants which increase the negative consequences and decrease the positive effects of culture travel. In this we followed the literature, although our own inclination has been to reverse the emphasis and dwell on how the positive effects might have increased and the negative ones decreased, a much more

constructive approach to this problem. The second half of the book
reflects this more optimistic orientation to culture stress.

Having established that culture travel is stressful, but not uniformly
across all instances of other-culture exposure, the obvious questions to
ask are, first, what are the determinants of this stress in general and,
second, why are there systematic variations in particular reactions to
unfamiliar environments? But before these questions could be considered,
certain taxonomies had to be established. In particular, it became
necessary to describe in more detail the various psychological reactions,
and to describe, categorize and distinguish between the various groups of
people who collectively make up the population of culture travellers.

Varieties of culture travellers

Although our starting point was the existing literature on cross-cultural
relations, our ultimate aim was to go beyond it and to develop a general
model of the sojourn. Initially, therefore, the book dealt with particular
groups of sojourners, such as overseas students, migrants, business
people, tourists, voluntary workers, and so forth. We then looked
behind these descriptive categories and teased out the psychological and
demographic attributes that characterize and distinguish each group.
This in turn provided us with a general schema that could be applied to
all categories of sojourners. For instance, although we were dealing with
vastly different sets of people, they all had motives for travelling
although their reasons differed according to whether they were students,
migrants or tourists; they all spent some time abroad, although this
might vary from a few days to a lifetime; they all had some form of
occupation, income and status, although this varied from low to high,
and so forth. This approach enabled us to develop hypotheses and draw
tentative conclusions about why some categories of sojourners cope
better than others. Rather than simply to assert that, for instance, tourists
and business travellers have it easier than migrants – which is true but
does not explain why – we were able to point to specific variables such as
relative social status, length of stay, observation versus participation, as
all implicated in how well a person will cope with a new environment.
We will not repeat the list of determinants here, as these have been dealt
with in previous sections, except to note some of the general principles
that emerged from this analysis. To the extent that one can generalize
about categories of culture travellers, the evidence indicates that the
distance between the culture of the sojourner and the culture of the host
country is a crucial determinant of stress *and* coping. Irrespective of how
culture distance is defined, whether in terms of social class, language,
religion, technological development, customs, communication patterns,
physical appearance, family structure, or any other of the salient
characteristics on which human groups differ, the data indicate that the

greater the differences between visitors and hosts, the greater the mutual problems encountered. This generalization, although primarily descriptive, carries within it the seeds of explanation, since it can generate a variety of testable hypotheses, many of which were dealt with in this book.

One area in which further work is required is to determine the relative importance of the various dimensions on which cultures differ, and how these dimensions affect each other in producing stress. For instance, do religious differences have a greater impact than, say, variations in family structure, and if the cultures differ on more than one dimension, are the consequences additive or, as is more likely, exponential in their effect?

Varieties of reactions to unfamiliar environments

As was the case with the taxonomy of sojourners, we started off by looking at how the literature had previously described the experience of culture stress, and then went beyond this to tease out some general principles and potential explanations. The literature has been dominated by the notion of 'culture shock', which among other things shows that social scientists, like the rest of humankind, are not immune to the influence of a snappy phrase. Still, the term does capture some of the flavour of coming into sudden contact with an alien environment, and as we saw, has been employed as a shorthand way of referring to the confusion, uncertainty and anxiety that travellers often experience. We criticized the use of the 'culture shock' label on the grounds that it provided very few leads as to what might determine the shock and was to some extent misleading since it obscured the very real differences in the amount of shock that different travellers experience under various conditions of contact.

Another major theme in the literature has been the notion of the U-curve of adjustment (or one of its variants, such as the W-curve), the basic idea being that adjustment or coping with a new culture is a sequential process following a series of stages that describe a U-shaped pattern. It has been repeatedly stated in the literature that travellers tend to start their sojourn with a positive, optimistic attitude but gradually become more and more despondent and distressed. If they survive this bad period, they will in due course emerge 'adjusted' and able to cope with their new environment. Presumably the bottom of the U-curve coincides with the period when culture shock is most acute. There are methodological problems with measuring these adjustment curves, and not all studies setting out to confirm the existence of the U-curve have found it. However, that was not our main criticism of this literature. As with the notion of culture shock, it struck us that the U-curve formulation was somewhat misleading because it obscured the existence of very real differences between the adjustment patterns of different groups of travellers, and it had not been sufficiently used to generate hypotheses about the determinants of patterns of adjustment in general, nor of different coping styles in particular.

Conceptual issues

In trying to go beyond the existing descriptive literature on culture shock in order to arrive at a general theory about its determinants, it became clear that a major, mostly unrecognized conceptual problem lurked in the background. The problem is not unique to this area but pervades the entire field of general psychology, and stems from the controversy about whether to locate the springs of behaviour primarily inside or outside the person. In an early statement of this issue, Mann (1969), using somewhat colloquial but nevertheless vivid language, distinguished within-skin from between-skin determinants of behaviour. The current formulation tends to use less flamboyant terms and is often referred to as the $P \times S$ (person by situation) debate (for a recent review, see Argyle, Furnham and Graham, 1981).

Traditional accounts of the antecedents of behaviour have tended to favour the within-skin approach. In concrete terms, if say a person had a successful career, coped well with stress, was likable, had a happy marriage and was a good parent, this was assumed to be due to the favourable inner qualities, character attributes, genetic endowment and enduring personality traits of the individual concerned. Likewise, people who are less successful in their lives are deemed to have failed because they possess less desirable personality traits. The within-skin model of human nature has been highly influential in psychology, stimulating eight decades of research into personality and its structure. Jung and Freud, in the early days, and more recently Cattell and Eysenck, are only some of the well-known scholars who have used this perspective in their work. The model also coincides with the implicit psychology of most lay persons who by and large explain each other's behaviour by referring to their respective enduring characteristics and personality traits, even though this often results in a tautology. Who has not overheard a conversation that goes something like this: 'Why does your neighbour beat the dog?' 'Because the person has an aggressive nature.' 'Ah, yes, that is it.'

One practical consequence of the within-skin approach has been the widespread practice of selecting people for a whole variety of tasks, from jobs in industry, recruiting soldiers in wartime, to matching marriage partners. The practice is based on the assumption that certain tasks require certain personality attributes for their successful performance, and psychology can assist by selecting the people that have those traits and screen out those individual who are temperamentally unsuitable. Although the idea has considerable face validity, the evidence, reviewed elsewhere in this book, indicates that scores on personality tests are not very good predictors of actual performance in the field (e.g. Guthrie, 1975, 1981; Mischel, 1984). Despite this, the use of personnel selection techniques has not diminished.

The between-skin approach plays down the role of enduring personality traits in the determination of behaviour and, in some more extreme versions of this model, does away with the trait concept altogether. Instead, the behaviour of individuals is regarded as resulting primarily from forces that are located outside the person, hence the 'between-skin' appellation. The main sources of influence include the groups that a person belongs to, the social roles they occupy and the norms and expectations that are associated with their behaviour settings. When it comes to fitting people to jobs, this model emphasizes training, the establishment of group norms and practices, and the provision of relevant social supports rather than selecting people on the basis of their character. The between-skin formulation of human nature arose out of the findings and constructs of social psychology.

Finally, a number of workers have tried to combine the two approaches, arguing that behaviour is the result of an interaction between what a person brings to the situation and the situation itself. The relative contribution of the person and the situation will vary with circumstances, and it then becomes an empirical matter to establish which aspect is more important under what conditions.

These basic conceptual issues were largely ignored in the literature on culture shock, mainly because the early workers influential in this field tended to be personality rather than social psychologists, which affected both their choice of dependent and independent variables. On the response side, culture shock was regarded as an internal reaction, like fear or anxiety (as opposed to an interpersonal response such as liking or communication skills). To the extent that there was any serious speculation about the determinants of culture shock, these too were regarded as basically within the make-up of the person. Typically, the variables included tolerance for ambiguity, rigidity and, in the mental health and migration literature, actual pathology or a constitutional predisposition to succumb to mental illness. In practical terms this led to attempts to select 'suitable' migrants, businesspersons, overseas students and volunteers; to screen out people deemed not to be able to withstand the rigours of second-culture exposure; and to use a counselling model in the treatment of those unable to cope.

It was the failure of the selection programme in the Peace Corps, despite its generous funding and expert staffing, that provided the impetus for a new approach. It was gradually acknowledged that how persons reacted to unfamiliar environments, including culture shock, depended greatly on the contemporary experiences of the travellers. Whatever the status of the within-skin hypothesis in general, in the area of culture stress, between-skin variables seemed to carry more weight than within-skin ones as far as coping with new environments was concerned. Once this was realized, theoretical models that departed from previous, trait-based formulations, began to appear. Much of the book has been concerned with developing such a social psychological model of culture shock, and its implications for intervention and remedial action.

A culture-learning/social-skills model

According to this model, 'culture shock' occurs when a sojourner is unfamiliar with the social conventions of the new culture, or if familiar with them, unable or unwilling to perform according to these rules. Several consequences follow from this construction, including the following. (1) Coping difficulties are attributed to a lack in appropriate skills rather than to some deficiency in the character of the sojourner; (2) The notion of 'adjustment' with its ethnocentric overtones is eliminated. Sojourners are not expected to adjust themselves to a new culture. Rather, they learn selected aspects of it for instrumental reasons. These new practices need not become part of the permanent repertoire of the person but will be discarded when they are not functional, as for instance when the sojourner is among fellow-nationals or after returning home. Unlike the concept of adjustment, culture-learning does not imply that a person must undergo a basic shift in values and conform to a new set of norms. Culture-learning makes a distinction between skills and values, between performance and compliance. (3) The technology exists for teaching second-culture skills, as an extension of the very well-developed field of intracultural social-skills training (SST). (4) Cultural SST is easier, more economic and more effective than remedial approaches based on counselling and psychotherapy. (5) SST can be specifically used to train people for bicultural competence, for which there will be an expanding demand as societies become increasingly multicultural.

Social-support systems

Most culture travellers are not provided with systematic training to prepare them for a sojourn in an unfamiliar environment. Despite this lack, the literature records big individual differences in how people acquire second-culture skills, some being much better at it than others. This led to theoretical as well as empirical speculation about what might contribute to effective unplanned culture-learning. The results of this analysis suggest that two interrelated conditions are important for culture-learning, whether planned or unplanned. The first is the availability of a 'culture friend' to serve as an unofficial tutor in cultural affairs. The evidence indicates that many sojourners lead lives that are relatively isolated from their host society. Those sojourners, whether students, business people or tourists, who do have some intimate contact with host members, seem to be more content, satisfied and successful than sojourners who have no such contact. This finding can be due to the 'training' role that such hosts perform or to the social and emotional support they provide, or to a combination of both factors. Whatever the actual mechanisms, there is no doubt that the presence or absence of a 'culture friend' makes a big difference to how a person copes in an unfamiliar environment.

The second condition contributing to effective culture-learning is the extent to which a sojourner can become a participant in the new society as distinct from being either an observer or excluded as an outsider. Clearly, if a newcomer is in the process of acquiring the skills of the host society and is 'sponsored' by a host member, becoming a participant will be facilitated, and once persons begin to participate they are in a better position to learn and rehearse their second-culture skills. This in turn makes participating easier, thus setting up a beneficial spiral. However, even such favourable conditions do not necessarily lead to a reduction of culture stress. For instance, there are societies, or sectors of societies, that will exclude even socially skilled and 'sponsored' sojourners because the newcomer's race, religion or other perceived attribute may be regarded as unacceptable. This brings us to our final point, an examination of the impact of culture-contact on cross-cultural understanding and inter-group harmony.

Inter-group relations

An underlying theme in the literature on culture shock has been the assumption, or at least the hope, that contact between culturally diverse people will reduce inter-group hostility and prejudice, and ultimately make a contribution to world peace simply as a by-product of that contact. As we have seen, a naive contact hypothesis cannot be sustained either empirically or theoretically. Empirically, the evidence indicates that under some conditions contact will lead to increased hostility and conflict (Amir, 1969, 1976).

Theoretically, virtually every one of the major theories in social psychology implies that people will prefer the company of others who are similar to themselves over those who are different. The theories, all of which have been supported by empirical evidence, include the belief-similarity hypothesis (Rokeach, 1961), the similarity-attraction hypothesis (Byrne, 1969); Tajfel's theory of positive social identity (Tajfel, 1970; Turner and Giles, 1981), attribution theory (Jaspars and Hewstone, 1982); balance theory (Heider, 1958; Newcomb, 1956); dissonance theory (Aronson, 1976; Festinger, 1957); social-learning theory (Guthrie, 1975); role theory (Triandis, Vassiliou, Vassiliou, Tanaka and Shanmugam, 1972); primary socialization (Deaux, 1976); stereotyping (Allport, 1954); social categorization (Sherif, 1970); the self-presentation hypothesis (Jones, 1964); and conformity to social norms (Kelman, 1958).

Cross-cultural contact almost always entails a meeting between individuals who are diverse in some important respect. Despite theoretical expectations, and unequivocal evidence about the existence of a powerful in-group bias, many instances of harmonious inter-group relations can be found world-wide, both within multicultural societies as well as between members of different societies. It is not often realized, or perhaps admitted, that this relatively happy state of affairs is contrary to traditional theoretical expectations. Consequently, rather than bemoan the breakdown of the contact hypothesis, one might instead marvel that so much cross-cultural good-will actually exists. To the extent that we are prepared to gaze into a crystal ball, it is our belief that the next major advance in this field will be directed at improving inter-group relations through a systematic application of the new models, ideas and techniques that are currently being developed.

Bibliography

Adams, W. (ed.) (1968) *The Brain Drain*, New York, Macmillan.

Adler, P. S. (1975) 'The transitional experience: an alternative view of culture shock', *Journal of Humanistic Psychology*, 15, 13–23.

Aiello, J. R. and Jones, S. E. (1971) 'Field study of the proxemic behavior of young school children in three subcultural groups', *Journal of Personality and Social Psychology*, 19, 351–6.

Alatas, S. H. (1972) 'The captive mind in development studies: some neglected problems and the need for an autonomous social science tradition in Asia', *International Social Science Journal*, 24, 9–25.

— (1975) 'The captive mind and creative development', *International Social Science Journal*, 27, 691–700.

Allport, G. W. (1954) *The Nature of Prejudice*, Garden City, NY, Doubleday Anchor.

— Vernon, P. and Lindzey, G. (1960) *A Study of Values*, Boston, Houghton Mifflin.

Amir, Y. (1969) 'Contact hypothesis in ethnic relations', *Psychological Bulletin*, 71, 319–42.

— (1976) 'The role of intergroup contact in change of prejudice and ethnic relations', in Katz, P. A. (ed.), *Towards the Elimination of Racism*, New York, Pergamon.

Ananth, J. (1978) 'Psychopathology in Indian females', *Social Science and Medicine*, 12, 177–8.

Antler, L. (1970) 'Correlates of home and host country acquaintanceship among foreign medical residents in the United States', *Journal of Social Psychology*, 80, 49–57.

Antonovsky, A. and Katz, A. (1979) *From the Golden to the Promised Land*, Jerusalem, PRA Press.

Anumonye, A. (1970) *African Students in Alien Cultures*, London, Black Academy Press.

Argyle, M. (1975) *Bodily Communication*, London, Methuen.

— (1979) 'New developments in the analysis of social skills', in Wolfgang, A. (ed.), *Non-verbal Behaviour*, London, Academic Press.

— (1980) 'Interaction skills and social competence', in Feldman, P. and

Orford, J. (eds), *Psychological Problems: The Social Context*, Chichester, Wiley.

— (1981) 'Inter-cultural communication', in Argyle, M. (ed.), *Social Skills and Work*, London, Methuen.

— (1982) 'Inter-cultural communication', in Bochner, S. (ed.), *Cultures in Contact: Studies in Cross-cultural Interaction*, Oxford, Pergamon.

— Furnham, A. and Graham, J. A. (1981) *Social Situations*, Cambridge, Cambridge University Press.

— and Kendon, A. (1967) 'The experimental analysis of social perform-ance', in Berkowitz, L. (ed.), *Advances in Experimental Social Psychology*, New York, Academic Press, vol. 3.

Aronson, E. (1976) *The Social Animal*, 2nd edn, San Francisco, W. H. Freeman.

Arredondo-Dowd, P. M. (1981) 'Personal loss and grief as a result of immigration', *Personnel and Guidance Journal*, 2, 376–8.

Astrup, C. and Ødegaard, O. (1960) 'Internal migration and mental disease in Norway', *Psychiatric Quarterly Supplement*, 34, 116–30.

Atkinson, J. W. (ed.) (1958) *Motives in Fantasy, Action, and Society*, Princeton, NJ, Van Nostrand.

Au, D. S. C. (1969) 'The influence of contact with host nationals on foreign students' attitudes', unpublished BA Honours thesis, University of New South Wales.

Averill, J. R. (1968) 'Grief: its nature and significance', *Psychological Bulletin*, 70, 721–48.

Babiker, I. E., Cox, J. L. and Miller, P. M. C. (1980) 'The measurement of culture distance and its relationship to medical consultation, symptomatology and examination performance of overseas students at Edinburgh University', *Social Psychiatry*, 15, 109–16.

Bagley, C. (1968) 'Migration, race and mental health: a review of some recent research', *Race*, 9, 343–56.

— (1969) 'A survey of problems reported by Indian and Pakistani immigrants in Britain', *Race*, 11, 65–78.

— (1971) 'Mental illness in immigrant minorities in London', *Journal of Biosocial Science*, 3, 449–59.

— and Greer, S. (1972) ' "Black suicide": a report of 25 English cases and controls', *Journal of Social Psychology*, 86, 175–9.

Ballard, C. (1971) Conflict, continuity and change: second-generation Asians in minority families in Britain', in Watson, J. L. (ed.), *Between Two Cultures*, London, Community Relations Commission Publica-tions.

Ball-Rokeach, S. J. (1973) 'From pervasive ambiguity to a definition of the situation'. *Sociometry*, 36, 3–13.

Banton, M. P. (1965) *Roles: An Introduction to the Study of Social Relations*, London, Tavistock.

— (1967) *Race Relations*, London, Tavistock.

Baranowski, T., Nader, P., Dunn, K. and Vanderpool, N. A. (1982) 'Family self-help: promoting changes in health behaviour', *Journal of Communication*, 32, 161–72.

Bardo, J. W. and Bardo, D. J. (1980) 'Sociodemographic correlates of adjustment for American migrants in Australia', *Journal of Social Psychology*, 112, 255–60.

Barker, R. G. (1968) *Ecological Psychology: Concepts and Methods for Studying the Environment of Human Behaviour*, Stanford, Calif., Stanford University Press.

— (1979) 'Settings of a professional lifetime', *Journal of Personality and Social Psychology*, 37, 2137–57.

Baron, R. C., Thacker, S. B., Gorelkin, L., Vernon, A. A., Taylor, W. R. and Choi, K. (1983) 'Sudden death among Southeast Asian refugees: an unexplained nocturnal phenomenon', *The Journal of the American Medical Association*, 250, 2947–51.

Barrera, M. and Ainlay, S. L. (1983) 'The structure of social support: a conceptual and empirical analysis', *Journal of Community Psychology*, 11, 133–43.

Bartel, A. (1979) 'The migration decision: what role does job mobility play?' *American Economic Review*, 69, 775–86.

Bar-Yosef, R. (1969) 'De-socialization and resocialization: the adjustment process of immigrants', *International Migration Review*, 3, 27–45.

Basker, C. and Dominguez, V. R. (1984) 'Limits of cultural awareness: the immigrant as therapist', *Human Relations*, 37, 693–719.

Batta, I. D., McCulloch, J. W. and Smith, N. J. (1975) 'A study of juvenile delinquency among Asians and half-Asians', *British Journal of Criminology*, 15, 32–42.

Baxter, J. C. (1970) 'Interpersonal spacing in natural settings', *Sociometry*, 33, 444–56.

Beels, C. C. (1981) 'Social support and schizophrenia', *Schizophrenia Bulletin*, 7, 58–72.

Bennett, J. W., Passin, H. and McKnight, R. K. (1958) *In Search of Identity: The Japanese Overseas Scholar in America and Japan*, Minneapolis, University of Minnesota Press.

Benyoussef, A., Cutler, J., Levine, A., Mansourian, P., Phan-Tan, T., Baylet, R., Collomb, H., Diaz, S., Lacombe, B., Ravel, J., Vaugelade, J., and Diebold, G. (1974) 'Health effects of rural–urban migration in developing countries – Senegal', *Social Science and Medicine*, 8, 243–54.

Berk, B. and Hirata, L. (1973) 'Mental illness among the Chinese: myth or reality?', *Journal of Social Issues*, 29, 145–60.

Berman, G. (1979) 'Why North Americans migrate to Israel', *Jewish Journal of Sociology*, 21, 135–44.

— (1981) 'Work satisfaction and general adjustment of migrants',

Sociology of Work and Occupations, 8, 417–38.

Bernard, W. S. (1976) 'Immigrants and refugees: their similarities, differences and needs', *International Migration*, 14, 267–81.

Berry, J. W. (1975) 'Ecology, cultural adaptation, and psychological differentiation: traditional patterning and acculturative stress', in Brislin, R. W., Bochner, S. and Lonner, W. J., (eds), *Cross-cultural Perspectives on Learning*, New York, Wiley.

— and Pleasants, M. (1984) 'Ethnic tolerance in plural societies', paper given at the International Conference on Authoritarianism and Dogmatism, Potsdam, New York.

Bettelheim, B. (1943) 'Individual and mass behavior in extreme situations', *Journal of Abnormal and Social Psychology*, 38, 417–52.

Bhatt, A. K. and Fairchild, H. H. (1984) 'Values of convergence for Indian students in the United States', *Psychological Reports*, 55, 446.

Bickley, V. C. (1982) 'Language as the bridge', in Bochner, S. (ed.), *Cultures in Contact: Studies in Cross-cultural Interaction*, Oxford, Pergamon.

Biegel, D., Naparstek, A. and Khan, M. (1980) 'Social support and mental health: an examination of interrelationships', paper presented at the meeting of the American Psychological Association in Montreal, Canada.

Bloom, L. (1971) *The Social Psychology of Race Relations*, London, Allen & Unwin.

Bochner, S. (1972) 'Problems in culture learning', in Bochner, S. and Wicks, P. (eds), *Overseas Students in Australia*, Sydney, New South Wales University Press.

— (1973) *The Mediating Man: Cultural Interchange and Transnational Education*, Honolulu, Culture Learning Institute, East–West Center.

— (1976) 'Religious role differentiation as an aspect of subjective culture', *Journal of Cross-Cultural Psychology*, 7, 3–19.

— (1979) 'Cultural diversity: implications for modernization and international education', in Kumar, K. (ed.), *Bonds without Bondage: Explorations in Transcultural Interactions*, Honolulu, University Press of Hawaii.

— (1980) 'Unobtrusive methods in cross-cultural experimentation', in Triandis, H. C. and Berry, J. W. (eds), *Handbook of Cross-cultural Psychology: Methodology*, Boston, Allyn and Bacon, vol. 2.

— (ed.) (1981) *The Mediating Person: Bridges between Cultures*, Cambridge, Mass., Schenkman.

— (1982) 'The social psychology of cross-cultural relations', in Bochner, S. (ed.), *Cultures in Contact: Studies in Cross-cultural Interaction*, Oxford, Pergamon.

— and Cairns, L. G. (1976) 'An unobtrusive measure of helping behaviour toward Aborigines', in Kearney, G. E. and McElwain, D. W., (eds), *Aboriginal Cognition: Retrospect and Prospect*, Canberra,

Australian Institute of Aboriginal Studies.

— and Harris, R. J. (1984) 'Sex differences in the attribution of socially desirable and undesirable traits to out-group members', *International Journal of Psychology*, 19, 207–15.

— and Ohsako, T. (1977) 'Ethnic role salience in racially homogeneous and heterogeneous societies', *Journal of Cross-Cultural Psychology*, 8, 477–92.

— and Orr, F. E. (1979) 'Race and academic status as determinants of friendship formation: a field study', *International Journal of Psychology*, 14, 37–46.

— and Perks, R. W. (1971) 'National role evocation as a function of cross-national interaction', *Journal of Cross-Cultural Psychology*, 2, 157–64.

— and Wicks, P. (eds) (1972) *Overseas Students in Australia*, Sydney, New South Wales University Press.

— Buker, E. A. and McLeod, B. M. (1976) 'Communication patterns in an international student dormitory: a modification of the "small world" method', *Journal of Applied Social Psychology*, 6, 275–90.

— Hutnik, N. and Furnham, A. (in press) 'The friendship patterns of overseas and host students in an Oxford student residence', *Journal of Social Psychology*.

— Lin, A. and McLeod, B. M. (1979) 'Cross-cultural contact and the development of an international perspective', *Journal of Social Psychology*, 107, 29–41.

— — — (1980) 'Anticipated role conflict of returning overseas students', *Journal of Social Psychology*, 110, 265–72.

— McLeod, B. M. and Lin, A. (1977) 'Friendship patterns of overseas students: a functional model', *International Journal of Psychology*, 12, 277–97.

Bock, P. (ed.) (1970) *Culture Shock: A Reader in Modern Anthropology*, New York, Alfred A. Knopf.

Boekestijn, C. (1984) 'Intercultural migration and the development of personal identity: the dilemma between identity maintenance and cultural adaptation', paper given at the Seventh International Congress of Cross-cultural Psychology, Acapulco.

Boker, W. (1981) 'Psycho(patho)logical reactions among foreign labourers in Europe', in Eitinger, L. and Schwarz, D. (eds), *Strangers in the World*, Bern, Hans Huber.

Boldt, E. D. (1978) 'Structural tightness and cross-cultural research', *Journal of Cross-Cultural Psychology*, 9, 151–65.

— and Roberts, L. W. (1979) 'Structural tightness and social conformity: a methodological note with theoretical implications', *Journal of Cross-Cultural Psychology*, 10, 221–30.

Bottoms, A. E. (1967) 'Delinquency among immigrants', *Race*, 8, 357–70.

Bourne, P. G. (1975) 'The Chinese student: acculturation and mental illness', *Psychiatry*, 38, 269–77.

Bowlby, J. (1960) 'Grief and mourning in infancy and early childhood', *Psychoanalytic Study of the Child*, 15, 9–52.

— (1961) 'Process of mourning', *International Journal of Psychoanalysis*, 42, 317–40.

— (1969) *Attachment and Loss*, London, Hogarth.

Boxer, A. H. (1969) *Experts in Asia: An Inquiry into Australian Technical Assistance*, Canberra, Australian National University Press.

Brein, M. and David, K. H. (1971) 'Intercultural communication and the adjustment of the sojourner', *Psychological Bulletin*, 76, 215–30.

Brett, J. M. (1982) 'Job transfer and well-being', *Journal of Applied Psychology*, 67, 450–63.

Brewin, C. (1980) 'Explaining the lower rates of psychiatric treatment among Asian immigrants to the United Kingdom: a preliminary study', *Social Psychiatry*, 15, 17–19.

Brislin, R. W. (1979) 'Orientation programs for cross-cultural preparation', in Marsella, A. J., Tharp, R. G. and Ciborowski, T. J. (eds), *Perspectives on Cross-cultural Psychology*, New York, Academic Press.

— (1980) 'Translation and content analysis of oral and written materials', in Triandis, H. C. and Berry, J. W. (eds), *Handbook of Cross-cultural Psychology: Methodology*, Boston, Allyn & Bacon, vol. 2.

— and Baumgardner, S. R. (1971) 'Non-random sampling of individuals in cross-cultural research', *Journal of Cross-Cultural Psychology*, 2, 397–400.

— and Pedersen, P. (1976) *Cross-cultural Orientation Programs*, New York, Gardner Press.

Britt, W. G. (1983) 'Pre-training variables in the prediction of missionary success overseas', *Journal of Psychology and Theology*, 11, 213–17.

Bronfenbrenner, U. (1961) 'The mirror image in Soviet–American relations: a social psychologist's report', *Journal of Social Issues*, 17, 45–56.

Brown, G. W. (1974) 'Meaning, measurement, and stress of life events', in Dohrenwend, B. S. and Dohrenwend, B. P. (eds), *Stressful Life Events: Their Nature and Effects*, New York, Wiley.

— and Harris, T. (1978) *Social Origins of Depression: A Study of Psychiatric Disorder in Women*, New York, Free Press.

— Bhrolchain, M. N. and Harris, T. (1975) 'Social class and psychiatric disturbance among women in an urban population', *Sociology*, 9, 225–54.

Brown, L. (1959) 'The differential job satisfaction of English immigrants and New Zealanders', *Occupational Psychology*, 33, 54–8.

— (1960) 'English migrants to New Zealand: the decision to move', *Human Relations*, 13, 167–74.

— and Holmes, J. (1971) 'Intra-urban migration lifelines: a spatial view', *Demography*, 8, 103–23.

Brownell, K. D., Heckerman, C. L., Westlake, R. J., Hayes, S. C. and Monti, P. M. (1978) 'The effect of couples training and partner co-operativeness in the behavioral treatment of obesity', *Behaviour Research and Therapy*, 16, 323–33.

Burke, A. G. (1977) 'Family stress and the precipitation of psychiatric disorder: a comparative study among immigrant West Indian and native British patients in Birmingham', *International Journal of Social Psychiatry*, 23, 35–40.

Burvill, P. W. (1984) 'Immigration and mental disease', in Messick, J. and Berganza, C. (eds), *Culture and Psychopathology*, New York, Columbia University Press.

Byrne, D. (1969) 'Attitudes and attraction', in Berkowitz, L. (ed.), *Advances in Experimental Social Psychology*, New York, Academic Press, vol. 4.

Byrnes, F. C. (1966) 'Role shock: an occupational hazard of American technical assistants abroad', *Annals of the American Academy of Political and Social Science*, 368, 95–108.

Cade, J. F. J. and Krupinski, J. (1962) 'Incidence of psychiatric disorders in Victoria in relation to country of birth', *Medical Journal of Australia*, 1, 400–8.

Caplan, G. (1974) *Support Systems and Community Mental Health*, New York, Behavior Publications.

Carey, A. T. (1956) *Colonial Students*, London, Secker & Warburg.

Carpenter, L. and Brockington, I. F. (1980) 'A study of mental illness in Asians, West Indians and Africans living in Manchester', *British Journal of Psychiatry*, 137, 201–10.

Cattell, R., Bruel, H. and Hartman, H. (1951) 'An attempt at a more refined definition of the cultural dimensions of syntality in modern nations', *American Sociological Review*, 17, 43–56.

— Graham, R. and Wolwer, R. (1979) 'A reassessment of the factorial cultural dimensions of modern nations', *Journal of Social Psychology*, 108, 241–58.

Cauce, A., Felner, R. and Primavera, J. (1982) 'Social support in high-risk adolescents: structural components and adaptive impact', *American Journal of Community Psychology*, 10, 417–28.

Chandra, S. (1975) 'Cognitive development of Indians and Fijians', in Berry, J. W. and Lonner, W. J. (eds), *Applied Cross-cultural Psychology*, Amsterdam, Swets & Zeitlinger.

Cheung, F. M. and Lan, B. W. K. (1982) 'Situational variations of help-seeking behaviour among Chinese patients', *Comprehensive Psychiatry*, 23, 252–62.

Chiu, E. (1977a) 'The plight of the mentally ill Chinese in Victoria, 1867 to 1879', *Medical Journal of Australia*, 17, 541–4.

— (1977b) 'More about the plight of mentally ill Chinese in Victoria,

1867–1879', *Medical Journal of Australia*, 17, 594–7.

Chu, G. C. (1968) 'Student expatriation: a function of relative social support', *Sociology and Social Research*, 52, 174–84.

Church, A. T. (1982) 'Sojourner adjustment', *Psychological Bulletin*, 91, 540–72.

Cleveland, H., Mangone, G. J. and Adams, J. G. (1960) *The Overseas Americans*, New York, McGraw Hill.

Cobb, S. (1976) 'Social support as a moderator of life stress', *Psychosomatic Medicine*, 3, 300–14.

Cochrane, R. (1977) 'Mental illness in immigrants to England and Wales: an analysis of mental hospital admissions, 1971', *Social Psychiatry*, 12, 25–35.

— (1979) 'Psychological and behavioural disturbance in West Indians, Indians and Pakistanis in Britain: a comparison of rates among children and adults', *British Journal of Psychiatry*, 134, 201–10.

— (1980) 'Mental illness in England, in Scotland and in Scots living in England', *Social Psychiatry*, 15, 9–15.

— (1983) *The Social Creation of Mental Illness*, London, Longman.

— and Robertson, A. (1973) 'The life events inventory: a measure of the relative severity of psychosocial stressors', *Journal of Psychosomatic Research*, 17, 215–18.

— and Sobel, M. (1980) 'Life stresses and psychological consequences', in Feldman, P. and Orford, J. (eds), *Psychological Problems: The Social Context*, Chichester, Wiley.

— and Stopes-Roe, M. (1977) 'Psychological and social adjustment of Asian immigrants to Britain: a community survey', *Social Psychiatry*, 12, 195–207.

— — (1979) 'Psychological disturbance in Ireland, in England and in Irish emigrants to England: a comparative study', *Economic and Social Review*, 10, 301–20.

— — (1980) 'Factors affecting the distribution of psychological symptoms in urban areas of England', *Acta Psychiatrica Scandinavia*, 61, 445–60.

— — (1981a) 'Psychological symptom level in Indian immigrants to England: a comparison with natives', *Psychological Medicine*, 11, 319–27.

— — (1981b) 'Social class and psychological disorder in natives and immigrants to Britain', *International Journal of Social Psychiatry*, 27, 173–82.

— Hashmi, F. and Stopes-Roe, M. (1977) 'Measuring psychological disturbance in Asian immigrants to Britain', *Social Science and Medicine*, 11, 157–64.

Coelho, G. V. (1958) *Changing Images of America*, Glencoe, Ill., Free Press.

Cohen, E. (1979) 'Rethinking the sociology of tourism', *Annals of Tourism Research*, 6, 18–35.

Cohen, S. and Hoberman, H. (1983) 'Positive events and social supports as buffers of life change stress', *Journal of Applied Social Psychology*, 13, 99–125.

Cole, J., Allen, F. and Green, J. (1980) 'Survey of health problems of overseas students', *Social Science and Medicine*, 14, 627–31.

Cole, M. (1975) 'An ethnographic psychology of cognition', in Brislin, R. W., Bochner, S. and Lonner, W. J. (eds), *Cross-cultural Perspectives on Learning*, New York, Wiley.

— Gay, J., Glick, J. and Sharp, D. (1971) *The Cultural Context of Learning and Thinking*, New York, Basic Books.

Collett, P. (1971) 'Training Englishmen in the non-verbal behaviour of Arabs: an experiment on intercultural communication', *International Journal of Psychology*, 6, 209–15.

— (1982) 'Meetings and misunderstandings', in Bochner, S. (ed.), *Cultures in Contact: Studies in Cross-cultural Interaction*, Oxford, Pergamon.

Collins, G. (1977) *You Can Profit from Stress*, Santa Anna, Calif., Vision House.

Cook, S. W. and Selltiz, C. (1955) 'Some factors which influence the attitudinal outcomes of personal contact', *International Social Science Bulletin*, 7, 51–8.

Cort, D. A. and King, M. (1979) 'Some correlates of culture shock among American tourists in Africa', *International Journal of Intercultural Relations*, 3, 211–25.

Crompton, J. (1979) 'Motivations for pleasure vacation', *Annals of Tourism Research*, 6, 408–24.

Crowley, M. (1978) 'The other side of the integration coin: level of worldmindedness of third-generation Australian children as a function of ethnic composition of friendship group, age, ethnic density of school and sex', unpublished honours thesis, School of Psychology, University of New South Wales.

Curle, A. (1970) *Educational Strategy for Developing Societies*, 2nd edn, London, Tavistock.

Dann, G. (1977) 'Anomie, ego-enhancement and tourism', *Annals of Tourism Research*, 4, 184–94.

Danziger, K. (1974) 'The acculturation of Italian immigrant girls in Canada', *International Journal of Psychology*, 9, 129–37.

Darnell, F. (ed.) (1972) *Education in the North*, Fairbanks, University of Alaska.

Davey, B. (1957) 'The disappointed undergraduate', *British Medical Journal*, 2, 547–50.

David, K. (1971) 'Culture shock and the development of self-awareness', *Journal of Contemporary Psychotherapy*, 4, 44–8.

Daws, G. (1968) *Shoal of Time: A History of the Hawaiian Islands*, Honolulu, University Press of Hawaii.

Deaux, K. (1976) *The Behavior of Women and Men*, Monterey, Calif., Brooks/Cole.

Deutsch, S. E. and Won, G. Y. M. (1963) 'Some factors in the adjustment of foreign nationals in the United States', *Journal of Social Issues*, 19 (3), 115–22.

DeVos, G. A. (1980) 'Ethnic adaptation and minority status', *Journal of Cross-Cultural Psychology*, 11, 101–24.

Di Marco, N. (1974) 'Stress and adaptation in cross-cultural transition', *Psychological Reports*, 35, 279–85.

Dohrenwend, B. P. and Dohrenwend, B. S. (1969) *Social Status and Psychological Disorder: A Causal Inquiry*, New York, Wiley.

— — (1974) 'Psychiatric disorders in urban settings', in Arietti, S. and Caplan, G. (eds), *American Handbook of Psychiatry*, New York, Basic Books.

— — (eds) (1974) *Stressful Life Events: their Nature and Effects*, New York, Wiley.

Draguns, J. G. (1980) 'Psychological disorders of clinical severity', in Triandis, H. C. and Draguns, J. G. (eds), *Handbook of Cross-cultural Psychology: Psychopathology*, Boston, Allyn & Bacon, vol. 6.

Du Bois, C. (1956) *Foreign Students and Higher Education in the United States*, Washington, DC, American Council on Education.

Duck, S. (1977) *The Study of Acquaintance*, London, Saxon House.

— and Craig, G. (1978) 'Personality similarity and the development of friendship: a longitudinal study', *British Journal of Social and Clinical Psychology*, 17, 237–42.

— and Spencer, C. (1972) 'Personal constructs and friendship formation', *Journal of Personality and Social Psychology*, 23, 40–5.

Duncan, S. (1969) 'Nonverbal communication', *Psychological Bulletin*, 72, 118–37.

Durkheim, E. (1897) *Suicide: A Study in Sociology*, Paris, Felix Alcan.

Dutton, D. G. (1971) 'Reactions of restaurateurs to blacks and whites violating restaurant dress requirements', *Canadian Journal of Behavioural Science*, 3, 298–302.

— (1973) 'Reverse discrimination: the relationship of amount of perceived discrimination toward a minority group on the behaviour of majority group members', *Canadian Journal of Behavioural Science*, 5, 34–45.

Eaton, W. W. and Lasry, J. C. (1978) 'Mental health and occupational mobility in a group of immigrants', *Social Science and Medicine*, 12, 53–8.

Edgerton, W. B. (1976) 'Who participates in education exchange?', *The Annals of the American Academy of Political and Social Science*, 424, 6–15.

Edwards, J. E. and Whitlock, F. A. (1968) 'Suicide and attempted suicide in Brisbane: 2', *Medical Journal of Australia*, 6, 989–95.

Eichenbaum, J. (1975) 'A matrix of human movement', *International*

Migration, 13, 21–41.

Eide, I. (ed.) (1970) *Students as Links between Cultures*, Paris, UNESCO.

Eitinger, L. and Schwarz, D. (eds) (1981) *Strangers in the World*, Bern, Hans Huber.

Ekman, P. and Friesen, W. V. (1972) 'Hand movements'. *The Journal of Communication*, 22, 353–74.

Eldridge, J. E. T. (1960) 'Overseas students at Leicester University: some problems of adjustment and communication', *Race*, 2, 50–9.

Ellis, R. and Whittington, D. (1981) *A Guide to Social Skills Training*, London, Croom Helm.

— — (1983) *New Directions in Social Skills Training*, London, Croom Helm.

El Sendiony, M., Abou-el-Azaer, M. and Luza, F. (1977) 'Culture change and mental illness', *International Journal of Social Psychiatry*, 23, 20–5.

Engel, G. (1970) 'Comparison between Americans living in Israel and those who returned to America', *Journal of Applied Psychology*, 76, 117–23.

European Value Systems Study Group (1982) *Main European Report*, Amsterdam.

Fayerweather, J. (1959) *The Executive Overseas: Administrative Attitudes and Relationships in a Foreign Culture*, Syracuse, Syracuse University Press.

Feather, N. T. (1970) 'Educational choice and student attitudes in relation to terminal and instrumental values', *Australian Journal of Psychology*, 22, 127–44.

— (1979) 'Assimilation of values in migrant groups', in Rokeach, M. (ed.), *Understanding Human Values: Individual and Societal*, New York, Free Press.

— (1980) 'Value systems and social interaction: a field study in a newly independent nation', *Journal of Applied Social Psychology*, 10, 1–19.

— (1981) 'Culture contact and national sentiment', *Australian Journal of Psychology*, 33, 149–56.

— (ed.) (1982) *Expectations and Actions: Expectancy-Value Models in Psychology*, Hillsdale, NJ, Erlbaum.

— and Hutton, M. A. (1973) 'Value systems of students in Papua New Guinea and Australia', *International Journal of Psychology*, 9, 91–104.

— and Rudzitis, A. (1974) 'Subjective assimilation among Latvian adolescents: effects of ethnic schools and perception of value systems', *International Migration*, 12, 71–87.

— and Wasejluk, G. (1973) 'Subjective assimilation among Ukrainian migrants: value similarity and parent–child differences', *Australian and New Zealand Journal of Sociology*, 9, 16–31.

Feldman, R. E. (1968) 'Response to compatriot and foreigner who seek assistance', *Journal of Personality and Social Psychology*, 10, 202–14.

Festinger, L. (1957) *A Theory of Cognitive Dissonance*, Evanston, Ill., Row, Peterson.

Fiedler, F. E., Mitchell, T. and Triandis, H. C. (1971) 'The culture assimilator: an approach to cross-cultural training', *Journal of Applied Psychology*, 55, 95–102.

Fiore, J., Becker, J. and Coppel, D. B. (1983) 'Social network interactions: a buffer or a stress', *American Journal of Community Psychology*, 11, 423–39.

Foa, U. G. and Chemers, M. M. (1967) 'The significance of role behavior differentiation for cross-cultural interaction training', *International Journal of Psychology*, 2, 45–57.

Fondacaro, M. and Heller, K. (1983) 'Social support factors and drinking among college student males', *Journal of Youth and Adolescence*, 12, 285–99.

Fowler, B., Littlewood, B. and Madigan, R. (1977) 'Immigrant school-leavers and the search for work', *Sociology*, 11, 65–85.

Freeman, L. C. and Winch, R. F. (1957) 'Societal complexity: an empirical test of a typology of societies', *American Journal of Sociology*, 62, 461–6.

Freud, S. (1957) *Mourning and Melancholia*, London, Hogarth.

Frost, I. (1938) 'Homesickness and immigrant psychoses', *British Journal of Psychiatry*, 84, 801–37.

Fulbright, J. W. (1976) 'The most significant and important activity I have been privileged to engage in during my years in the Senate', *The Annals of the American Academy of Political and Social Science*, 424, 1–5.

Furnham, A. (1979) 'Assertiveness in three cultures: multidimensionality and cultural differences', *Journal of Clinical Psychology*, 35, 522–7.

— (1982) 'Why are the poor always with us? Explanations for poverty in Britain', *British Journal of Social Psychology*, 21, 311–22.

— (1983a) 'Situational determinants of social skill', in Ellis, R. and Whittington, D. (eds), *New Directions in Social Skill Training*, London, Croom Helm.

— (1983b) 'Research in social skills training: a critique', in Ellis, R. and Whittington, D. (eds), *New Directions in Social Skill Training*, London, Croom Helm.

— (1983c) 'Social difficulty in three cultures', *International Journal of Psychology*, 18, 215–28.

— (1984a) 'Personality and values', *Personality and Individual Differences*, 5, 483–5.

— (1984b) 'Tourism and culture shock', *Annals of Tourism Research*, 11, 41–57.

— (1985a) 'Why do people save? Attitudes to, and habits of, saving money in Britain', *Journal of Applied Social Psychology*, 15, 354–73.

— (1985b) 'Unemployment', in van Raaij, W. F., van Veldhoven, G. M., Verhallen, T. M. M. and Warneryd, K. E. (eds), *Handbook of*

Economic Psychology, Amsterdam, North Holland.
— (1986a) 'Explanations for immigration to, and emigration from Britain', *New Community*. (in press)
— (1986b) 'Economic locus of control', *Human Relations*, 39, 29–43.
— and Alibhai, N. (1985a) 'The friendship networks of foreign students', *International Journal of Psychology*, 20, 709–22.
— and Alibhai, N. (1985b) 'Value differences in foreign students', *International Journal of Intercultural Relations*, 9, 365–75.
— and Bochner, S. (1982) 'Social difficulty in a foreign culture: an empirical analysis of culture shock', in Bochner, S. (ed.), *Cultures in Contact: Studies in Cross-cultural Interaction*, Oxford, Pergamon.
— and Henry, J. (1980) 'Cross-cultural locus of control studies: experiment and critique', *Psychological Reports*, 47, 23–9.
— and Trezise, L. (1981) 'The mental health of foreign students', *Social Science and Medicine*, 17, 365–70.
— King, J. and Pendleton, D. (1980) 'Establishing rapport: interaction skills and occupational therapy', *British Journal of Occupational Therapy*, 43, 322–5.

Gallimore, R., Boggs, J. W. and Jordan, C. (1974) *Culture, Behavior and Education: A Study of Hawaiian-Americans*, Beverly Hills, Calif., Sage.
Garza-Guerrero, A. C. (1974) 'Culture shock: its mourning and the vicissitudes of identity', *Journal of the American Psychoanalytic Association*, 22, 408–29.
Gish, D. (1983) 'Sources of missionary stress', *Journal of Psychology and Theology*, 11, 243–50.
Gordon, M. M. (1964) *Assimilation in American Life*, London, Oxford University Press.
Gudykunst, W. B. (1983) 'Toward a typology of stranger–host relationships', *International Journal of Intercultural Relations*, 7, 401–13.
Gullahorn, J. T. and Gullahorn, J. E. (1963) 'An extension of the U-curve hypothesis', *Journal of Social Issues*, 19 (3), 33–47.
Gunn, A. (1970) *The Privileged Adolescent*, Aylesbury, Medical and Technical Publications.
— (1979) 'National health problems in student care', *Journal of the American College Health Association*, 27, 322–3.
Gupta, Y. (1977) 'The educational and vocational aspirations of Asian immigrant and English school-leavers: a comparative study', *British Journal of Sociology*, 28, 199–225.
Guthrie, G. M. (1966) 'Cultural preparation for the Philippines', in Textor, R. B. (ed.), *Cultural Frontiers of the Peace Corps*, Cambridge, Mass., MIT Press.
— (1975) 'A behavioral analysis of culture learning', in Brislin, R. W., Bochner, S. and Lonner, W. J. (eds), *Cross-cultural Perspectives on Learning*, New York, Wiley.

266   *Culture Shock*

— (1981) 'What you need is continuity', in Bochner, S. (ed.), *The Mediating Person: Bridges between Cultures*, Boston, Schenkman.
— and Zektick, I. N. (1967) 'Predicting performance in the Peace Corps', *Journal of Social Psychology*, 71, 11–21.

Hall, E. T. (1959) *The Silent Language*, Garden City, NY, Doubleday.
— (1966) *The Hidden Dimension*, Garden City, NY, Doubleday.
Hall, J. and Beil-Warner, D. (1978) 'Assertiveness of male Anglo- and Mexican-American college students', *Journal of Social Psychology*, 105, 175–8.
Hammer, M. (1981) 'Social supports, social networks and schizophrenia', *Schizophrenia Bulletin*, 7, 45–57.
Harding, R. K. and Looney, J. G. (1977) 'Problems of Southeast Asian children in a refugee camp', *American Journal of Psychiatry*, 134, 407–11.
Harris, J. G., Jr. (1973) 'A science of the South Pacific: analysis of the character structure of the Peace Corps Volunteer', *American Psychologist*, 28, 232–47.
Hartley, E. L. and Thompson, R. (1967) 'Racial integration and role differentiation', *Journal of the Polynesian Society*, 76, 427–43.
Hashmi, F. (1968) 'Community psychiatric problems among Birmingham immigrants', *British Journal of Social Psychiatry*, 2, 196–201.
Hays, R. D. (1972) 'Behavioral issues in multinational operations', in Hays, R. D. (ed.), *International Business: An Introduction to the World of the Multinational Firm*, Englewood Cliffs, NJ, Prentice Hall.
Heider, F. (1958) *The Psychology of Interpersonal Relations*, New York, Wiley.
Heiss, J. (1963) 'Sources of satisfaction and assimilation among Italian immigrants', *Human Relations*, 17, 165–77.
— and Nash, D. (1967) 'The stranger in laboratory culture revisited', *Human Organization*, 26, 47–51.
Helson, H. (1964) *Adaptation-Level Theory*, New York, Harper & Row.
Hemsi, L. K. (1967) 'Psychiatric morbidity of West Indian immigrants', *Social Psychiatry*, 2, 95–100.
Henderson, S. (1984) 'Interpreting the evidence on social support', *Social Psychiatry*, 19, 1–4.
— and Byrne, D. G. (1977) 'Towards a method for assessing social support systems', *Mental Health and Society*, 4, 164–70.
— Byrne, D. G., Duncan-Jones, P., Adcock, S., Scott, R. and Steele, G. P. (1978) 'Social bonds in the epidemiology of neurosis: a preliminary communication', *British Journal of Psychiatry*, 132, 463–6.
Hendrie, J. C., Lachan, D. and Lennox, K. (1975) 'Personality trait and symptom correlates of life change in a psychiatric population', *Journal of Psychosomatic Research*, 19, 203–8.
Hertz, D. G. (1981) 'The stress of migration: adjustment reactions of

migrants and their families', in Eitinger, L. and Schwarz, D. (eds), *Strangers in the World*, Bern, Hans Huber.

Higginbotham, H. H. (1979) 'Culture and mental health services', in Marsella, A. J., Tharp, R. G. and Ciborowski, T. J. (eds), *Perspectives on Cross-Cultural Psychology*, New York, Academic Press.

Hinkle, L. (1974) 'The effect of exposure to culture change, social change and changes in interpersonal relationships on health', in Dohrenwend, B. S., and Dohrenwend, B. P., (eds), *Stressful Life Events: Their Nature and Effects*, New York, Wiley.

Hirsch, B. J. (1979) 'Psychological dimensions of social networks: a multimethod analysis', *American Journal of Community Psychology*, 8, 159–72.

Hitch, P. J. and Clegg, P. (1980) 'Modes of referral of overseas immigrants and native-born first admissions to psychiatric hospitals', *Social Science and Medicine*, 14, 369–74.

— and Rack, P. A. (1980) 'Mental illness among Polish and Russian refugees in Bradford', *British Journal of Psychiatry*, 137, 206–11.

Hofstede, G. (1984) *Culture's Consequences: International Differences in Work-Related Values*, Beverly Hills, Calif., Sage.

Holahan, C. J., Betak, J. F., Spearly, J. L. and Chance, B. J. (1983) 'Social integration and mental health in a biracial community', *American Journal of Community Psychology*, 11, 301–11.

— and Moos, R. H. (1981) 'Social support and psychological distress: a longitudinal analysis', *Journal of Abnormal Psychology*, 90, 365–70.

— and Moos, R. H. (1982) 'Social support and adjustment: predictive benefits of social climate indices', *American Journal of Community Psychology*, 10, 403–14.

— and Moos, R. H. (1983) 'The quality of social support: measures of family and work relationships', *British Journal of Clinical Psychology*, 22, 157–62.

Holmes, T. H. and Masuda, M. (1974) 'Life change and illness susceptibility', in Dohrenwend, B. S. and Dohrenwend, B. P. (eds), *Stressful Life Events: Their Nature and Effects*, New York, Wiley.

— and Rahe, R. H. (1967) 'The social readjustment rating scale', *Journal of Psychosomatic Research*, 11, 213–18.

Hopkins, J., Malleson, N. and Sarnoff, I. (1957) 'Some non–intellectual correlates of success and failure among university students', *British Journal of Sociology*, 9, 25–36.

House, J. S. (1981) *Work Stress and Social Support*, Reading, Mass., Addison-Wesley.

Huang, K. (1977) 'Campus mental health: the foreigner at your desk', *Journal of the American College Health Association*, 25, 216–19.

Hui, C. H. (1982) 'Locus of control: a review of cross-cultural research', *International Journal of Intercultural Relations*, 6, 301–23.

— and Triandis, H. C. (1983) 'Multi-strategy approach to cross-cultural research: the case of locus of control', *Journal of Cross-Cultural Psychology*, 13, 65–83.

Hurst, M. W. (1979) 'Life changes and psychiatric symptom development: issues of content, scoring and clustering', in Barrett, J. E. (ed.), *Stress and Mental Disorder*, New York, Raven.

Inkeles, A. (1975) 'Becoming modern: individual change in six developing countries', *Ethos*, 3, 323–42.

Jacobson, E. H. (1963) 'Sojourn research: a definition of the field', *Journal of Social Issues*, 19 (3), 123–9.

Jaspars, J. and Hewstone, M. (1982) 'Cross-cultural interaction, social attribution and inter-group relations', in Bochner, S. (ed.), *Cultures in Contact: Studies in Cross-Cultural Interaction*, Oxford, Pergamon.

Jenkins, H. M. and Associates (1983) *Educating Students from Other Nations*. San Francisco, Jossey-Bass.

Jensen, A. R. (1969) 'How much can we boost IQ and scholastic achievement?' *Harvard Educational Review*, 39, 1–123.

Jones, E. E. (1964) *Ingratiation: A Social Psychological Analysis*, New York, Appleton-Century-Crofts.

Jones, S. E. (1971) 'A comparative proxemics analysis of dyadic interaction in selected subcultures of New York City', *Journal of Social Psychology*, 84, 35–44.

Jordan, C. and Tharp, R. G. (1979) 'Culture and education', in Marsella, A. J., Tharp, R. G. and Ciborowski, T. J. (eds), *Perspectives on Cross-cultural Psychology*, New York, Academic Press.

Kahn, R. L. and Antonucci, T. (1980) 'Convoys over the life cycle: attachment roles and social support', in Baltes, P. B. and Brim, O. (eds), *Lifespan Development and Behavior*, Boston, Lexington, vol. 3.

Kalin, R. and Berry, J. W. (1980) 'Geographic mobility and ethnic tolerance', *Journal of Social Psychology*, 112, 129–34.

Kapur, R., Kapur, M. and Carstairs, G. (1974) 'Indian psychiatric survey schedule', *Social Psychiatry*, 9, 61–76.

Katz, P. A. (ed.) (1976) *Towards the Elimination of Racism*, New York, Pergamon.

Kearney, G. E. and McElwain, D. W. (eds) (1976) *Aboriginal Cognition: Retrospect and Prospect*, Canberra, Australian Institute of Aboriginal Studies.

Kelman, H. C. (1958) 'Compliance, identification, and internalization: three processes of attitude change', *Journal of Conflict Resolution*, 2, 51–60.

Kelvin, R. P., Lucas, C. J. and Ojha, A. B. (1965) 'The relation between personality, mental health and academic performance in university students', *British Journal of Social and Clinical Psychology*, 4, 244–53.

Kidd, C. B. (1965) 'Psychiatric morbidity amongst students', *British Journal of Preventive and Social Medicine*, 19, 5–9.

Kiev, A. (1965) 'Psychiatric morbidity of West Indian immigrants in an urban group practice', *British Journal of Psychiatry*, 111, 51–6.

Kikuchi, A. and Gordon, L. (1966) 'Evaluation and cross-cultural application of a Japanese form of the survey of interpersonal values', *Journal of Social Psychology*, 69, 189–95.

Kim, Y. (1977) 'Communication patterns of foreign immigrants in the process of acculturation', *Human Communications Research*, 4, 66–77.

Kinzie, J. D. (1981) 'Evaluation and psychotherapy of Indochinese refugee patients', *American Journal of Psychotherapy*, 35, 251–61.

— Tran, K. A., Breckenridge, A. and Bloom, J. D. (1980) 'An Indochinese refugee psychiatric clinic: culturally accepted treatment approaches', *American Journal of Psychiatry*, 137, 1429–32.

Klineberg, O. (1971) 'Black and white in international perspective', *American Psychologist*, 26, 119–28.

— (1976) *International Educational Exchange: An Assessment of Its Nature and Prospects*, Paris, Mouton.

— (1981) 'The role of international university exchanges', in Bochner, S. (ed.), *The Mediating Person: Bridges between Cultures*, Boston, Schenkman.

— (1982) 'Contact between ethnic groups: a historical perspective of some aspects of theory and research', in Bochner, S. (ed.), *Cultures in Contact: Studies in Cross-cultural Interaction*, Oxford, Pergamon.

— and Hull, W. F. (1979) *At a Foreign University: An International Study of Adaptation and Coping*, New York, Praeger.

Kosa, J. (1957) *Land of Choice*, Toronto, University of Toronto Press.

Krau, E. (1982) 'The vocational side of a new start in life: a career model of immigrants', *Journal of Vocational Behaviour*, 20, 313–30.

Kraus, J. (1969) 'Some social factors and the rates of psychiatric hospital admissions of immigrants in New South Wales', *Medical Journal of Australia*, 56, 17–19.

Krause, N. and Carr, L. G. (1976) 'The effects of response bias in the survey assessment of the mental health of Puerto Rican migrants', *Social Psychiatry*, 13, 167–73.

Krause, N. and Hoelter, J. W. (1983) 'Race comparisons on Rotter's I–E scale: difference in locus of control or in concept being measured?', *Quality and Quantity*, 17, 225–37.

— and Stryker, S. (1984) 'Stress and well-being: the buffering role of locus of control beliefs', *Social Science and Medicine*, 18, 783–90.

Krech, D., Crutchfield, R. S. and Ballachey, E. L. (1962) *Individual in Society*, New York, McGraw-Hill.

Krupinski, J. (1975) 'Psychological maladaptation in ethnic concentrations in Victoria, Australia', in Pilowsky, I. (ed.), *Cultures in Collision*, Adelaide, Australian National Association for Mental Health.

— (1984a) 'Changing patterns of migration to Australia and their influence on the mental health of migrants', *Social Science and Medicine*, 18, 927–37.

— (1985) 'On the relationship between expectation and adaptation', personal communication.

— and Stoller, A. (1965) 'Incidence of mental disorders in Victoria, Australia, according to country of birth', *Medical Journal of Australia*, 52, 265–9.

— — (1971) *Health of a Metropolis: Health and Social Survey of a Melbourne Metropolitan Area*, Melbourne, Heinemann.

— Schaechter, F. and Cade, J. F. J. (1965) 'Factors influencing the incidence of mental disorders among migrants', *Medical Journal of Australia*, 7, 269–77.

— Stoller, A. and Wallace, L. (1973) 'Psychiatric disorders in Eastern European refugees now in Australia', *Social Science and Medicine*, 7, 31–50.

Kubler-Ross, E. (ed.) (1975) *Death: The Final Stage of Growth*, Englewood, NJ, Prentice-Hall.

Kumar, K. (ed.) (1979) *Bonds without Bondage: Explorations in Transcultural Interactions*, Honolulu, University Press of Hawaii.

Kuo, W. (1976) 'Theories of migration and mental health: an empirical testing on Chinese-Americans', *Social Science and Medicine*, 10, 297–306.

— Gray, R. and Lin, N. (1976) 'Locus of control and symptoms of psychological distress among Chinese-Americans', *International Journal of Social Psychiatry*, 22, 176–87.

L'Abate, L. and Milan, M. (eds) (1985) *Handbook of Social Skills Training and Research*, New York, Wiley.

LaFromboise, T. D. and Rowe, W. (1983) 'Skills training for bicultural competence: rationale and application', *Journal of Counselling Psychology*, 30, 589–95.

Lambert, R. D. (1966) 'Some minor pathologies in the American presence in India', *Annals of the American Academy of Political and Social Science*, 368, 157–70.

— and Bressler, M. (1956) *Indian Students on an American Campus*, Minneapolis, University of Minnesota Press.

Lambo, T. (1960) *A Report on the Study of Social and Health Problems of Nigerian Students in Britain and Ireland*, Nigerian Government Printer.

Langer, T. S. and Michael, S. T. (1963) *Life Stresses and Mental Health: The Midtown Study*, Glencoe, Ill., Free Press.

Lansing, J. B. and Mueller, E. (1967) *The Geographic Mobility of Labor*, Ann Arbor, University of Michigan.

Lasry, J. C. (1977) 'Cross-cultural perspective on mental health and immigrant adaptation', *Social Psychiatry*, 12, 49–55.

Leavy, R. L. (1983) 'Social support and psychological disorder: a review', *Journal of Community Psychology*, 11, 3–21.
— (1983) 'Social support and compliance: a selective review and critique of treatment integrity and outcome measurement', *Social Science and Medicine*, 17, 1329–35.
Leff, J. (1977) 'The cross-cultural study of emotions', *Culture, Medicine and Psychiatry*, 1, 317–50.
Lesser, S. O. and Peter, H. W. (1957) 'Training foreign nationals in the United States', in Likert, R. and Hayes, S. P. (eds), *Some Applications of Behavioural Research*, Paris, UNESCO.
LeVine, R. and Campbell, D. T. (1972) *Ethnocentrism*, New York, Wiley.
— and Bartlett, K. (1984) 'Pace of life, punctuality and coronary heart disease in six countries', *Journal of Cross-Cultural Psychology*, 15, 233–55.
— West, L. J. and Reis, H. T. (1980) 'Perceptions of time and punctuality in the United States and Brazil', *Journal of Personality and Social Psychology*, 38, 541–50.
Lewin, K. (1941) 'Self-hatred among Jews', *Contemporary Jewish Record*, 4, 219–32.
Lewinsohn, P., Sullivan, M. and Grosscup, S. (1980) 'Changing reinforcement events: an approach to the treatment of depression', *Psychotherapy: Theory, Research and Practice*, 17, 332–34.
Liem, N. D. (1980) 'Vietnamese-American crosscultural communication', *Bilingual Resonances*, 3 (2), 9–15.
Lin, K., Tazuma, L. and Masuda, M. (1979) 'Adaptational problems of Vietnamese refugees: I. Health and mental status', *Archives of General Psychiatry*, 36, 955–61.
Lin, L. and Ensel, W. M. (1984) 'Repression-mobility and its social ecology: the role of life events and social support', *Journal of Health and Social Behaviour*, 25, 176–88.
— Simeone, R. S., Ensel, W. M. and Kuo, W. (1979) 'Social support, stressful life events and illness: a model and an empirical test', *Journal of Health and Social Behaviour*, 20, 108–19.
Lindemann, E. (1944) 'Symptomatology and management of acute grief', *American Journal of Psychiatry*, 101, 141–8.
Lipset, S. (1963) 'The value patterns of democracy: a case study in comparative analysis', *American Sociological Review*, 28, 515–91.
Littlewood, R. and Lipsedge, M. (1982) *Aliens and Alienists: Ethnic Minorities and Psychiatry*, Harmondsworth, Penguin.
Lucas, C. J., Kelvin, R. P. and Ojha, A. B. (1966) 'Mental health and student wastage', *British Journal of Psychiatry*, 112, 277–84.
Lundstedt, S. (1963) 'An introduction to some evolving problems in cross-cultural research', *Journal of Social Issues*, 19 (3), 1–9.
Lysgaard, S. (1955) 'Adjustment in a foreign society: Norwegian

Fulbright grantees visiting the United States', *International Social Science Bulletin*, 7, 45–51.

Machlis, G. E. and Burch, W. R., Jr. (1983) 'Relations between strangers: cycles of structure and meaning in tourist systems', *Sociological Review*, 31, 666–92.

McKenzie, I. K. (1984) 'Psychology and police education: a reply to Taylor', *Bulletin of the British Psychological Society*, 37, 145–7.

Malleson, N. (1954) 'The mental health of students', in Malleson, N. (ed.), *Health at the University*, Paris, International University Bureau.

Malzberg, B. (1936) 'Mental disease among native and foreign-born whites in New York State', *American Journal of Psychiatry*, 93, 127–37.

— (1940) *Social and Biological Aspects of Mental Disease*, New York, State Hospital Press.

— (1955) 'Mental disease among native and foreign-born white populations of New York State, 1933–1941', *Mental Hygiene*, 34, 545–61.

— (1962) 'Migration and mental disease among the white population of New York State, 1949–1951', *Human Biology*, 39, 89–98.

— (1964) *Internal Migration and Mental Disease in Canada, 1950–1952*, Albany, NY, Research Foundation for Mental Hygiene.

— (1968) *Migration in Relation to Mental Disease*, Albany, NY, Research Foundation for Mental Hygiene.

— (1969) 'Are immigrants psychologically disturbed?', in Plog, S. C. and Edgerton, R. B. (eds), *Changing Perspectives in Mental Illness*, New York, Holt, Rinehart & Winston.

— and Lee, E. (1956) *Migration and Mental Disease*, New York, Social Science Research Council.

Mann, J. (1973) 'Status: the marginal reaction – Mixed-Bloods and Jews', in Watson, P. (ed.), *Psychology and Race*, Harmondsworth, Penguin.

Mann, L. (1969) *Social Psychology*, Sydney, Wiley.

Marsella, A. J. (1979) 'Cross-cultural studies of mental disorders', in Marsella, A. J., Tharp, R. G. and Ciborowski, T. J. (eds), *Perspectives on Cross-cultural Psychology*, New York, Academic Press.

Maslow, A. (1966) *The Psychology of Science*, New York, Harper & Row.

Masuda, M., Lin, K. and Tazuma, L. (1980) 'Adaptation problems of Vietnamese refugees: II. Life changes and perception of life events', *Archives of General Psychiatry*, 37, 447–50.

May, R. (1970) 'The nature of anxiety and its relation to fear', in Elbing, A. O. (ed.), *Behavioral Decisions in Organizations*, New York, Scott, Foresman & Co.

Mechanic, D. (1974) 'Social structure and personal adaptation: some neglected dimensions', in Coelho, G. V., Hamburg, D. A., and Adams, J. E. (eds), *Coping and Adaptation*. New York, Basic Books.

— and Greenley, J. R. (1976) 'The prevalence of psychological distress and help-seeking in a college student population', *Social Psychiatry*, 11, 1–10.

Mehrabian, D. (1972) *Nonverbal Communication*, Chicago, Aldine.

Merton, R. (1938) 'Social structure and anomie', *American Sociological Review*, 3, 672–82.

Mischel, W. (1973) 'Toward a cognitive social learning reconceptualization of personality', *Psychological Review*, 80, 252–83.

— (1984) 'Convergences and challenges in the search for consistency', *American Psychologist*, 39, 351–64.

Mitchell, I. S. (1968) 'Epilogue to a referendum', *Australian Journal of Social Issues*, 3 (4), 9–12.

Monroe, S. M. (1982) 'Life events and disorder: event–symptom associations and the course of disorder', *Journal of Abnormal Psychology*, 91, 14–24.

— (1983) 'Social support and disorder: toward an untangling of cause and effect', *American Journal of Community Psychology*, 11, 81–97.

— Imhoff, D. F., Wise, B. D. and Harris, J. E. (1983) 'Prediction of psychological symptoms under high-risk psychosocial circumstances: life events, social support and symptom specificity', *Journal of Abormal Psychology*, 92, 338–50.

Morgan, P. and Andrushko, E. (1977) 'The use of diagnosis-specific rates of mental hospitalization to estimate underutilization by immigrants', *Social Science and Medicine*, 11, 611–18.

Morris, D., Collett, P., Marsh, P. and O'Shaughnessy, M. (1979) *Gestures: Their Origins and Distribution*, London, Jonathan Cape.

Morris, R. T. (1960) *The Two-Way Mirror*, Minneapolis, University of Minnesota Press.

Morrison, S. D. (1973) 'Intermediate variables in the association between migration and mental illness', *International Journal of Social Psychiatry*, 19, 60–5.

Mortimer, R. (1973) 'Aiding the "underdeveloped" countries', *Australia's Neighbours*, 4 (85), 1–5.

Muhlin, G. (1979) 'Mental hospitalization of the foreign-born and the role of cultural isolation', *International Journal of Social Psychiatry*, 28, 258–67.

Munoz, L. (1980) 'Exile as bereavement: socio-psychological manifestations of Chilean exiles in Great Britain', *British Journal of Medical Psychology*, 53, 227–32.

Murphy, H. B. M. (1961) 'Social change and mental health', in Murphy, H. B. M. (ed.), *Causes of Mental Disorder: A Review of Epidemiological Knowledge*, New York, Milbank Memorial Foundation.

— (1965) 'Migration and the major mental disorders: a reappraisal', in Kantor, M. B. (ed.), *Mobility and Mental Health,* Springfield, Ill., C. C. Thomas.

— (1973) 'Migration and the major mental disorders: a reappraisal', in

Zwingmann, C. A. and Pfister-Ammende, M. (eds), *Uprooting and After*, New York, Springer Verlag.
— (1977) 'Migration, culture and mental health', *Psychological Medicine*, 7, 677–84.

Naamary, S. N. (1971) 'Attitude towards migration among rural residents: stages and factors involved in the decision to migrate', unpublished doctoral dissertation, University of Kentucky.
Nash, D. (1967) 'The fact of Americans in a Spanish setting: a study of adaptation', *Human Organization*, 26 (3).
— and Wolfe, A. (1957) 'The stranger in laboratory culture', *American Sociological Review*, 22, 149–67.
Nathanson, C. (1980) 'Social roles and health status among women: the significance of employment', *Social Science and Medicine*, 14A, 463–71.
Nehru, J. (1936) *An Autobiography*, London, Bodley Head (reprinted 1958).
Nelson, D. W. and Cohen, L. H. (1983) 'Locus of control and control perceptions and the relationship between life stress and psychological disorder', *American Journal of Community Psychology*, 11, 705–22.
Newcomb, T. M. (1956) 'The prediction of interpersonal attraction', *American Psychologist*, 11, 575–86.
Ng, S. H., Hossain, A. B. M., Ball, P., Bond, M., Hayashi, K., Lim, S., O'Driscoll, M., Sinha, D. and Yang, K. (1982) 'Human values in nine countries', in Rath, R., Asthara, H. S., Sinha, D. and Sinha, J. B. H. (eds), *Diversity and Unity in Cross-cultural Psychology*, Lisse, Swets & Zeitlinger.
Nicassio, P. M. (1983) 'Psychosocial correlates of alienation: study of a sample of Indochinese refugees', *Journal of Cross-cultural Psychology*, 337–51.
— (1985) 'The psychosocial adjustment of the Southeast Asian refugee: an overview of empirical findings and theoretical models, *Journal of Cross-cultural Psychology*, 16, 153–73.
— and Pate, J. K. (1984) 'An analysis of problems of resettlement of the Indochinese refugees in the United States', *Social Psychiatry*, 19, 135–41.
Noesjirwan, J. (1978) 'A rule-based analysis of cultural differences in social behaviour: Indonesia and Australia', *International Journal of Psychology*, 13, 305–16.
Norman, B. (1974) 'Suicide rates in Sweden', unpublished paper.
Noudehou, A. (1982) 'Déracinés avant d'être partis', *Journal de Genève*, 213–15.

Oberg, K. (1960) 'Cultural shock: adjustment to new cultural environ-ments', *Practical Anthropology*, 7, 177–82.
O'Cuneen, P. J. (1984) 'Culture shock and coping strategies in short-

term multiple sojourners', BSc. dissertation, University of Zimbabwe.

Ødegaard, O. (1932) 'Emigration and insanity', *Acta Psychiatrica et Neurologica*, supplement 4.

— (1945) 'The distribution of mental diseases in Norway', *Acta Psychiatrica et Neurologica*, 20, 247–84.

O'Neil, M. K., Lance, W. J. and Freeman, S. J. (1984) 'Help-seeking behaviour of depressed students', *Social Science and Medicine*, 18, 511–14.

Packard, V. (1972) *A Nation of Strangers*, New York, McKay.

Padesky, C. A. and Hammen, C. L. (1981) 'Sex differences in depressive symptom expression and help-seeking among college students', *Sex Roles*, 7, 309–17.

Park, R. E. (1928) 'Human migration and the marginal man', *American Journal of Sociology*, 33, 881–93.

Parker, F. (1965) 'Government policy and international education: a selected and partially annotated bibliography', in Fraser, S. (ed.), *Government Policy and International Education*, New York, Wiley.

Parker, S. and Kleiner, R. (1966) *Mental Illness in the Urban Negro Community*, Glencoe, Free Press.

— Kleiner, R. and Needelman, B. (1969) 'Migration and mental illness: some reconsiderations and suggestions for further analysis', *Social Science and Medicine*, 3, 1–9.

Parkes, C. M. (1965) 'Bereavement and mental illness', *British Journal of Medical Psychology*, 36, 1–11.

— (1975) *Bereavement: Studies of Grief in Adult Life*, Harmondsworth, Penguin.

Pearce, P. L. (1981) ' "Environmental shock": a study of tourists' reactions to two tropical islands', *Journal of Applied Social Psychology*, 11, 268–80.

— (1982a) *The Social Psychology of Tourist Behaviour*, Oxford, Pergamon.

— (1982b) 'Tourists and their hosts: some social and psychological effects of inter-cultural contact', in Bochner, S. (ed.), *Cultures in Contact: Studies in Cross-cultural Interaction*, Oxford, Pergamon.

— and Caltabiano, N. J. (1982) 'Gesture decoding and encoding in children: the effects of ethnicity, age and sex', *Australian Journal of Psychology*, 34, 17–24.

Pedersen, P., Lonner, W. J. and Draguns, J. G. (eds) (1976) *Counseling across Cultures*, Honolulu, University Press of Hawaii.

Pelto, P. J. (1968) 'The difference between "tight" and "loose" societies', *Transaction*, 5, 37–40.

Penalosa, F. (1971) 'Post-migration experiences and assimilation of Latin Americans in Israel', *Jewish Social Studies*, 33, 165–71.

Peterson, W. (1958) 'A general typology of migration', *American Sociological Review*, 23, 260–76.

Pettigrew, T. F. (1964) *A Profile of the Negro American*, Princeton, NJ, D. Van Nostrand.

— (1969) 'Racially separate or together?' *Journal of Social Issues*, 25 (1), 43–69.

Phillips, S. L. (1981) 'Network characteristics related to the well-being of normals: a comparative base', *Schizophrenia Bulletin*, 7, 117–24.

Pope, H. G. (1983) 'Migration and manic–depressive illness', *Comprehensive Psychiatry*, 24, 158–65.

Porritt, D. (1979) 'Social support in crises: quantity or quality?' *Social Science and Medicine*, 13, 715–21.

Price, C. A. (1966) *Australian Immigration: A Bibliography and Digest*, Canberra, Australian National University Press.

— (ed.) (1970) 'Australian immigration: a bibliography and digest. No. 2', Canberra, Australian National University, Department of Demography.

Price, G. (1913), 'Discussion on the causes of invaliding from the tropics', *British Medical Journal*, 2, 1290–7.

Prokop, H. (1970) 'Psychiatric illness of foreigners vacationing in Innsbruck', *Neurochirugie und Psychiatrie*, 107, 363–8.

Rack, P. (1982) *Race, Culture and Mental Disorder*, London, Tavistock.

Rahe, R. H., Looney, J. G., Ward, H. W., Tung, T. M. and Liu, W. T. (1978) 'Psychiatric consultation in a Vietnamese refugee camp', *American Journal of Psychiatry*, 135, 185–90.

— McKean, J. D. and Arthur, R. J. (1967) 'A longitudinal study of life-change and illness patterns', *Journal of Psychosomatic Research*, 10, 355–66.

— Meyer, M., Smith, M., Kjaer, G. and Holmes, T. H. (1964) 'Social stress and illness onset', *Journal of Psychosomatic Research*, 8, 35–44.

Reich, J. W. and Zantra, A. (1981) 'Life events and personal causation: some relationships with satisfaction and distress', *Journal of Personality and Social Psychology*, 41, 1002–12.

Reverson, T. A., Wollman, C. A. and Felton, B. (1983) 'Social supports as stress buffers for adult cancer patients', *Psychosomatic Medicine*, 45, 321–31.

Richardson, A. (1974) *British Immigrants and Australia: A Psycho-social Inquiry*. Canberra, Australian National University Press.

Rim, Y. (1970) 'Values and attitudes', *Personality*, 1, 243–50.

Ritchie, J. E. (1981) 'Tama tu, tama ora: mediating styles in Maori culture', in Bochner, S. (ed.), *The Mediating Person: Bridges between Cultures*, Cambridge, Mass., Schenkman.

Roberts, C. R., Roberts, R. E. and Stevenson, J. M. (1982) 'Women, work, social support and psychiatric morbidity', *Social Psychiatry*, 17, 167–73.

Roberts, R. E. (1980) 'Prevalence of psychological distress among

Mexican Americans', *Journal of Health and Social Behaviour*, 21, 134–45.

Robertson, A. and Cochrane, R. (1976) 'Attempted suicide and cultural change: an empirical investigation', *Human Relations*, 9, 863–83.

Robertson, J. W. (1903) 'Prevalence of insanity in California', *American Journal of Insanity*, 60, 81–2.

Rokeach, M. (1961) 'Belief versus race as determinants of social distance: comment on Triandis' paper', *Journal of Abnormal and Social Psychology*, 62, 187–8.

— (1973) *The Nature of Human Values*, New York, Free Press.

— and Parker, S. (1970) 'Values as social indicators of poverty and race relations in America', *Annals of the American Academy of Political and Social Science*, 388, 97–111.

Rook, P. (1954) 'Student suicides', *British Medical Journal*, 1, 599–603.

Rose, E. and Felton, W. (1955) 'Experimental histories of culture', *American Sociological Review*, 20, 383–92.

Rosenthal, D. A. (1984) 'Intergenerational conflict and culture: a study of immigrant and nonimmigrant adolescents and their parents', *Genetic Psychology Monographs*, 109, 53–75.

— Moore, S. M. and Taylor, M. J. (1983) 'Ethnicity and adjustment: a study of the self-image of Anglo-, Greek- and Italian-Australian working-class adolescents', *Journal of Youth and Adolescence*, 12, 117–35.

Ross, C. E. and Mirowsky, J. (1984) 'Socially desirable response and acquiescence in a cross-cultural survey of mental health', *Journal of Health and Social Behaviour*, 25, 189–97.

— Mirowsky, J. and Cockesham, W. C. (1983) 'Social class, American culture and fatalism: their effects on psychological distress', *American Journal of Community Psychology*, 11, 383–98.

Rossi, P. (1955) 'Why families move', in Lazarsfeld, L. and Rosenberg, M. (eds), *The Language of Social Research*, Glencoe, Free Press.

Rotter, J. B. (1966) 'Generalized expectancies for internal versus external control of reinforcement', *Psychological Monographs*, 80 (whole no. 609).

Ruse, R. (1960) 'Epidemiology of mental health in college', *Journal of Psychology*, 49, 235–48.

Rust, R. (1960) 'Epidemiology of mental health in college', *Journal of Psychology*, 49, 235–48.

Rutter, M., Yule, W., Berger, M., Yule, B., Morton, J. and Bagley, C. (1974) 'Children of West Indian immigrants: I. Rates of behavioural deviance and of psychiatric disorder', *Journal of Child Psychology and Psychiatry*, 15, 241–62.

Sandler, I. N. and Lakey, B. (1982) 'Locus of control as a stress moderator: the role of control perceptions and social support',

American Journal of Community Psychology, 10, 65–80.

Sarason, I. G., de Monchaux, C. and Hunt, T. (1975) 'Methodological issues in the assessment of life stress', in Levi, L. (ed.), *Emotions: Their Parameters and Measurement*, New York, Raven.

Schaechter, F. (1965) 'Previous history of mental illness in female migrant patients admitted to the psychiatric hospital, Royal Park', *Medical Journal of Australia*, 6, 277–9.

Scherer, S. E. (1974) 'Proxemic behaviour of primary school children as a function of their socioeconomic class and subculture', *Journal of Personality and Social Psychology*, 29, 800–5.

Schild, E. O. (1962) 'The foreign student, as stranger, learning the norms of the host culture', *Journal of Social Issues*, 18 (1), 41–54.

Schwartz, A. (1980) 'Inaccuracy and uncertainty in estimates of college suicide rates', *Journal of the American College Health Association*, 28, 201–4.

Scott, F. D. (1956) *The American Experience of Swedish Students: Retrospect and Aftermath*, Minneapolis, University of Minnesota Press.

Scott, W. A. and Scott, R. (1982) 'Ethnicity, interpersonal relations, and adaptation among families of European migrants to Australia', *Australian Psychologist*, 17, 165–80.

— and Stumpf, J. (1984) 'Personal satisfaction and role performance: subjective and social aspects of adaptation', *Journal of Personality and Social Psychology*, 47, 812–27.

Seeman, M. (1959) 'On the meaning of alienation', *American Sociological Review*, 24, 783–91.

Seidel, G. (1981) 'Cross-cultural training procedures: their theoretical framework and evaluation', in Bochner, S. (ed.), *The Mediating Person: Bridges between Cultures*, Boston, Schenkman.

Seligman, M. E. P. (1975) *Helplessness: On Depression, Development and Death*, San Francisco, W. H. Freeman.

Selltiz, C. and Cook, S. W. (1962) 'Factors influencing attitudes of foreign students towards the host country', *Journal of Social Issues*, 18 (1), 7–23.

— Christ, J. R., Havel, J. and Cook, S. W. (1963) *Attitudes and Social Relations of Foreign Students in the United States*, Minneapolis, University of Minnesota Press.

Sewell, W. H. and Davidsen, O. M. (1961) *Scandinavian Students on an American Campus*, Minneapolis, University of Minnesota Press.

— Morris, R. T. and Davidsen, O. M. (1954) 'Scandinavian students' images of the United States: a study in cross-cultural education', *Annals of the American Academy of Political and Social Science*, 295, 126–35.

Sharma, S. M. (1984) 'Assimilation of Indian immigrant adolescents in British society', *Journal of Psychology*, 118, 79–84.

Shaw, M. E. and Costanzo, P. R. (1970) *Theories of Social Psychology*, New York, McGraw Hill.

Shaw, R. P. (1975) *Migration Theory and Fact: A Review and Bibliography of Current Literature*, Philadelphia, Regional Sciences Research Institute.

Sherif, M. (1970) *Group Conflict and Co-operation: Their Social Psychology*, London, Routledge & Kegan Paul.

Shields, J. J. (1968) 'A selected bibliography', in Scanlon, D. G. and Shields, J. J. (eds), *Problems and Prospects in International Education*, New York, Teachers College Press.

Shimoda, K., Argyle, M. and Ricci Bitti, P. (1978) 'The intercultural recognition of emotional expression by three national groups – English, Italian and Japanese', *European Journal of Social Psychology*, 8, 169–79.

Shumaker, S. and Stokols, D. (1982) 'Residential mobility as a social issue and research topic', *Journal of Social Issues*, 38, 1–19.

Sillitoe, A. (1973) *Britain in Figures: A Handbook of Social Statistics*, Harmondsworth, Penguin.

Singh, A. K. (1963) *Indian Students in Britain*, Bombay, Asia Publishing House.

Skinner, W. (1968) *American Industry in Developing Economies: The Management of International Manufacturing*, New York, Wiley.

Smalley, W. (1963) 'Culture shock, language shock, and the shock of self-discovery', *Practical Anthropology*, 10, 49–56.

Smith, C. R. (1975) 'Bereavement: the contribution of phenomenological and existential analysis to a greater understanding of the problem', *British Journal of Social Work*, 5, 75–92.

Smith, M. B. (1966) 'Explorations in competence: a study of Peace Corps teachers in Ghana', *American Psychologist*, 21, 555–66.

Smith, R. E., Johnson, J. H. and Sarason, I. G. (1978) 'Life change, the sensation seeking motive, and psychological distress', *Journal of Consulting and Clinical Psychology*, 46, 348–9.

Smither, R. and Rodriguez-Giegling, M. (1969) 'Marginality, modernity, and anxiety in Indochinese refugees', *Journal of Cross-Cultural Psychology*, 10, 469–78.

Sommer, R. (1969) *Personal Space: The Behavioural Basis of Design*, Englewood Cliffs, NJ, Prentice-Hall.

Spence, S. (1980) *Social Skills Training with Children and Adolescents: A Counsellor's Manual*, Windsor, NFER.

Steinkalk, E. and Taft, R. (1979) 'The effect of a planned intercultural experience on the attitudes and behaviour of the participants', *International Journal of Intercultural Relations*, 3, 187–98.

Stevens, F. S. (ed.) (1971) *Racism: The Australian Experience: Vol. 1, Prejudice and Xenophobia*, Sydney, Australia & New Zealand Book Company.

— (ed.) (1972) *Racism: The Australian Experience: Volume 2, Black versus White*, Sydney, Australia & New Zealand Book Company.

Still, R. (1961) 'Mental health in overseas students', *Proceedings of the British Health Association*.

Stokols, D. and Shumaker, S. (1982) 'The psychological context of residential mobility and well-being', *Journal of Social Issues*, 38, 149–71.

— Shumaker, S. A. and Martinez, J. (1983) 'Residential mobility and personal well-being', *Journal of Environmental Psychology*, 3, 5–19.

Stoller, A. (ed.) (1966) *New Faces: Immigration and Family Life in Australia*, Melbourne, Cheshire.

— (1981) 'A migrating world: migrants and refugees, some facts, patterns and figures', in Eitinger, L. and Schwarz, D. (eds), *Strangers in the World*, Bern, Hans Huber.

— and Krupinski, J. (1973) 'Immigration to Australia: mental health aspects', in Zwingmann, C. and Pfister-Ammende, M. (eds), *Uprooting and After*, Berlin, Springer-Verlag.

Stonequist, E. V. (1937) *The Marginal Man*, New York, Scribner.

Stoner, J. A., Aram, J. D. and Rubin, J. M. (1972) 'Factors associated with effective performance in overseas work assignments', *Personnel Psychology*, 25, 303–18.

Suzuki, P. T. (1981) 'Psychological problems of Turkish migrants in West Germany', *American Journal of Psychotherapy*, 35, 187–94.

Syrotuik, J. and D'Arcy, C. (1984) 'Social support and mental health: direct, protective and compensatory effects', *Social Science and Medicine*, 18, 229–36.

Taft, R. (1961) 'The assimilation of Dutch male immigrants in a Western Australian community', *Human Relations*, 14, 265–81.

— (1963) 'The assimilation orientation of immigrants and Australians', *Human Relations*, 16, 279–93.

— (1966) *From Stranger to Citizen*, London, Tavistock.

— (1973) 'Migration: problems of adjustment and assimilation in immigrants', in Watson, P. (ed.), *Psychology and Race*, Harmondsworth, Penguin.

— (1977) 'Coping with unfamiliar cultures', in Warren, N. (ed.), *Studies in Cross-cultural Psychology*, London, Academic Press, vol. 1.

— (1981) 'The role and personality of the mediator', in Bochner, S. (ed.), *The Mediating Person: Bridges between Cultures*, Cambridge, Mass., Schenkman.

— (1985) 'The psychological study of the adjustment and adaptation of immigrants in Australia', in Feather, N. T. (ed.), *Survey of Australian Psychology: Trends in Research*, Sydney, George Allen & Unwin.

— and Doczy, A. G. (1962) 'The assimilation of intellectual refugees in Western Australia', *REMP Bulletin*, 10, 1–82.

Tajfel, H. (1970) 'Experiments in intergroup discrimination', *Scientific American*, 223 (5), 92–102.

— (1981) *Human Groups and Social Categories*, Cambridge, Cambridge University Press.

— and Dawson, J. L. (1965) (eds), *Disappointed Guests*, London, Oxford University Press.

Taylor, M. (1983) 'Psychology and police education', *Bulletin of the British Psychological Society*, 36, 406–8.

Taylor, R. C. (1966) *The Implications of Migration from the Durham Coal Fields: An Anthropological Study*, unpublished doctoral dissertation, University of Durham.

Terhune, K. W. (1964) 'Nationalism among foreign and American students: an exploratory study', *Journal of Conflict Resolution*, 8, 256–70.

Textor, R. B. (ed.) (1966) *Cultural Frontiers of the Peace Corps*, Cambridge, Mass., MIT Press.

Thoits, P. A. (1981) 'Life stress, social support, and psychological vulnerability: epidemiological considerations', *Journal of Community Psychology*, 10, 341–62.

— (1982) 'Conceptual, methodological and theoretical problems in studying social support as a buffer against life stress', *Journal of Health and Social Behaviour*, 23, 145–59.

Throssell, R. P. (1981) 'Toward a multi-cultural society: the role of government departments and officials in developing cross-cultural relations in Australia', in Bochner, S. (ed.), *The Mediating Person: Bridges between Cultures*, Cambridge, Mass., Schenkman.

Tietze, C., Lemkau, P. and Cooper, M. (1942) 'Personality disorder and spatial mobility', *American Journal of Sociology*, 48, 29–39.

Torbiorn, I. (1982) *Living Abroad: Personal Adjustment and Personnel Policy in the Overseas Setting*, Chichester, Wiley.

Trevelyan, G. M. (1947) *English Social History*, London, Longmans, Green & Co.

Trevino, F. M., Bruhn, J. G. and Burce, H. (1977) 'Utilization of community mental health services in a Texas–Mexico border city', *Social Science and Medicine*, 13, 331–4.

Triandis, H. C. (1967) 'Interpersonal relations in international organizations', *Organizational Behavior and Human Performance*, 2, 26–55.

— (1975) 'Culture training, cognitive complexity and interpersonal attitudes', in Brislin, R. W., Bochner, S. and Lonner, W. J. (eds), *Cross-cultural Perspectives on Learning*, New York, Wiley.

— and Brislin, R. W. (1984) 'Cross-cultural psychology', *American Psychologist*, 39, 1006–16.

— Vassiliou, V., Vassiliou, G., Tanaka, Y. and Shanmugam, A. V. (1972) *The Analysis of Subjective Culture*, New York, Wiley.

Trimble, J. E. (1976) 'Value differences among American Indians: concerns for the concerned counselor', in Pedersen, P. Lonner, W. J. and Draguns, J. G. (eds), *Counseling across Cultures*, Honolulu, University Press of Hawaii.

Trower, P., Bryant, B. and Argyle, M. (1978) *Social Skills and Mental Health*, London, Methuen.

Turner, J. C. and Giles, H. (1981) *Intergroup Behaviour*, Oxford, Blackwell.

Turner, R. (1949) 'Migration to a medium-sized American city: attitudes, motives, and personal characteristics revealed by an open-ended interview methodology', *Journal of Social Psychology*, 30, 229–49.

Useem, J. and Useem, R. H. (1967) 'The interfaces of a binational third culture: a study of the American community in India', *Journal of Social Issues*, 23 (1), 130–43.

— and Useem, R. H. (1968) 'American-educated Indians and Americans in India: a comparison of two modernizing roles', *Journal of Social Issues*, 24 (4), 143–58.

— Useem, R. H. and Donoghue, J. (1963) 'Men in the middle of the third culture: the roles of American and non-western people in cross-cultural administration', *Human Organization*, 22, 169–79.

— Useem, R. H. and McCarthy, F. E. (1979) 'Linkages between the scientific communities of less-developed and developed nations: a case study of the Philippines', in Kumar, K. (ed.), *Bonds without Bondage: Explorations in Transcultural Interactions*, Honolulu, University Press of Hawaii.

— Useem, R. H., Othman, A. H. and McCarthy, F. E. (1981) 'Trans-national networks and related third cultures: a comparison of two Southeast Asian scientific communities', *Research in Social Movements, Conflict and Change*, 4, 283–316.

Veroff, J. (1963) 'African students in the United States', *Journal of Social Issues*, 19, 48–60.

Vignes, A. J. and Hall, R. C. W. (1979) 'Adjustment of a group of Vietnamese people to the United States', *American Journal of Psychiatry*, 136, 442–4.

Wade, N. (1975) 'Third World: science and technology contribute feebly to development', *Science*, 189, 770–6.

Wallendorf, M. and Reilly, M. O. (1983) 'Ethnic migration, assimilation and consumption', *Journal of Consumer Research*, 10, 292–300.

Wallis, C. P. and Maliphant, R. (1972) 'Delinquent areas in the county of London', in Barron, M. J. (ed.), *Juvenile Delinquency, the Family and the Social Group*, London, Longman.

Walvin, J. (1984) *Passage to Britain*, Harmondsworth, Penguin.

Ward, L. (1967) 'Some observations of the underlying dynamics of conflict in a foreign student', *Journal of the American College Health Association*, 10, 430–40.

Watson, J. L. (ed.) (1977) *Between Two Cultures: Migrants and Minorities in Britain*, Oxford, Blackwell.

Watson, O. M. (1970) *Proxemic Behavior: A Cross-cultural Study*, The Hague, Mouton.

— and Graves, T. D. (1966) 'Quantitative research in proxemic behavior', *American Anthropologist*, 68, 971–85.

Weiner, B. (1980) *Human Motivation*, New York, Holt, Rinehart & Winston.

Welford, A. T. (1981) 'Social skill and social class', *Psychological Reports*, 48, 847–52.

Westermeyer, J., Neider, J. and Vang, T. F. (1984) 'Acculturation and mental health: a study of Hmong refugees at 1.5 and 3.5 years postmigration', *Social Science and Medicine*, 18, 87–93.

— Vang, T. F. and Neider, J. (1983) 'Refugees who do and do not seek psychiatric care: an analysis of premigratory and postmigratory characteristics', *The Journal of Nervous and Mental Disease*, 171, 86–91.

White, N. R. and White, P. B. (1983) 'Evaluating the immigrant presence: press reporting of immigrants to Australia, 1935–1977', *Ethnic and Racial Studies*, 6, 284–307.

Williams, A. W., Ware, J. E. and Donald, C. A. (1981) 'A model of mental health life events, and social supports applicable to general populations', *Journal of Health and Social Behavior*, 22, 324–36.

Williams, C. L. and Westermeyer, J. (1983) 'Psychiatric problems among adolescent Southeast Asian refugees', *The Journal of Nervous and Mental Disease*, 171, 79–84.

Willmuth, L., Weaver, L. and Donland, S. (1975) 'Utilization of medical services by transferred employees', *Archives of General Psychiatry*, 2, 182–9.

Wills, T. A. (1984) 'Supportive functions of interpersonal relationships', in Cohen, S. and Syme, L. (eds), *Social Support and Health*, New York, Academic Press.

Wilson, A. T. M. (1961) 'Recruitment and selection for work in foreign cultures', *Human Relations*, 14 (1), 3–21.

Witkin, H. A. and Berry, J. W. (1975) 'Psychological differentiation in cross-cultural perspective', *Journal of Cross-Cultural Psychology*, 6, 4–87.

Wohlwill, J. F. and Kohn, I. (1973) 'The environment as experienced by the migrant: an adaptation-level view', *Representative Research in Social Psychology*, 4, 135–64.

Wolpert, J. (1965) 'Behavioral aspects of the decision to migrate', *Regional Science Association Papers*, 15, 159–69.

Yao, E. L. (1979) 'The assimilation of contemporary Chinese immigrants', *Journal of Psychology*, 101, 107–13.

Yap, P. M. (1951) 'Mental diseases peculiar to certain cultures', *Journal of Mental Science*, 97, 313–27.

Zaidi, S. M. H. (1975) 'Adjustment problems of foreign Muslim students in Pakistan', in Brislin, R. W., Bochner, S. and Lonner, W. J. (eds), *Cross-cultural Perspectives on Learning*, New York, Wiley.

Zantra, A. and Reich, J. W. (1980) 'Positive life events and reports of well-being: some useful distinctions', *American Journal of Community Psychology*, 8, 657–70.

Zavalloni, M. (1980) 'Values', in Triandis, H. C. and Brislin, R. W., (eds), *Handbook of Cross-cultural Psychology: Vol. 5, Social Psychology*, Boston, Allyn & Bacon.

Zuckerman, M. (1981) 'Sensation seeking and psychopathy', in Hare, R. and Shalling, D. (ed.), *Psychopathic Behavior*, New York, Wiley.

Zwingmann, C. A. A. and Gunn, A. D. G. (1983) 'Uprooting and health: psycho-social problems of students from abroad', Geneva, World Health Organization, Division of Mental Health.

Name index

Adams, W. 30, 40, 114
Adler, P. S. 50, 130, 131
Aiello, J.R. 207
Aislay, A.L. 186
Alatas, S.H. 30, 40
Alibhai, N. 14, 129, 194
Allport, G.W. 189, 251
Amir, Y. 30, 39, 251
Ananth, J. 169
Andrushko, E. 93, 106
Antler, L. 128
Antonovsky, A. 44
Antonucci, T. 186
Anumonye, A. 119
Argyle, M. 14, 15, 138, 200–7 *passim*, 210, 216, 226, 248
Aronson, E. 25, 251
Arredondo-Dowd, P.M. 221
Atkinson, J.W. 35, 173
Averill, J.R. 163, 165

Babiker, I.E. 121–2
Bagley, C. 77–9
Ball-Rokeach, S.J. 49
Ballachey, E.L. 209
Ballard, C. 85
Banton, M.P. 233
Bar-Yosef, R. 95
Baranowski, T. 188
Bardo, J.W. and D. J. 69, 74–5
Barker, R.G. 19
Baron, R.C. 103
Barrera, M. 186
Bartel, A. 37
Bartlett, K. 209
Basker, C. 96
Batta, I.D. 85
Baumgardner, S.R. 12
Baxter, J.C. 207
Beels, C.C. 186

Beil-Warner, D. 15, 201
Bennett, J.W. 11
Benyoussef, A. 105
Berk, B. 88–9
Berman, G. 44–5, 95
Berry, J. W. 20, 230, 233
Bettelheim, B. 26
Bhatt, A.K. 221
Bickley, V.C. 32
Biegel, D. 187
Bloom, J.D. 100
Bloom, L. 30, 233
Bochner, S. 12, 233; on communication differences 209; on culture-learning and social skills 13, 14, 15, 209, 215–16, 235, 239–40; on motives 35, 38–9; on refugees 100; on social psychology of encounter 202; on social relations 213, 215–16; on students 11, 16, 20, 38–9, 113–14, 122, 125, 128–9, 132–3, 215; on tourism 143, 149
Bock, P. 49
Boekestijn, C. 230, 231
Boggs, J.W. 214, 233
Boker, W. 22, 95, 233
Boldt, E.D. 20
Bottoms, A.E. 85
Bourne, P.G. 121
Bowlby, J. 163–4
Boxer, A.H. 40, 151, 233,
Breckenridge, A. 100
Brein, M. 206, 207, 208
Bressler, M. 11
Brett, J. M. 152–3
Brewin, C. 84
Brislin, R.W. 12, 18, 211, 221, 231, 233
Britt, W.G. 228–9

Subject index

abbreviated grief 165
aboriginal inhabitants *see under*
  Australia; North America
academic problems of students 120–1,
  125
accent problems 23
accountability of students 125–6
acculturation 69; *see also* assimilation
achievement motivation and tourism
  36
adaptation: mental illness and 75–6;
  predicted 170; psycho-social, of
  refugees 100–4
adjustment 14, 131; problems of
  concept 234–5; problems of
  students 120, 125; *see also* culture
  shock; U-curve
affective dimensions of support 186
affective disorders: migrants and 77,
  80–1, 93; *see also* emotional
  problems
Africa: adjustment undesirable in 235;
  black–white relations 19, 22, 24,
  210; business visitors in 152;
  business visitors from 151;
  diplomats in 229; emigration from
  79, 116, 117–21, 123; grief in 166;
  missionaries in 174; tourists in 143,
  146; values in 194; aid, international
  17, 223; *see also* students
alcoholism 73, 80–1, 83, 145–6
alienation 49; index 104
ambiguity, pervasive 49
anger and loss 164, 166
anomie 49; escape from 36
anticipatory grief 165
anxiety: in culture shock 48, 49; loss
  and 164, 166; of tourists 143, 145–6;
  see also stress
Arab countries 148, 207, 238

assertion programme 241
assimilation 24, 25, 26, 27, 32; types
  and rates of migrant 68–70, 73, 86,
  90
assimilation, culture (learning manual)
  238
attribution theory 36, 250; training 230
attrition rates of voluntary workers
  137
Australia: aborigines 19, 24, 233;
  immigrants 16, 44, 64, 68–76, 97,
  100, 110, 128, 172, 208; integration
  24; refugees in 97, 100; students in
  114, 117–18, 189; tourists in 147;
  values and communication in 189,
  193–4, 208, 210–11
Austria 93–4, 145
awareness, cultural 230

balance theory 250
Bali 148
Bangladesh 189
Barbados 36
behaviour: modification training 230;
  role-related of tourists 143–5
Belgium 92, 192
belief-similarity hypothesis 250
bereavement *see* grief
between-skin approach 248, 249
bewilderment of tourists 143, 145
bicultural: social networks 16, 127;
  SST approach 240–1, 242, 243
bilinguality 32
black people in USA 67, 91–2, 185;
  passing selves off as whites 29; *see
  also* South Africa
bodily contact 207
bolstering factor in migration 44
boredom of tourists 145–6
'brain drain' 40, 114

294   *Index*

Hawaii (*con't*)
  integration in 24, 28; orientation
    programmes in 238; social relations
    in 214; students in 127
heterocultural, becoming 31–2
heterogeneity of societies 19–20, 230
high contact tourists 141–2
Hmong, emigrants from 90–1, 102
homogeneity of societies 19, 26
honeymoon stage in culture shock 131
Hong Kong 98, 118
hostility 146
hosts 21, 22–4; business people and
    157; guest workers and 22, 95;
    migrants and 45; psychology of
    229–31; status of 22–3; students
    and 22, 39, 117, 118, 124–5, 215–16;
    tourists and 18, 143, 147–8;
    typology of relationships with 57
Hungary, emigration from 69, 93, 181
hypochondria 104, 118–19, 123
hysteria, diagnosis of 52

Iceland 148
identification 69
identity, ethnic 19–20; changes 29; loss
    of 25
identity, positive social 230, 250; *see
    also* individual; personal; self
immigration: policies 47, 173; *see also*
    migration
impotence feelings in culture shock 48
inadequacy, social 14–15, 200–17
    passim
independence 130
India: emigration from 22, 78–87, 110,
    116, 118, 172, 175; fatalism in
    169–70; segregation in 24; values in
    189–90
Indians *see under* North America
indigenous inhabitants *see* hosts *and
    under* Australia; North America
indignation in culture shock 48
individual effects of contact 25, 29–31;
    see also identity; personal; self
individualism dimension of cultural
    differences 191
Indo-Chinese migrants 90–1, 97–105,
    111, 175
Indonesia 209, 210–11
inferiority feelings 26
information giving in training 230,
    236–7

informational dimensions of support
    186
in-group, attitudes of 23–4; *see also*
    hosts
inhibited grief 165
innovating migration 43
instrumental: dimensions of support
    186; values 193
instrumentalism, fatalism as opposite
    167
integration 24, 27–8
intensity of grief 165
interaction 230; *see also under* social
    interaction; social skills
intercultural contact *see* motives;
    processes and outcomes
inter-group relations 251–2
internal: approach 248–9; control and
    fatalism 167; determinants of
    conflict 203–4, 212; homogeneity of
    societies 19; migration 65, 105–6
international: agencies 17, 18, 24; aid
    17, 233; education 11–16; relations,
    improved, hope for 39; *see also*
    global; migrants; sojourners;
    tourists
interpersonal factors xx; *see also* social
    support
intimacy 21; *see also* friendship; social
    support
intrapersonal factors xix
intrinsic cultural traits 90
inverted U-curve 49
involuntary migration *see* refugees
involvement, type of in cross-cultural
    contact 21
Iran 118
Iraq 118
Ireland: emigration from 79, 80–3,
    93–4, 110; religious conflict in 19;
    see also Britain
isolation 79, 89, 93–4, 121
isomorphic attributions as culture-
    training technique 237–8
Israel: immigrants 16, 44, 95, 97, 117;
    mental illness in 106; tourists in 147;
    values in 193
Italy: emigration to Australia 68, 69,
    73–4, 208; emigration to Britain
    80–1, 86; emigration to North
    America 93–4; punctuality in 209

Japan 19; emigration from 22; values
    in 189–90, 192, 209, 235